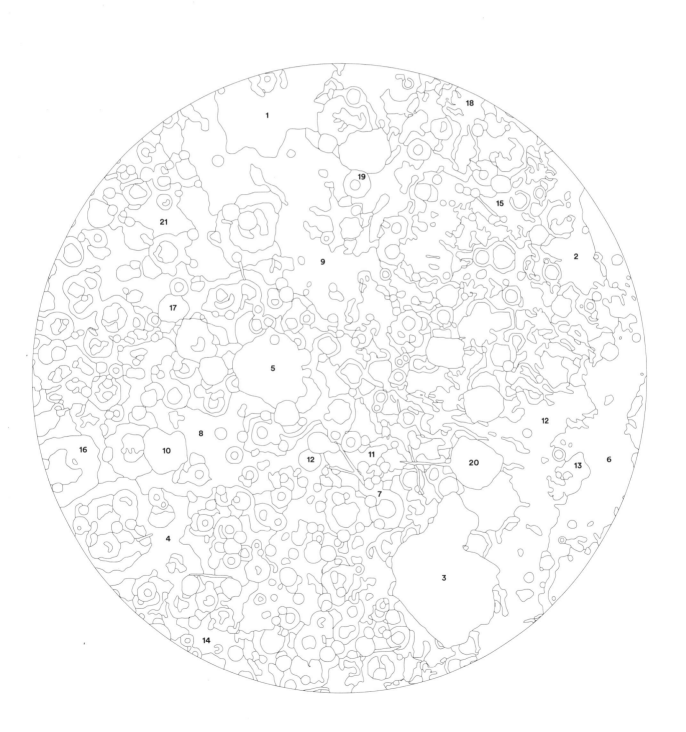

Plastic

Foreword

Plastics have shaped our daily lives on a scale like no other material, from food containers to electronic devices, from furniture to cars, from fashion to prefab buildings. With almost limitless malleability, versatility, and low-cost production, plastics have fired the imagination of designers and consumers alike for decades. But our experiences of plastics vary as much as its applications, and those experiences themselves often mask the complexity of this pressing issue. As much an outcome of Western colonialization and exploitation as scientific development, the convenience of plastic has in the past been associated with progress, even a culture and design revolution, but today it is most conspicuous as the waste that is a key factor in the global environmental crisis that has plastic at its core. The effects of both the production of plastic, which is reliant on the oil industry, and plastic waste are being felt by everyone, especially people in the Global South, and it is painfully clear that the days of unconscious plastic consumption are limited. But completely abolishing plastics seems unthinkable—at least in the mid-term—so finding different ways of producing, using, designing, and valuing them is of existential importance for our future and that of the planet.

What strategies exist for the responsible and ecologically sustainable use of plastics? How are design, industry, research, engineering, politics, and behaviour intertwined when it comes to solving the problem of plastic? Why has plastic been so important in the history of the modern world, and why is it so difficult to replace? What contributions can designers, manufacturers, governments, policymakers, industry, companies, and consumers make towards tackling the massive problems resulting from the production and use of plastic?

To address these and other questions head on, the Vitra Design Museum, the V&A in London and Dundee, and the Museum of Art, Architecture and Technology in Lisbon have teamed up. We have gathered expertise from numerous institutions and research areas: from museum collections holding some of the most spectacular examples of plastic design from the past 120 years to first-hand insights into the plastics industry, from scientific research to activists, policy makers, and critical or experimental approaches from avant-garde designers and artists.

The results of this collaboration are presented in the exhibition *Plastic: Remaking Our World* and in this accompanying book. Both examine the rise of plastic over the course of the twentieth century, analyse its environmental impact, and present current research and design projects geared towards a radical change of the status quo and new, more sustainable uses of plastic. Our heartfelt thanks go to the brilliant team of curators from these four institutions who have put their knowledge and energy into gathering this wealth of information and who have developed a concept which clearly states the problems associated with plastic while also addressing constructive approaches for improvements and solutions. We also thank the sponsors, lenders, contributors, and partners who have made this exhibition and book possible.

Being able to connect the present with a wider historical and societal perspective is a strength of design museums, which can bridge the gap to the future by bringing together different perspectives to generate solutions for the urgent challenges of our times. We believe that cross-disciplinary discourse is key to tackling the plastics problem, and we hope that *Plastic: Remaking Our World* will bring forward perspectives and ideas that contribute to a more sustainable future.

Mateo Kries, Director, Vitra Design Museum
Leonie Bell, Director, V&A Dundee
Beatrice Leanza, Director, Museum of Art, Architecture and Technology

When Mateo Kries and his team presented their vision for *Plastic: Remaking Our World*, the concept immediately excited us. For us, this represents a very special opportunity to show so much of what moves us in the context of plastics. To understand, to categorize, and, yes, to rethink.

BASF is a plastics pioneer. We have always been fascinated by the possibilities of these materials from a design, economic, and social perspective.

We want to inspire designers, engineers, and consumers with our materials. For more than a century, we have been pushing the performance limits and applications of materials, and we participate in solving practical issues with as much enthusiasm as we bring to creating visions with plastics. In the present, however, plastics are at a crossroads. They are an integral part of our modern lives. They make cars more efficient. They help us to build more sustainably. They are irreplaceable in medicine and keep our food fresh. And they are critical to the success of the energy transition. They are an enormously valuable resource. But plastic waste has become a global problem. Despite its value, plastic is too often disposed of negligently and in an environmentally harmful way, endangering people, the oceans, plants, and animals.

One thing is clear: we need to change how we use plastics, to think in circles. The way there leads through the interfaces between science and design, industry and society. Together we are on a journey to find solutions to the challenges around plastics. At BASF, we ensure that this journey reaches its destination faster. We develop high-performance materials that extend the service life of products. We use recycled and waste-based raw materials to conserve fossil-based raw materials. And by 2050, we want to make our entire production CO_2-neutral.

At BASF, we create chemistry for a sustainable future. So let's rethink plastics—and thus, our world—together.

We look forward to it.

Martin Jung
BASF Performance Materials

Nike exists to innovate, to unlock human potential, and to advance the progression of sport. The athletes we serve never stop striving for better, so neither do we. As a company, we're constantly responding to the dynamic requirements of sport. Every design throughout our history is encoded with the ambition to evolve and improve. Fifty years on, we are still in pursuit. In essence, we maintain plasticity.

Design at Nike is a practice of optimistic speculation: of intuiting, identifying, and, ideally, solving problems that inhibit a more desirable future. Increasingly, the design solutions we propose must extend beyond a single purpose, beyond a single lifetime. Our solutions should be complete but never final. They should celebrate being done and then undone. Our products often elicit wonder and desire. At their best, they're an invitation to the future.

The possibilities of plastic lie not just in what can be made from it, but in what can be unmade and remade from it. It's a material that, while imperfect, invites imagination and demands intention. Without it, sport would be less fluid, expressive, and empowered. Being both pliable and lightweight, plastic is perhaps the most symbiotic known extension of an athlete's anatomy. When used purposefully, it can channel and return biomechanical energy, providing propulsion far beyond human ability alone.

Take Nike Air as an example. It continues to push athletic performance to new heights while humbly providing haptic feedback that makes us all more aware of our literal impact on the planet. This enduring invention is also our most elemental: air encapsulated in plastic—a technological feat that initially needed to be seen to be believed.

Embracing this material's future responsibly means investigating its plasticity further—its ability to be returned, reimagined, and reincarnated—while continuing the search for reformulations and alternatives. At the 2000 Sydney Summer Olympics, Nike debuted its first running singlet made from recycled plastic bottles. What was "unbelievable" then is standard practice now. In fact, we divert more than one billion plastic bottles from landfill and waterways annually. But this is only one leg of the race. It's progress, just as the footwear concept presented in the *Plastic: Remaking Our World* exhibition is the latest stop on a much longer journey. It's a mindset shift towards making matter matter more and designing products not just for what they will be in the beginning, but more importantly, what they will be in the end.

John Hoke III
Chief Design Officer, Nike, Inc.

Introduction

Plastic. It's everywhere. It's the fabric of everyday life. Applied, used, and experienced differently across the globe as both product and waste, it is essential yet superfluous, life-saving and life-threatening, seductive but dangerous. The material's contested status stands as the starting point for the exhibition and accompanying catalogue *Plastic: Remaking Our World.*

Now, in the first decades of the twenty-first century, people experience plastic pollution in dramatically different ways and disagree vehemently about the solutions. Is there a place for plastic in this world or should it be banned? Is it to be better valued or rejected? Such questions and debates, like plastic, are ever-present: at almost every step along the supermarket aisle, in the news, on social media, when wearing a face mask, or when earning a living. Those who have contributed least to the plastic problem are the worst affected in society across the globe, while the phrase "plastic problem" generates over three billion search results on Google. Although very far from clear, the answers to these questions will shape our future, for better or worse.

*
**

Never has there been a more urgent time to understand the story of this man-made material, to look back on plastic's more than 150-year history, and to unpack this wonderous, yet cautionary tale and the cast of characters that shaped it. *Plastic: Remaking Our World* charts the material's unparalleled rise—its vast popularity and the dawning realization of its destructive power over the relatively short time of its existence—and probes design's role within this story. How has the history of plastic—the innovation, production, application, consumption, and disposal of this material—enabled new ways of living and contributed to the inescapable crisis of plastic pollution today?

This publication brings together essays, historical texts, a portfolio of images that relate to plastic in a visual chronology, and a series of conversations and roundtable discussions to tell the story of plastic's production, consumption, and its threat to the environment. Multiple voices from across the globe—including designers, manufacturers, policymakers, and activists—consider the promises and problems of plastic over the course of its history and address the areas of primary concern today, including legislation, climate justice, recycling, and the potential of a post-plastic future. In bringing together these many standpoints, the objective is to stimulate discussion and debate around plastic's role in society and to advocate for collective action and meaningful, long-term change.

While it is possible to point to potential solutions to the problems associated with plastic in terms of new legislation, material innovations, experimental approaches, as well as changing attitudes and behaviours, the exhibition and this book seek to offer a broad reach across the subject and via a range of different views. The field is ever-changing and fizzes with opinions, which makes it difficult to pin down where it is likely to go next. As such, the sharing of historical perspectives alongside expressions of new scientific discoveries and expertise, of worry and hope as well as a selection of future-facing ideas, is intended to offer nuanced and balanced insights.

*
**

To build a picture of the history and development of plastics, this book features three essays that take the reader from the origins of the first man-made plastics in the 1850s to the issue of plastic waste today. "From Natural to Man-made" by Mark Miodownik (pp. 16–21) investigates how the nineteenth-century search for plasticity revolved around the natural world. Horn, ivory, shellac, rubber, gutta-percha, and tortoiseshell were sought-after materials the trade of which was enabled by the colonial exploitation of people, animals, and land. At the same time, scientists and opportunists were conducting experiments in laboratories and workshops to make synthetic materials of similar qualities, leading to the first man-made plastics such as Parkesine, celluloid, and, later, Bakelite. In "Love in the Age of Plastic", Susan Freinkel (pp. 22–31) looks at the petrochemical industry as the source of supply for plastic production and its role in building the modern-day dependency on throwaway, single-use plastic. In the twenty-first century, the ubiquity of plastic enables many everyday conveniences, from our daily routines of consumption to aspects of personal hygiene. Nanjala Nyabola's essay, "Homo Plasticus" (pp. 32–39), explores this new reality by looking at the prevalence of single-use plastics in Kenya. Over the last 30 years, Kenya, like so many other countries, has moved from an economy almost devoid of single-use plastic, to one highly dependent and blighted by it—and is now seeking to free itself through far-reaching legislation.

"Images of Plastic 1850–Today" (pp. 40–91) documents the changing perceptions of plastic over time through a selection of promotional and educational leaflets, advertisements, and other ephemera from the Global North. From the celebratory, innovative, and alluring to the doom-laden and threatening, the chronology gives shape to the key material protagonist of the twentieth century and to the evermore real climate crisis to which it has contributed in the twenty-first. Alongside this, a selection of reprints of historical and contemporary articles document changing attitudes to plastic (pp. 92–111). These include Alexander Parkes' speech about Parkesine to the Royal Society for the Encouragement of Arts in 1865; a chapter on plastic from Roland Barthes' Mythologies of 1957; and a text by Max Liboiron from 2018 about plastic pollution and colonialism. Some are often quoted, some overlooked, and others offer new and pressing perspectives. These visual and written markers through the passage of time are further complimented by a select catalogue of objects from museums and private collections (pp. 112–49) that chart the application of plastic from the seventeenth century to today. They include portable rather than disposable cutlery, buttons made from milk, and a plastic aircraft cockpit hood through to the brilliantly inexpensive Monobloc chair, a bespoke set of vases made from used household product bottles, and the facemask that has become a defining object of the early 2020s.

Lastly, this volume features a series of conversations (pp. 150–83) and roundtable discussions (pp. 184–223) with individuals involved in the field of plastics past, present, and future. Together, this series serves as a platform to give voice and space to debate for those who enable and fight for justice alongside those who call out the potential obstacles to change. This section is complimented by a set of infographics (pp. 224–45) that provide facts and figures detailing the increased presence of plastics and, with it, the urgent problem plastic has created in today's world. And while it is acknowledged that the statistics given will shift and change rapidly, they nonetheless provide a tool to understand how the world has become overrun by plastic waste.

Concerns about overconsumption and living beyond the means of the planet are not new. In *The Man Who Never Threw Anything Away* of 1978, the artist Ilya Kabakov writes: "The whole world, everything which surrounds me here, is to me a boundless dump with no ends or borders, an inexhaustible diverse sea of garbage. [...] This whole dump is full of twinkling stars, reflections and fragments of culture [...] an enormous past rises up behind these crates, vials and sacks, all forms of packaging which were ever needed by man have not yet lost their shape, they did not become something dead once they were discarded."[1]

1. Ilya Kabakov, *The Man Who Never Threw Anything Away*. New York: Harry N. Abrams, 1996/1978, p. 22.

Almost 50 years later, this world of waste is even more entrenched in the plastic detritus of the twentieth and twenty-first centuries. This build-up stands as a material mirror to the motivations and methods of production and their inextricable links to patterns of consumption and disposal.

There is no single solution that is going to be able to deal with this changed reality, but the exhibition and book *Plastic: Remaking Our World* seek to make clear the need for change on both an individual and societal level and local and global scale. To unravel this tightly wound and destructive interdependence, attitudes to production, consumption, and product life cycles need to shift radically. The value of objects needs to be fully appreciated—the way a product is brought to life, the materials it is made from, how it evolves and degrades, and its potential reuse—because, in such a revaluation, a more sustainable, circular economy can be enacted.

Individuals and collectives, activists and designers, manufacturers and waste pickers, scientists and consumers, businesses and legislators, everyone can bring about change across disciplines and industries in the fight to reduce reliance on plastic. Lobbying for restrictions on the exportation of plastic waste, pressurizing corporations to divest from fossil fuels, considering material alternatives to plastic, and consuming less and in a more careful manner, must all be part of this call to action.

In offering insight into how the world has become so filled with plastic, *Plastic: Remaking Our World* sets out to spark a revaluation of the material, to see it not as disposable or throwaway but as something remarkable once again, to be used selectively in the ways it is most useful—and thereby least harmful—for global society and planetary health.

Johanna Agerman Ross, Lauren Bassam, Jochen Eisenbrand, Corinna Gardner, Charlotte Hale, Mea Hoffmann, Anniina Koivu

Essays

14–1 Detail of the Blow Chair (1967) designed by Jonathan de Pas, Donato D'Urbino, Paolo Lomazzi, and Carla Scolari.

From Natural to Man-made

Mark Miodownik

The citizens of Europe and North America saw their everyday lives transforming rapidly in the nineteenth century. Old ways of doing things were giving way to industrialization, changing the types of jobs that were available: factory work was common, but also, increasingly, clerical and professional jobs were in reach for agricultural workers who relocated to the cities. This created a growing middle class, who acquired houses and celebrated their new wealth and improved status by filling their homes with stuff—tables, chairs, cutlery, cushions, crockery, mirrors, hairbrushes, and all manner of other things. The resin, ivory, ebony, rubber, and other materials used in these produces had their origins in the vast trading network that saw European states benefit, directly and indirectly, from the uneven and exploitative colonial relationships they had developed around the world. This trading network—a type of global capitalism developed by Western European countries—used military power to access natural resources, to acquire colonies, and to enslave local populations. A show of naval strength was used to project power and maintain the colonies, but also to protect the merchant ships importing these materials to the western ports of London, Amsterdam, and Boston.

This exploitative trading network, giving European powers access to the natural materials that became increasingly important for the new technologies, in turn, helped underpin their economies. For instance, the trade in gutta-percha—a type of rubber obtained from the sap of the *Palaquium gutta* tree [43–1] that the people of Malaysia had been using for centuries to make knife handles and walking sticks—boomed when the electric telegraph was invented. This technology allowed messages and news to be encoded into electrical signals that could then be transmitted along wires to connect towns, cities, and countries. The first commercial electric telegraph was developed in 1837, but the copper wires needed to be insulated from the environment to stop disruption of the electrical signals. What was required was a tough, corrosion-resistant, mouldable, flexible, and waterproof electrical insulator. Finding a material that could do all of these things was particularly challenging. Gutta-percha was one of the few materials that fulfilled these requirements: once extracted from the tree bark through boiling, it hardened into a plastic material that was found to be both flexible and electrically non-conductive. By 1850, the world's first undersea telegraph cable was laid between Britain and France, and all 25 miles of it was coated in gutta-percha.[1] By 1858, a similar but much longer cable linked Europe and America, again coated in this natural rubber. The extreme usefulness of this technology to the colonial powers led to rapid expansion, and the global cable network grew from 15,000 to over 200,000 nautical miles between 1866 and 1900[2] [44–1]. This expansion required the production of vast amounts of gutta-percha that all needed to be shipped around the world. Since every 10,000 miles of cable required approximately a million trees to be felled, this boom in demand led to the destruction of the forest habitat on a vast scale, so much so that by the late nineteenth century, the *Palaquium gutta* faced extinction in some regions of Southeast Asia.[3]

1. See the text on sea cables in this book, p. 116.

2. John Tully, "A Victorian Disaster: Imperialism, the Telegraph, and Gutta-Percha", *Journal of World History*, vol. 20, no. 4 (2009), pp. 559–79.

3. Rebecca Altman, "The Myth of Historical Bio-Based Plastics", *Science*, vol. 373, no. 6550 (2021), pp. 47–49.

Other materials such as ivory, horn, and tortoiseshell were also imported by the imperialist powers for use in making items for the home, including hairbrushes and combs, eyeglass frames, piano keys, and billiard balls.[4] As the colonizing powers grew richer, the growing middle classes in these countries acquired more everyday and luxury household items. As these uneven trade relations continued in the latter part of the nineteenth century, the number of wild animals shot or trapped for their horn or shell started to lead to shortages and price increases. This led some manufacturers to consider the possibility of creating synthetic versions of these materials that would lead to a more reliable and controllable supply. The desire for a synthetic ivory was even expressed publicly in the early 1860s in an advertisement in the *New York Times* that promised a reward of 10,000 dollars in gold to anyone who could invent a new material for billiard balls.[5]

Chemists in the nineteenth century, aware that material objects were made up of atoms and molecules, were building a catalogue of all the different types of atoms, the Periodic Table of Elements. It is natural to assume that the more complex an object is the larger the number of different types of atoms needed to build it. But analysis of living organisms such as plants, animals, and bacteria confound this notion. Organisms comprise few ingredients, mostly carbon, hydrogen, and oxygen, with small amounts of other elements. This raises the question, then, how it is that hard, tough ivory, while made mostly from the same stuff as bouncy, stretchy rubber, has radically different properties? The answer is that these materials are built of long chains of carbon atoms in which the same unit of molecular structure is repeated. Combining the Greek word *poly* meaning many and *mer* meaning unit, polymers describe the small change in the repeating unit or the length or scale of the chain that yields vastly different properties, from rubberiness to hardness. The magical way in which the use of a few different ingredients can alter the material properties of something is the secret of our bodies too; our skin, organs, and our teeth are all built using polymers. Thus, chemists reached the conclusion in the early twentieth century that the trick to creating synthetic versions of ivory and rubber was to master polymer chemistry. While progress had been made before this time, it was mostly through trial and error.

Alexander Parkes made the first experimental breakthrough [46–1]. He took the plant extract cellulose and treated it with nitric acid and a solvent to create a plastic material that had many of the characteristics of ivory. He called it Parkesine and exhibited it at the World's Fair in London in 1862, wowing the crowds with the material's beauty and its versatility. Parkes did not have a fundamental understanding of the chemistry involved, but he did know how to manufacture objects with his new material. He heated up the Parkesine to make it plastic and used moulds to form it into imitation ivory combs, boxes, pens, knife handles, and art objects. Unfortunately, he was unable to commercialize the process successfully; making the material required expensive solvents, and the production process was labour intensive. As a result, the manufacture of Parkesine ceased when the costs of industrializing production spiralled out of control.

4. See, for example, the object entries about tortoiseshell and horn in this book, p. 114 and p. 115.

5. Susan Freinkel, *Plastic: A Toxic Love Story*. New York: Houghton Mifflin Harcourt, 2011, pp. 15–17. See also the text on billiard balls in this book, p. 119.

Mark Miodownik

6. Clive Everton, *The Story of Billiards and Snooker*. London: Cassell, 1979, p. 53.

Others took up the challenge. Celluloid—a plastic manufactured with very similar ingredients to Parkesine—was introduced by the Americans John Wesley Hyatt and his brother Isaiah in their attempt to win the *New York Times'* prize for the invention of a new material to replace ivory for billiard balls.[6] Celluloid succeeded first as a material for dentures and then increasingly as a replacement for horn and ivory in the everyday domestic products flowing into Western middle-class homes. Its versatility arises from its chemical structure: the long-chain polymer molecules that comprise celluloid are not strongly bonded to each other, so, when heated up they become mobile and can be moulded into any shape. This ability to be thermally moulded makes celluloid a thermoplastic suitable for mass production, since moulds could be used again and again. This had the potential to make imitation ivory very cheap, but like Parkesine, it didn't quite work out that way. The costs of the solvents required for mass manufacture were high, and the material properties of celluloid did not match those of ivory, which continued to be imported. The major significance of celluloid was the discovery of its other properties, its flexibility and transparency when produced in thin strips. Thus, celluloid had an unexpected and radical effect on photographic technology as a suitable replacement for the heavy glass plates used to hold the photographic emulsion.

In the early days of photography, camera bodies were bulky, because they needed to be strong enough to hold the glass plates; this made taking photographs a cumbersome activity. But the American George Eastman saw the potential of the new plastic to change this. Celluloid, like glass, was transparent, but it was also much lighter and could be moulded into a thin strip of plastic. By putting photographic emulsion on this much lighter, flexible material, Eastman invented photographic film. A further bonus was that celluloid film could be rolled up, and a single film roll could potentially take many photographs. By making cameras lighter, the whole business of taking a photograph was made easier since photographers no longer had to carry stacks of glass plates. Once roll film existed, it then became clear that a sequence of photographs taken in quick succession, when played back through a projector, appeared to make the picture move. This opened the door to a type of camera designed to take a large number of sequential photos per second. The invention of motion pictures introduced a new mode of storytelling. This new visual culture was named after the plastic that created it; early movies were called celluloid [49–1, 49–2].

At the turn of the twentieth century, the possibilities of plastics seemed endless, and chemists dedicated themselves to understanding polymer science and making synthetic versions of natural materials. Perhaps the most iconic of these was Bakelite. Named after its inventor, Leo Baekeland [50–1], it was manufactured from liquid synthetic ingredients which, when cast in a mould, set into a solid shape through a polymer reaction. Called a thermoset plastic, it was comprised of long chains of carbon molecules all chemically bonded together to make the whole structure rigid. Unlike thermoplastics such as celluloid, this made Bakelite heat resistant and therefore both stronger and more durable.

The inventor of thermoset plastics, Baekeland, originally set out to create a replacement for shellac, a natural resin obtained from lac beetle known as *kerria lacca* found in tropical countries such as India and Thailand. The beetles suck tree sap and excrete a sticky resin. In swarms, they can reach numbers high enough to cover entire trees in resin [42–1]. The material is itself a natural plastic, and the practice of scraping it off trees to use as an adhesive or as a varnish has been going on for thousands of years. In the late nineteenth century, with the emergence of the phonograph, shellac was used to produce gramophone discs.[7] Like the wax and rubber alternatives, it had the capacity to be heated, moulded, and stamped with fine grooves to hold the imprint of an audio soundtrack. What made it superior to the alternatives was its surface finish and hardness, which yielded better sound quality. As audio technology improved and the gramophone gave way to the record player, shellac maintained its position as the best material for music discs, with the 78 rotations per minute (rpm) gramophone record being made from this natural material. By the 1930s, half of the global production of shellac was used to make gramophone records, and this was the market that Leo Baekeland had hoped his Bakelite would provide a synthetic replacement for.[8] He was, however, unsuccessful in this ambition, since the moulds were incapable of imprinting the fine indentations that correspond to audio soundtracks.

Although Baekeland had failed to create a replacement for shellac, Bakelite found huge success through other applications. Its hardness, strength, and fine surface finish meant that objects which were previously carved from wood or other hard materials could now be mould-cast and mass produced. Even complicated shapes could be standardized, such as door handles. It also meant that colour could be introduced as a variant, changing the design potential of household products entirely. Because it was an electrical insulator, it was also perfect for the manufacture of the modern electrical gadgets that were coming on to the market at the beginning of the twentieth century, such as telephones, radios, and televisions. So versatile was Bakelite that it was marketed as "the material of a thousand uses" [51–1]. Its popularity made it the iconic modernist material and ushered in the electronic age.

Eventually, synthetic plastic replaced shellac in record production. When plastic, 33 rpm records superseded the shellac 78s in 1948, they were made from a new thermoplastic called polyvinyl chloride, or vinyl for short. This truly modern plastic was less brittle than shellac and had better acoustic properties. It is still used today. Vinyl was developed and manufactured using the now fundamental understanding of polymer chemistry. With particular applications in mind, chemists had gained the ability to apply theory to the design of new plastics that had specific mechanical, electrical, or acoustic properties. Polymer chemistry had shifted from trial-and-error experimentation to a theory-led science, and a cornucopia of new plastics designed for twentieth-century living then emerged.

7. See the text on shellac records in this book, p. 118.

8. Freinkel, *Plastic: A Toxic Love Story*, pp. 22–24.

Mark Miodownik

Love in the Age of Plastic

Susan Freinkel

In the early days of World War II, a pair of British chemists published a slim volume called *Plastics*. Victor Yarsley and Edward Couzens were plastics pioneers, eager to advance the then-young industry. Most of the book is a dry read for anyone who's not a polymer chemist—that is, until the final chapter. There, the two vividly described their vision for the future once the "dust and smoke of the present conflict clear away": a utopia they dubbed the "Plastic Age".

"Let us try to imagine a dweller in the Plastic Age", they wrote. "This Plastic man will come into a world of colour and bright shining surfaces." He will grow up surrounded by unbreakable toys, rounded corners, scuff-proof walls. There will be no sharp edges or splintering surface, no rot or decay. Clothes will repel dirt and wrinkles. He will travel in lightweight cars, boats and planes, be entertained by shows on plastic film, listen to plastic-encased radios. He'll wear plastic glasses to correct failing vision and plastic dentures to replace lost teeth, and, when death comes, he'll be buried in a hygienically sealed coffin made of plastic. "How much brighter and cleaner a world he has lived in than that which preceded the plastics age. It is a world free from moth and rust and full of colour", they concluded. A built-to-order world of unprecedented abundance in which "man like a magician, makes what he wants for almost every need".[1]

This, of course, is the world we inhabit today, surrounded by plastic from cradle to grave. Because of its eerie accuracy, a book that otherwise would languish in obscurity is often quoted. It was cited in the preface to a 2009 set of landmark scientific papers documenting how plastics pollute oceans and landscapes and even our bodies.[2] The journal *Nature* included it in a recent round-up of seven classic books that "speak to us now".[3] Given all that is now known about the dark consequences of plastics' ubiquity, the optimism of the authors' vision for a plastic-stuffed future can be easy to dismiss. Yet, reading it now is like reading an early love letter from a romance gone terribly bad. It helps remind us why people fell in love in the first place.

The roots of the affair go back to the mid-nineteenth century, when inventors began concocting new semi-synthetic substances from plants to replace scarce natural materials. The first to become a commercial success was celluloid. It was created as a substitute for ivory, then in such high demand it was feared elephants were being hunted to extinction. John Wesley Hyatt's 1869 creation went far beyond the capabilities of those much-sought-after tusks. Celluloid could be made hard as horn or malleable as rubber. It could be cut, polished, moulded, carved, or coloured. It shrugged off water and spills. Best of all, it could be rendered to look like ivory, but also tortoiseshell, coral, ebony, or other luxe materials, at a fraction of what the real thing would cost. Thanks to celluloid's power of imitation, even a lowly secretary or shop worker could afford a "tortoiseshell" comb or an "ivory" dresser set. As the historian Jeffrey Meikle notes,

1. Victor E. Yarsley and Edward G. Couzens, *Plastics*. Harmondsworth: Penguin Books, 1941, pp. 154–58.

2. Theme issue devoted to the impacts of plastics, complied by R. C. Thompson et al., "Plastics, The Environment and Human Health", *Philosophical Transactions of the Royal Society B*, vol. 364, no. 1526 (2009).

3. Freeman Dyson, et al., "Books for Our Time: Seven Classics that Speak to us Now", *Nature*, vol. 576, no. 7787 (2019), pp 374–78.

"By replacing materials that were hard to find or expensive to produce, celluloid democratized a host of goods for an expanding consumption-oriented middle class."[4] In North America, it was the first plastic to level the playing field for consumption. It would be far from the last.

For all its symbolic significance, celluloid had a fairly modest place in the material world of the early twentieth century—limited mainly to novelties and small items of utility. The next plastic to come along, Bakelite, was far more influential. Invented in 1907, Bakelite was the product of Belgian inventor Leo Baekeland's quest for something new to insulate electrical wire. (The existing insulator, shellac, was made from a resin excreted by lac beetles, who could never generate enough to sustain the burgeoning electrical industry.) Unlike celluloid, which was made from plant cellulose, Bakelite was a fully human-made creation, conjured by applying heat and pressure to phenol (a coal derivative) and formaldehyde. Or, as *Time* magazine poetically put it, "born of fire and mystery" [50–1].[5]

Dark, rugged, never to be disguised, Bakelite introduced us to the beauty of frank artificiality, an aesthetic that would become even more emphatic in the brightly coloured, multivariate plastics to come. Moulded or machined into sleek, curvy forms, Bakelite expressed, said one designer, "the vernacular of the twentieth century […] the language of invention and synthesis".[6] It evoked a spirit of modernity, especially when wrapped around new devices like telephones or radios that were fast becoming essential accoutrements of middle-class life.

Yet the texture of daily life was still largely made up of the natural materials that had sustained humans for centuries. For the first few decades of the twentieth century, production of plastic was minuscule, compared to the production of glass, cotton, or iron. This reflected the limitations of the materials themselves—like celluloid's extreme flammability—and still fairly primitive processing technologies. But it also had to do with their manufacturing DNA: celluloid and Bakelite were created by lone inventors seeking a replacement for a natural material in short supply. They had a problem they were trying to solve, a need in mind.

The plastics that would stock Yarsley and Couzens' utopia, the ones that would change the world, were born in a very different milieu.

Once upon a time, it is said, John D. Rockefeller stood looking out over one of his refineries and noticed blue flames flaring from some smokestacks. "What's that burning?" he asked, and someone explained the flares were burning off by-products of the refining process that had no use. "Let's find something to do with them", Rockefeller snapped. "I don't believe in wasting anything." That something became plastic.

The story is almost certainly apocryphal, an oil-age fairy tale. But like all fairy tales, it contains a kernel of truth. It captures the brutal, beautifully efficient nature of an industry organized on the principle that no hydrocarbon sucked from the ground should ever go to waste.[7] What is true is that, in 1913, Rockefeller's company figured out a way to

4. Jeffrey Meikle, *American Plastic: A Cultural History*. New Brunswick, NJ: Rutgers University Press, 1997, p. 14. See also Robert Friedel, *Pioneer Plastic: The Making and Selling of Celluloid*. Madison, WI: University of Wisconsin Press, 1983.

5. Quoted from Bill Bregar, "100 years later, Bakelite shines", *Plastics News*, 9 August 2007. The 1937 film produced by the Bakelite Corporation, *The Fourth Kingdom: The Story of Bakelite Resinoid* (narrated by Lowell Thomas), boasted that Bakelite had transcended the classical taxonomies of the animal, mineral, or vegetable kingdoms: "Chemical research has taken the three kingdoms […] and created a fourth kingdom, whose boundaries are unlimited."

6. Paul T. Frankl, quoted from Meikle, *American Plastic*, p. 108.

7. Source unknown. Interestingly the same insight came from Dmitri Mendeleev, the Russian chemist who created the Periodic Table of the Elements. Mendeleev had a keen interest in petroleum. He recognized that crude oil contained a bounty of compounds that could be raw materials for the chemical industry. To just burn oil for fuel, he warned, "would be akin to firing up a kitchen stove with bank notes". Quoted from Christopher Flavin, *The Future of Synthetic Materials: The Petroleum Connection*. Washington, DC: Worldwatch Institute, April 1980, p. 7.

Susan Freinkel

8. Herman Francis Mark, *Giant Molecules*. New York: Time Life Books, 1966, p. 104.

9. An ICI researcher, quoted from Meikle, *American Plastic*, p. 189.

10. William S. Dutton, "A Drama of Opportunity", in *The Wonder World of Chemistry: New York World's Fair ... 1939*, p. 5, online: https://www.1939nyworldsfair.com/ftp/Dupont-Chemistry-1939.pdf, accessed 30 August 2021.

11. Stephen Fenichell, *Plastic: The Making of a Synthetic Century*. New York: Harper Collins, 1996, pp. 145–46.

12. Ibid., p. 132.

13. Quoted in an advert headlined "Du Pont Announces for the World of Tomorrow... a new word and a new material: NYLON", which ran in "The Woman's Forum", *New York Herald Tribune* (30 October 1939), online: https://digital.sciencehistory.org/works/02870v94c/viewer/g445cd45k, accessed 6 October 2021.

multiply the value of crude oil. Through a process called cracking, the company was able to isolate and capture hydrocarbons in raw crude, such as ethylene, propylene, and benzene. When petroleum and chemical companies began to align and integrate, these once-discarded by-products became the principal raw materials, or feedstocks, of the emerging petrochemical industry—and the starting ingredients of the plastics that would enrapture and envelop us over the next century.

In the 1920s and '30s, armed with a growing understanding of polymer science, industrial chemists at major petrochemical companies began trying to construct new substances out of those by-products. The team of white-coated scientists at IG Farben was so creative that between 1929 and 1932, they were averaging a new polymer a day. Their discoveries included polystyrene, polyvinyl, and polyacrylic.[8] DuPont's research and development programme, led by a brilliant chemist, Wallace Carruthers, synthesized one new polymer after another: neoprene in 1930; nylon in 1935; and Teflon in 1938. An experiment gone awry at England's Imperial Chemical Industries (ICI) led to the discovery of polyethylene. The chemists were so stumped by the tough mystery material in their leaking reactor vessel that at first, as one recalled, "no one could envisage a use for it".[9] Most of these new polymers were "thermoplastics", versatile shape-shifters that were even better suited than Bakelite or celluloid to mass production.

Unlike the inventors of early plastics, the goal now was "improving on Nature's products", as DuPont announced in a promotional brochure for its 1939 World's Fair exhibit. Countless new compounds had been developed, with countless more to come, DuPont promised. "It is as if a wholly new continent had been discovered containing riches of which nobody had dreamed."[10] [60–1]

Crowds thronged DuPont's *Wonder World of Chemistry* exhibit at the World's Fair, oohing and aahing at those riches, most of which were not yet available. Here was a huge sparkling "diamond" cut from a hunk of acrylic. There, a giant steel ball crashed into a sheet of glass every ten minutes, but the glass just bowed instead of breaking, because it was laminated with polyvinyl butyral. In another display, a machine spat out sweets individually wrapped in the miraculous new packaging film, cellophane.[11] Cellophane was truly a wonder: transparent as glass, but thin as tissue, clean and waterproof [68–1]. American songwriter Cole Porter spoke for many when he wrote the line in the song, "You're the Top", "You're cellophane". In a 1940 poll by a Texas newspaper asking people what they considered the most beautiful-sounding word in the English language, cellophane came in third, after "motherhood" and "memory".[12]

But the star of the show was nylon, "so new a material that a new name had to be coined [for it]", as DuPont boasted.[13] A floodlit courtyard displayed thousands of nylon filaments arranged in a synthetic fountain that shimmered under a spotlight. Visitors could watch a nylon stocking take shape in a knitting machine and then see one put to the test by a pair of mechanical hands that stretched it out and let it snap back into shape. Models played tug of war with a stocking to show off its amazing strength and elasticity. Nearby on a plastic podium, another model posed as the show's mascot, Miss Chemistry, her long shapely legs sheathed in the lustrous sheer fibre touted as "strong as steel, and as fine as the spider's web".[14]

Nylon was the answer to a longstanding dream that went back to the eighteenth century for a synthetic silk. For twentieth-century women, it would be a welcome alternative to the existing choices in hosiery: costly delicate silk, saggy rayon, or durable, but distinctly unsexy cotton. Unlike many other plastic products that would later come along, nylon stockings were something people already wanted. Still, DuPont masterfully stoked that longing to a fever pitch. The company waited a year to release the first nylon stockings. After a few test sales in its hometown of Wilmington, Delaware—where supplies were snapped up in a matter of hours—the company designated 16 May 1940, as "Nylon Day" for a national release through a select number of stores. The four million pairs—priced at about a dollar 15 cents apiece, the equivalent of more than 21 dollars today—sold out within two days.[15]

Yet, it would still be a while before nylon, or any other polymer marvels would become part of our daily lives. The reason: World War II.

What few plastics existed were quickly diverted to military needs. In an effort to conserve strategic materials such as rubber, brass, silk, or steel and free itself of dependence on imports, the US military turned to the nascent plastics industry to supply alternatives. It was a challenge, but the industry complied, finding ways to make everything from whistles and helmets to bazooka barrels, bomber turrets, and mortar fuses. Nylon was severely rationed and diverted into the manufacturing of parachutes,[16] tyre cords, rope, fuel tanks, shoelaces, mosquito netting, and hammocks [62–1]. The hard-rubber combs issued to every GI were replaced with plastic ones. A Chicago toymaker quickly turned out some 200,000 plastic bugles to stand in for the traditional brass instruments used to rouse soldiers with reveille each morning.[17] The shift to plastics gave the US a leg-up in building its military capabilities.

The plastics industry matured under the pressure to produce, improving and refining its processing and manufacturing capabilities [63–1]. The demands of war also created uses for plastics that until then had confounded chemists. Polyethylene, it turned out, was an excellent insulator of electrical current. That attribute, combined with its featherweight nature, enabled the British to create radar stations light enough to be mounted in planes. Airborne radar gave the British a critical advantage in the war. While the Germans eventually acquired radar, they didn't have polyethylene.[18] Teflon, too, found a purpose for the first time when scientists involved in the Manhattan Project deployed its supreme resistance to corrosion to make containers for the volatile gasses used in constructing the first atomic bomb.[19]

14. DuPont vice president Charles Stine, quoted from Meikle, *American Plastic*, p. 141.

15. Emily Spivak, "Stocking Series Part 1: Wartime Rationing and Nylon Riots", *Smithsonianmag.com* (4 September 2012), online: https://www.smithsonianmag.com/arts-culture/stocking-series-part-1-wartime-rationing-and-nylon-riots-25391066/, accessed 30 August 2021.

16. See the text on parachute nylon in this book, p. 129.

17. Fenichell, *Plastic: The Making of a Synthetic Century*, pp. 203–05.

18. Ibid., pp. 202–03.

19. John Emsley, *Molecules at an Exhibition: The Science of Everyday Life*. Oxford: Oxford University Press, 1998, p. 33.

Susan Freinkel

20. Meikle, *American Plastic*, p. 125.

21. Quoted from ibid., p. 6.

22. "Hosts of New Uses in Plastics Shown", *New York Times*, 23 April 1946.

Plastics production leaped to keep up with the surging military demand. Between 1939 and 1945, production quadrupled from nearly 213 million pounds (c. 96.6 million kilograms) to 818 million pounds (c. 371 million kilograms) annually.[20]

The stage was set for plastics to take off once the war ended. A consuming public that had scrimped through nearly two decades of economic depression and war would soon be flush with an unprecedented level of disposable income. To meet that demand was a much more mature industry with a vastly ramped-up production capacity and no intention to stop growing. The industry shifted its focus from the military market to household goods. As one plastics executive recalled, "In 1946, virtually nothing was made of plastic and *anything* could be."[21] (Including the pink flamingo lawn decorations that his company would later produce.)

Just months after the war's end, thousands of people lined up for blocks to get into the first National Plastics Exposition in New York City, a showcase of the new plastics that had proven themselves on the battlefield. For a public weary of two decades of scarcity, the show was dazzling. There were window screens in every colour of the rainbow that would never need to be painted. Suitcases light enough to lift with a finger but strong enough to hold a load of bricks. Nylon fishing lines that would hold against even the biggest fish. A prosthetic hand that looked and moved like a real one. Acrylic flowers that looked as if they'd been cut from glass. A plastic toy that made other plastic toys metaphorized the coming synthetic tidal wave: "Nothing can stop plastics", the chairman of the exposition crowed.[22]

Nothing that is, except the industry itself. Manufacturers were still on the steep side of the learning curve and, in the immediate post-war years, mistakes abounded: plates that softened in hot water, ashtrays that melted under cigarettes, vinyl raincoats that got clammy and sticky in wet weather. Polymer technology would improve as manufacturers figured out how to make better plastics and to better match the right polymer with the right application. Those early experiences left an indelible stain on plastic's cultural reputation.

Nonetheless, plastic became the shiny face of a post-war economic boom fuelled by America's copious supplies of cheap petroleum. Petrochemical companies were growing so fast they were soon among the biggest contributors to the GDP of the United States. Shell Oil sought to remind the public of its debt to oil in a 1949 film *Petroleum: "Oil for Aladdin's Lamp"*, which offered a new twist on the classic children's story. "We know the true genie of the lamp was the oil that provides its light", the narrator proclaimed, "for from humble commonplace oil has come enduring miracles beyond Aladdin's wildest dreams." The film followed a husband and wife through their morning routine, noting all the items they touched and used that had a petroleum base. That included the plastic items—the vinyl seat cushions, his fake-leather shoes, her synthetic silk dressing gown—as well as the fertilizer used to grow their breakfast oranges, the pectin in their jam, the ink in the morning newspaper, and, of course, the petrol in their car.[23]

As went petrochemicals, so went the plastics industry, their fortunes now inextricably linked. (Until the war, coal was a significant source of feedstock for plastics. Post-war, the industry became entirely reliant on oil and natural gas. [64–1, 65–1]) The flow of oil fuelled an entire culture based on consumption of new plastic products. Plastics production skyrocketed 500 per cent in the decade after the war (and has continued to ascend steadily to this day).

The first significant incursion came in durable goods, such as refrigerators, housewares, furniture, textiles, electronics, cars. There was no effort to disguise plastic's presence; it was part of the appeal. "Christmas is more fun at our house with toys made of Styron", ran one of the many Dow Chemical adverts pushing its new brand of polystyrene.

The industry partnered with the press to promote plastic's virtues. A 1946 *Life* magazine piece featured a photo of three children up to mischief: one boy was drawing on the walls, another was trying to set fire to the drapes, while a little girl was dumping a bowl of food onto an armchair. "If this were the usual kind of living room, the children would be doing $150 damage", the caption read. No such problem with synthetics. In 1947, *House Beautiful* ran an elaborate 50-page issue titled "Plastics: A Way to a Better, More Carefree Life"; Plastics, it promised, "are here to free you from drudgery".[24]

These weren't entirely empty promises. Formica counters and vinyl wallpaper were bright, durable, and easily cleaned with the proverbial damp cloth. Wash 'n' wear fabrics like Orlon or Dacron meant no more tiresome ironing. Baby-boom children enjoyed an endless stream of new types of fun—Barbie, Lego,[25] the hula hoop, and Frisbee—and as teens, their lives would be rocked by the new sounds coming from vinyl discs and cassette tapes. The post-war return of nylon stockings thrilled women around the world and sparked riots in several American cities, as crowds mobbed stores to get their hands on—or legs into— the first limited supplies.

Designers were enthralled by the arrival of such accommodating materials. Dream up a shape and some machine could mould or extrude or blow or press it into being in any hue desired (especially as processing technology improved). No need for a chair to have four legs, it could be a one-piece shiny swoop, a bag filled with little plastic beads, a balloon-like inflatable. A dress could be a chain mail of spangles. An entire home could be made without a single right-angle, like the spaceship-shaped "House of the Future" Monsanto created, or Buckminster Fuller's Geodesic dome.[26] Plastic made it possible to break old rules and blow past the innate limitations of natural materials.

23. Shell Oil, *Petroleum: "Oil for Aladdin's Lamp"*, 1949, updated version of the 1933 film version, restored and online (Jeff Quitney): https://vimeo.com/328982142, accessed 30 August 2021.

24. "Plastics: A Way to a Better, More Carefree Life", *House Beautiful*, vol. 89, no. 2 (1947) pp. 121–66.

25. See the object texts on Barbie and Ken, and Lego in this book, p. 135 and p. 138.

26. See text on Buckminster Fuller's Geodesic domes in this book, p. 140.

Susan Freinkel

Medicine was revolutionized by new plastic devices too, like vinyl blood bags and IV tubing, artificial joints and organs, dialysis machines, and cosy incubators for premature babies. (The surgeon who implanted the first artificial human heart said it snapped into place "just like closing Tupperware".[27]) Plastic helped space exploration move from dream to reality.

The flow of new products and applications was so constant, it was hard to remember life pre-plastic. It seemed Tupperware[28] had always existed, alongside faux-mahogany bedside tables, red acrylic tail lights, vinyl siding, polyester slacks, acrylic carpets, Naugahyde chairs, melamine plates, Astroturf, Band-Aids, and countless other synthetic things that filled our lives.

This never-ending smorgasbord of affordable goods vastly accelerated the democratizing effect celluloid had introduced decades before. Everyone could share in the comforts and conveniences of modern life. Just as Yarsley and Couzens had promised, plastics were providing abundance on the cheap. Of course, we all fell for the stuff.

It would take time for a romance that started in the US, Europe, and Japan to spread to the rest of the world. But by the end of the twentieth century as the industry spread, plastics had reached every corner of the globe. Gaining new strongholds and markets, consumers in countries with lesser developed economies sought the benefits polymers had to offer.

"Your future is in the garbage wagon", a speaker told an audience of American plastics' manufacturers in 1956.[29] What he meant was there were only so many cars and couches and refrigerators that people were going to buy. To keep growing, new markets were needed. The obvious solution was disposables. After years of promoting the strength and durability of its polymer products, the industry was taking a fateful turn [70–1].

Soon, many of the long-lasting materials developed to withstand the hardships of wartime were being turned to short-lived peacetime convenience items. The amazingly buoyant and insulating Styrofoam that the US Coast Guard had used for life rafts found new life in picnic cups and coolers. The vinyl-based compound Saran, which had proved so useful in protecting ships and planes from corrosive seawater and air, was redeployed to the short-term protection of leftovers [69–1]. Polyethylene found a booming new career in packaging.

Disposability was a hard sell at first—at least for the generation that lived through the Depression and wartime-scrap drives with the mantra "use it up, wear it out, make it do or do without". When the first coffee-vending machines were introduced, people tended to hang on to the plastic cups to reuse them. They had to learn—and be taught—to throw away.[30]

But we quickly absorbed the lesson, aided by an ever-expanding array of disposable plastic products. Some were designed for single-use, like squeeze bottles[31] [71–1] or plastic bags[32] or disposable nappies (which pundits declared were responsible for the baby boom). Others,

27. Susan Freinkel, *Plastic: A Toxic Love Story*. New York: Houghton Mifflin Harcourt, 2011, p. 126.

28. See the text on Tupperware in this book, p. 130.

29. "Plastics in Disposables and Expendables", *Modern Plastics* (April 1957), pp. 93–94.

30. Heather Rogers, *Gone Tomorrow: The Hidden Life of Garbage*. New York: New Press, 2005, p. 109.

31. See text on squeeze bottles in this book, p. 133.

32. See text on the plastic "T-shirt bag" in this book, p. 136.

like cigarette lighters or ballpoint pens, were short-term versions of items that once might have lasted a person's lifetime. Marketing for the products emphasized their low cost and convenience, like an advert for Scott's disposable plastic cups "at toss-away prices".[33] The pairing of cost and convenience was seductive, so few people thought twice about the consequences of making ephemera from molecules engineered to endure.

In the face of rare resistance, the marketing could get quite aggressive. When the first plastic carrier bags were introduced in 1976, neither grocers nor shoppers liked them, dubious that such flimsy bags could hold as much as the weight of paper. The budding carrier bag industry recognized that to win over consumers, it first would have to win over the stores. One American trade group, the Flexible Bag Association, launched a public relations campaign urging grocers to "Check out the Sack. It's Coming on Strong".[34] Bag manufacturers created educational programmes for grocers, showing them how best to pack the bags and teach store checkout staff not to lick their fingers when pulling a new bag off a stack. But in the end, the bags' success came down to simple arithmetic: plastic was considerably cheaper than paper.[35]

Plastic didn't create the throwaway lifestyle. There were much larger social and economic forces pulling consumers in that direction. The rise of self-serve grocery stores and prepared foods made it all the more important for packaging that would catch a shopper's eye. The growing dominance of cars helped spawn a fast-food nation, with its regalia of wrappers, straws, cups, and clamshells. In the US, the building of a national highway system helped usher in the end of returnable glass bottles, because bottlers were no longer restricted to regional networks. But, single-use bottles got a push in 1971 too when DuPont engineer Nathaniel Wyeth, brother of the famed painter Andrew Wyeth, invented a plastic bottle that could hold pressurized carbonated drinks without exploding. (It only took him 10,000 tries!) Within a few years, we were producing, consuming, and tossing away plastic bottles by the bazillions. Cheap, lightweight plastics, like the polyethylene terephthalate (PET) that Wyeth invented, helped speed us toward a thoroughly linear economy that started at the oil well and ended at the rubbish dump.[36]

It's hard to say exactly when the rapture with plastic began to fade in the US and Europe. It was surely on the wane by 1967 when the American film *The Graduate* came out. College graduate Benjamin Braddock is repelled at the career advice of a family friend: "I just want to say one word… Plastics!" Audiences understood his revulsion. By then, plastic no longer evoked a rich world of possibility, but one as airless and empty as a box of Styrofoam peanuts.

Somewhere along the line—aided surely by the flood of throwaways—we'd stopped seeing plastic as a marvel or a treasure. Indeed, we stopped seeing it at all. It had become so ubiquitous as to be invisible.

33. XiaoZhi Lim, "How Postwar Ads Got Us Hooked On 'Disposable' Single-Use Plastic", *HuffPost US* (16 May 2019), online: https://www.huffpost.com/entry/vintage-ads-plastic_n_5cdb1768e-4b01e9bd3540ffa, accessed 1 October 2021.

34. Quoted from Laura Bix and John J McKeon, *An Industry Takes Shape: The FPA Story, 1950–2000*. Washington, DC: Flexible Packaging Association, 2000, n. p.

35. Freinkel, *Plastic: A Toxic Love Story*, pp. 143–45.

36. See text on PET bottle in this book, p. 143.

Susan Freinkel

37. Edward J. Carpenter and K. L. Smith Jr., "Plastics on the Sargasso Sea Surface", *Science*, vol. 175, no. 4027 (1972), pp. 1240–41; Boyce Rensberger, "Plastic is Found in Sargasso Sea", *New York Times*, 19 March 1972. Reprinted in this book, see pp. 102–03.

38. J. B. Buchanan, "Pollution by Synthetic Fibres", *Marine Pollution Bulletin*, vol. 2, no. 2 (1971), p. 23.

39. Quoted from Patrick G. Ryan, "A Brief History of Marine Litter Research", in Melanie Bergmann, et al. (eds), *Marine Anthropogenic Litter*. Switzerland: Springer, 2015.

40. Gary B. Clark and Burt Kline, "Impact of Oil Shortage on Plastic Medical Supplies", *Public Health Reports*, vol. 96, no. 2 (1981), pp. 111–15, here p. 112.

41. Victor Cohn, "Plastics Residues Found in Blood-streams", *Washington Post*, 18 January 1972, p. 3.

Around the time of *The Graduate*, the first scientific reports of plastic in the ocean were starting to trickle in. Two research biologists from the Woods Hole Oceanographic Institution were conducting a routine sampling of marine life in the Sargasso Sea and were surprised to see hundreds of pieces of plastic, including pre-production pellets, and clumps of oil littering their nets.[37] A British scientist found plastic fibres "in embarrassing proportions" in plankton samples he pulled from the North Sea.[38] On his 1970 Ra expedition across the Atlantic, Thor Heyerdahl noted that "scarcely a day passed without some form of plastic container, beer-can, bottle […] and some other rubbish drifting close by".[39] Meanwhile, researchers from New Zealand to Newfoundland were finding plastic fragments in the stomachs of seabirds, and there were scattered dispatches about sea turtles, seals, and other marine animals being entangled in the nylon fishing lines and nets that had begun to replace jute.

In 1969, an oil rig six miles offshore from Santa Barbara, California, blew out, spewing millions of gallons of crude oil into the ocean. The spill created an oil slick nearly 30 miles wide, killing thousands of seabirds, and fouling miles of coastline. It was the biggest oil spill in US waters up to that point. People were sickened and outraged by the front-page photos of oil-slick-blackened beaches and dead and dying birds. We understood now that Aladdin's magic lamp could blow up in our faces.

That sense of vulnerability sharpened during the oil crisis of 1973–74. For six months, the Arab oil-producing countries embargoed exports to the US and other countries in retaliation for their support of Israel in the Yom Kippur War. Oil prices doubled, then quadrupled, sending shockwaves through entire national economies and disrupting the supply chains of oil-dependent industries, like plastics, which at the time accounted for about 5 per cent of petroleum use in the United States [80–1, 81–1].[40]

Such revelations would help spark the modern environmental movement and awareness of the many ways in which our reliance on oil and plastic was deeply problematic. Not that such awareness diminished our dependence. Production and consumption of plastic would continue to rise and spread throughout the world. In 1979, plastics production surpassed that of steel. The age of plastic had officially arrived, but the phrase had taken on a whole new more sinister meaning. For by then, scientists had begun detecting traces of plastics chemicals in human blood. As a journalist wrote in reporting the first finding in 1972 for the *Washington Post*: "Humans are just a little bit plastic now."[41]

Homo *Plasticus* and the Paradox of Plastic

Nanjala Nyabola

I can't tell you exactly when single-use plastic, in the form of plastic bottles and plastic bags, arrived in Kenya. But I can tell you that it happened within my lifetime. Anyone born as late as the 1980s is old enough to remember when going to the corner shop or the supermarket meant taking out the family shopping basket or a large jute sack—*kikapu* or *gunia* respectively in Kiswahili—depending on whether you were headed to the market for a weekly or monthly vegetable haul. Well into the 1990s, different types of baskets were common even in the capital Nairobi, with women balancing overloaded *vikapu* on their heads or *kiondo* on their backs, pulling taut the single leather strap by leaning forward at their waist. If you forgot your basket, you simply had to carry your shopping in your hands. The only plastics that we regularly interacted with was in sweet wrappers and in the sachets of frozen ice lollies that were ubiquitous in urban communities.

Today, Kenya, like so many countries around the world, is drowning in plastic. Indeed, perhaps no other material has as significant an impact on our relationship to each other and to the natural environment as plastic. By looking at the case of Kenya, and specifically the introduction of single-use plastics, this essay will explore the paradox of plastic, the contradictions of a material so thoroughly incorporated into our daily lives that it has altered our perception of and relation with the natural environment, the detrimental impact of which is devastating and will last for generations.

The increasing popularity of plastics in Kenya began slowly, as corner shops began charging ten Kenyan shillings and then five for carrier bags—the price decreasing as large chain supermarkets began giving them away for free and corner shops tried to retain vital customers. Carrying your shopping in a basket became old fashioned and out of touch. Suddenly, sometime between 1995 and 2005, plastic bags were everywhere. This peaked around 2017 when Kenyans were estimated to use 24 million plastic bags a month.[1]

This period also saw the increasing popularity of plastic bottles. As the urban water quality deteriorated due to economic collapse and severe cuts in public services, plastic water bottles grew common, first in supermarkets and then in corner shops. Hotels would hand them out at conferences, and families that could afford it would buy and dispose of multiple bottles in a day. It was easier and felt cheaper than boiling litres of drinking water, because the municipal water was no longer regularly available, and when it did show up, the city council could not guarantee that it was safe to drink. Until the end of the twentieth century, if you wanted a soft drink in Kenya, you would take your reusable glass bottle to the shop and swap it for a new one—a system that still endures for beers—but today all soft drinks come in single-use plastic bottles.

It didn't help that communities found multiple uses for plastic bottles and bags, creating a difficult paradox of an incredibly useful material

1. BBC News report, "Kenya plastic bag ban comes into force after years of delays", *BBC News* (28 August 2017), online: https://www.bbc.co.uk/news/world-africa-41069853, accessed 15 September 2012.

that is killing us slowly. Plastic bags became central to the hygiene systems in informal urban settlements. In these crowded hamlets of paper and corrugated iron with high insecurity and limited sanitation facilities, "flying toilets" allowed people to urinate and defecate within their own four walls at night and then throw the offending bags onto neighbourhood roofs in the morning. Plastic bottles made it possible for people to buy home brews and paraffin in smaller and smaller quantities, keeping Kenya's prodigious *kadogo* (that is, small quantity, the buying of expensive commodities in small quantities rather than in bulk) economy going. Discarded plastic soon became just as valuable as brand-new plastic, reincarnated multiple times across a multitude of households before winding up in the rapidly overfilling landfill sites all across the country.

Even with this reuse, plastic still eventually ends up in the natural environment as non-biodegradable waste. As late as the 1980s, it was still safe to fish and swim in Nairobi's rivers. Today, Kenyan rivers are choking in plastic. Islands of plastic collect at bottlenecks or bends in the rivers and turn into putrid festering breeding grounds for mosquitoes and other disease-bearing insects. The roofs of informal settlements are littered with it. Plastic is carried in from the high seas and washes in to litter our beaches faster than we can destroy it. In a country known internationally for its natural environment, and in less than a single generation, plastic has gone from a somewhat rare commodity to an incredibly useful material that is simultaneously the bane of Kenya's natural environment.

*
**

Archaeologists argue that East Africa, and Kenya specifically, is the cradle of mankind. In evolutionary terms, the remains of the oldest humanoid species have been discovered in the country, and there are several archaeological sites of major significance dotted across the area. For example, *Kenyanthropus platyops*—living around 3.5 million years ago—was found on the shores of Lake Turkana, the second largest freshwater lake in the country. When giving names to these different species of hominids, anthropologists often connect the name to a key characteristic that distinguishes that particular species from others. So, *Homo habilis* literally means skilful human because it was the first species to use tools, and *Homo erectus* means upright human because this was the first human predecessor to walk upright. Arguably, plastic has had enough of an impact on modern man for this to be considered the age of *Homo plasticus*, and the case of Kenya is a particularly poignant place to start to understand the ways that plastic has transformed and deformed the species.

Certainly, plastic is by many metrics the defining human invention of the last 100 years, the one that has done the most to improve the quality of human life while simultaneously promising to destroy it. The

Nanjala Nyabola

first synthetic plastic was produced in 1907, but for much of the twentieth century, it remained a somewhat niche commodity. However, after World War II, the popularity of plastic exploded, particularly in Western countries. According to *Our World in Data*, annual plastic production grew nearly 200-fold between 1950 and 2015 to nearly 381 million tons a year. Today, plastic is everywhere and in everything, used by everyone; it is in toothbrushes, pens, computers, cars, feminine hygiene products, fabrics, windowpanes, microbeads in facial cleansers, cars, and door handles. No one, however lofty they may feel their environmental credentials are, is living a plastic-free life, and so the twentieth century really did begin the age of *Homo plasticus*.

The big selling point of plastic is that it is a more durable and accessible alternative to other materials. Indeed, the word "plastic" is derived from the Greek word *plastikos*, meaning "pliable and easily shaped", qualities that made it a more sustainable alternative to scarce natural materials. Prior to World War II, far too many common household goods like combs or ashtrays were made from animal products like ivory, whale bone, and tortoiseshell, contributing to the intense hunting of several species.[2] Plastic was supposed to be the better choice for the natural environment. Yet perhaps the inventors of plastic did not predict that our appetite for plastic would so quickly outpace our ability to manage plastic waste, a short-sighted view even if we are being generous. Plastic as a material was created for its durability, but many plastic products designed today are inherently single-use, or our relationships with the items it's now used in have changed so dramatically that we are throwing away what we previously would have used many times.

Feminine hygiene products are an excellent example of how the usefulness of plastic stunted creativity around sustainability and contributed to the ongoing environmental disaster. Menstruation is a fact of *Homo sapiens* life—most people with uteruses bleed. In Kenya's traditional communities, women would often be separated from the rest of their families during their period. Where I come from, my grandmother tells me that there was a dedicated area in the homestead, usually in the hut, that unmarried women in the family shared with a matriarch. At that time of the month, the eldest active woman in the family—a grandmother or an aunt who was in charge of teaching women the cultural and social rites of womanhood—would turn over a mound of loose earth, and the menstruating girl or woman would sit there until her period ended. Other women in the family would bring her food or sit with her to entertain her. The girl or woman would only get up periodically to go and bathe. The boys and men knew it was happening and knew to avoid interfering with women during this time. There was no shame in a natural human process that was a sign of fertility and life.

The British colonization of Kenya brought with it gendered, restrictive, and stifling customs on purity. Anything to do specifically with

2. Thomas Hainschwang and Laurence Leggio, "Characterization of Tortoise Shell and its Limitations", *Gems & Gemology*, vol. 42, no. 1 (2006), pp. 35–52.

women was shrouded in shame and hidden away from the mainstream. But women also began working in offices and attending mixed-gender schools. You couldn't spend a day or two a month sequestered from the rest of society without explanation. So young girls would reuse old fabrics and clothes to fashion sanitary towels, changing them often or simply enduring the stigma of bleeding through their clothes. In Kenya as late as the 1990s, using a pad meant using a maxi-pad—a wad of compressed cotton wrapped in a light fabric that only really worked if your period was light and predictable. They were large, indiscreet nappies that not only infantilized the user but were also difficult to handle and dispose of. Then came the plastic pads and tampons with plastic applicators, and everything changed.

The advent of disposable sanitary napkins undoubtedly solved many problems for girls and women; they are more absorbent, they're smaller and more discreet, and they can address the unwarranted shame that girls and women endure around their period. The plastic objects do a better job of preventing leaks and by extension not just the associated shame but also the damage to your clothes. The aspirational value of being the woman in white riding a horse or a bicycle in the Always commercials is difficult to overstate. But one study found that these premium disposable pads are composed of up to 90 per cent plastic and that a pack of menstrual pads is equivalent to four plastic bags.[3] Moreover, most women will dispose of used menstrual products in a plastic bag.

The first plastic tampon applicator was invented in 1933, and by 1973, 70 per cent of women in the US used tampons.[4] Only the head of the tampon is made from organic material (cotton, whose modern production process is a separate environmental calamity). But modern tampons with applicators are wrapped in plastic, inserted using a plastic applicator, and pulled out using a string reinforced using plastic. In the rest of the world, women are more likely to use sanitary pads, even while the majority of the world's women who live in rural areas still rely on old methods of sequestration and old fabrics. India's National Family Health Survey of 2015–16 found that only 36 per cent of women in India use sanitary napkins, which are at the same time the most frequently used type of feminine hygiene product.[5] Data is scarce in Kenya, but an admittedly small study indicated that 65 per cent of schoolgirls still rely on homemade alternatives to pads, while 75 per cent of women in rural Western Kenya use commercial pads, with premium disposable pads commanding 62 per cent of the market.[6] Basically, women who have money tend to spend it on pads; girls who don't have access to their own money make do with what they have.

Can a material object alter the evolutionary arc of a species? Stone tools made *Homo habilis* distinct from his forebears, because it allowed him to hunt bigger animals and crush open brittle nuts and seeds, thereby enriching his diet and increasing his odds of survival.[7] Objects can change our perception of time by extending the life of

3. Heidi Ringshaw, "Plastic periods: Menstrual products and plastic pollution", *Friends of the Earth* (15 October 2018), online: https://friendsofth-eearth.uk/sustainable-living/plastic-periods-menstrual-products-and-plastic-pollution, accessed 15 September 2021.

4. Alejandra Borunda, "How Tampons and Pads Became so Unsustainable", *National Geographic* (6 September 2019), online: https://www.nationalgeographic.com/environment/article/how-tampons-pads-became-unsustainable-story-of-plastic, accessed 15 September 2021.

5. Aishwarya Upadhyay, "Menstrual Hygiene Day Facts: Only 36 Percent Of The Women In India Use Sanitary Pads During Periods", *NDTV* (28 May 2019), online: https://swachhindia.ndtv.com/menstrual-hygiene-day-facts-26-percent-use-sanitary-pads-periods-34309/, accessed 15 September 2021.

6. "Menstrual Health in Kenya: Country Landscape Analysis. Research sponsored by the Bill and Melinda Gates Foundation", *FSG* (May 2016), online: https://menstrualhygieneday.org/wp-content/uploads/2016/04/FSG-Menstrual-Health-Landscape_Kenya.pdf, accessed 15 September 2021.

7. "Homo habilis", *Smithsonian Natural Museum of History* (last updated 22 January 2021), online: https://humanorigins.si.edu/evidence/human-fossils/species/homo-habilis, accessed 15 September 2021.

Nanjala Nyabola

things in daily use or dramatically shortening it. They can change our relationship to the natural environment by making us less reliant on certain materials and therefore less reverent of them. When the cost of manufacturing objects is mostly in externalities that cannot be quantified in monetary or individual terms, we tend to think that no one is paying for it. If all that happens is that a factory which we never see pumps millions of gases into the atmosphere or a turtle that we have only read about in books chokes on a plastic flip-flop, we may find it hard to connect our actions to these consequences.

And this is so with plastic. No one is saying that plastic doesn't improve our quality of life, but as the case of feminine hygiene products demonstrates, we have simply failed to think about what will happen with the plastic once we are finished with it. Yet plastic has arguably changed our relationship to time, cost, and consequences, even when the evidence of the tremendous harm that the last 50 years have caused to the natural environment is all around us.

*
**

Kenya in particular has a reason to desire the end of the era of *Homo plasticus*—the country's economic dependence on the natural environment for its survival. In 2019, tourism contributed 7.9 billion US dollars to the country's GDP, stagnant from 2018 but the highest volume since 2009.[8] This amounts to 8.5 per cent of the country's GDP, making it the largest part of the country's dominant service-sector economy. Much of this tourism hinges on visiting Kenya's lush and varied landscape, and keeping these areas pristine is not just an environmental imperative but an economic one as well. And plastic also affects agriculture, the largest subsector of the economy. For instance, a study by the National Environmental Management Authority found that 50 per cent of cattle near urban areas had plastic bags in their stomach.[9]

This explains why Kenya took the unprecedented step of banning single-use plastic bags in the country in 2017. It is now illegal to manufacture, sell, or bring them into the country.[10] Anyone found selling, manufacturing, or carrying plastic bags faces a fine of up to 38,000 US dollars (alternatively a four-year prison sentence), or the lesser eight months in prison for "possession". It remains the harshest prohibition of plastics in the world. And in June 2020, the government took prohibition further by banning single-use plastics—bags, bottles, and any other items—within the country's national parks, which amount to 8 per cent of the national landmass. Reusable glass water bottles are now common in supermarkets again.

The results of the bans have been mixed. Yes, there is less plastic in circulation in Kenya than there was before 2017, and that is a net good. Driving through the city, you are less likely to be confronted by errant piles of discarded plastic bags filled with unidentifiable waste. But the

8. Julia Faria, "Contribution of travel and tourism to GDP in Kenya 2009–2020", *Statista* (10 August 2021), online: https://www.statista.com/statistics/1219642/contribution-of-travel-and-tourism-to-gdp-in-kenya/, accessed 15 September 2021.

9. BBC News Reality Check Team, "Has Kenya's plastic bag ban worked?", *BBC News* (28 August 2019), online: https://www.bbc.com/news/world-africa-49421885, accessed 15 September 2021.

10. Ibid.

underlying issues suggest that the victory might be short term and illusory. For one, the reliance on prisons and punishment rather than education betrays a policy failure to communicate the urgency of the plastic disaster in the country and the importance of halting it. Fines and prison sentences are unevenly distributed too, with poor people being more likely to receive harsher punishments than wealthy people. By 2019, about 300 people had been fined and some even sentenced to jail.[11] But paper remains an inconvenient and equally cumbersome alternative with questionable environmental credentials around virgin pulp, and many people are still using plastic in other ways—like hygiene products.

It is worth pointing out, however, that for all of these challenges, Kenya is by no means the most egregious offender when it comes to the manufacture and disposal of plastic. Industrial countries produce far more plastic waste and compound the problem by exporting it to poor countries under the guise of recycling. In 2010, China produced 59.08 million metric tons of plastic waste, while the US produced 37.83 million. In contrast, Kenya only produced 407,506 metric tons. The big challenge is that plastic consumption in poor countries is growing fast while it is not decreasing in rich countries, and poor countries have less capacity to develop elaborate plastic-waste management systems. So according to *Our World in Data*, East Asia and the Pacific mismanage 60.1 per cent of their plastic waste while sub-Saharan Africa mismanages 10.6 per cent of its plastic waste, and North America only mismanages 0.5 per cent of its plastic waste. But crucially, 0.5 per cent of a volume of waste that is larger by an order of magnitude of millions is still a significantly larger amount of plastic waste overall. North American countries simply produce far more waste, so that even 0.5 per cent is far more in absolute terms than the 60.1 per cent in East Asia or the 10.6 per cent in sub-Saharan Africa.

At the same time, the illusion of recycling has been shattered in recent years, with revelations that many of the items dutifully sorted into variously coloured bins still end up in landfill, incinerators, or the ocean. For decades, China was the hub for global recycling, accepting waste from developed countries and turning it into energy by incineration. In 2016, the US exported 16 million tons of waste to China, but 30 per cent of these materials were poorly sorted, and an estimated 1.3 to 1.5 billion metric tons ended up in the ocean.[12] Thus, in 2018, China banned the import of plastic waste from countries that don't meet their standards of sorting and has increasingly been turning to poor countries in Africa and Asia to provide plastic waste for their incinerators. Poor people and poor countries are simply more efficient at sorting waste, because there is an underclass of people who need to keep the materials in use to their end-of-life and who will sort through waste by hand to collect it for resale. Madagascar has built a growing industry around selling its plastic waste to China. Meanwhile, the US still ships over one million tons of plastic waste abroad to countries like... Kenya.[13]

11. Ibid.

12. Renee Cho, "Recycling in the U.S. Is Broken. How Do We Fix It?", *Columbia Climate School News* (13 March 2020), online: https://news.climate.columbia.edu/2020/03/13/fix-recycling-america/, accessed 15 September 2021.

13. Ibid.

Nanjala Nyabola

In 2021, the world was suffocating in a succession of natural disasters: flooding, forest fires, and famines triggered by climate change, all occurring under the cloud of the Covid-19 pandemic. As a species, it should have been an urgent reminder to review and reset our relationship with fossil fuels more broadly, but especially with plastic and plastic waste. *Homo plasticus*' dependence on the material, however, remained unflinching and unwavering. In fact, *Homo plasticus* is distinct from their forebears because of the way plastic has changed our relationship to each other and with the natural environment. It is no coincidence that the world's biggest producers of plastic waste are also the biggest producers of carbon dioxide (CO_2) emissions. Plastic is a by-product of the manufacture of oil, and the consumption of one is intricately connected to the production of the other, and yet it seems to have dampened our instinct for collective survival.

Still, the war on plastic in Kenya is a sign that *Homo plasticus* might be on the cusp of transformation. In Kenya, small companies are producing reusable sanitary products and encouraging the use of environmental alternatives like menstrual cups or reusable period underwear, not just for environmental reasons but also because they are cheaper and more convenient for people who live in remote rural communities. It is still too early to tell if the profound dependency on plastic that has emerged in the last 30 years can be overcome, but you could say that the recent bans and laws are an indication of a society that is ready to make the change.

Countries like Kenya are increasingly working to disentangle themselves from the paradox of plastic, but we need a global concerted effort to make the change stick. Shuffling around plastic waste between rich and poor countries is simply not a sustainable solution. The resistance of richer countries, those with a greater share of the responsibility for the global environmental disaster that plastic is causing, suggests that victory is hardly guaranteed. Faced by the choice between the vast environmental challenges that plastic presents and the convenience that it offers, they are routinely choosing the latter, suggesting that some kind of link between *Homo sapiens* and the rest of the natural environment has shifted. It is hard to imagine another species continuing to return to an object that causes it so much harm and threatens its survival. Other animals commonly learn to avoid trouble, but human beings, allegedly endowed with a higher capacity for rational thought, cannot seem to wean themselves off plastic.

Images of Plastic 1850– Today

40–1 Detail of Smoker's Cabinet (1916) designed by Charles Rennie Mackintosh.

TACHARDIA LACCA

42–1 Shellac is produced by a female scale lac beetle native to South and Southeast Asia. The beetles feed on the sap of certain trees on whose branches they secrete a resinous substance to protect the eggs they deposit. For shellac extraction, the branches are harvested and the lacquer scraped off. Plate from Harold Maxwell-Lefroy, *Indian Insect Life*, Kolkata/Simla, 1909.

Fig. 27.
Dichopsis gutta (Palaquium gutta; Isonandra gutta).

43–1 Branches, leaves, and seeds of *Palaquium gutta* (*Isonandra gutta* and *Dichopsis gutta*) from which gutta-percha is harvested. Illustration from Franz Clouth, *Gummi, Guttapercha und Balata*, Leipzig, 1899. To obtain gutta-percha, the trees were felled, then semicircles were drawn in the bark at intervals of 30 to 50 cm., in whose grooves the gutta-percha milk collected, which could then be turned into a kneadable mass in hot water.

43–2 Page from a photograph album entitled *Products of the Gutta Percha Company, 1860–1869.*

43–3 Etching by George Sala from his book *The Great Exhibition "Wot is to Be"*—a satirical look at the forthcoming Great Exhibition of 1851 in London. The cartoon-like drawing predicts future uses of gutta-percha for ear trumpets, "whales weals", cricket balls, "magical spectacles", "a lady and gentleman manufactured, top to toe, entirely from gutta-percha".

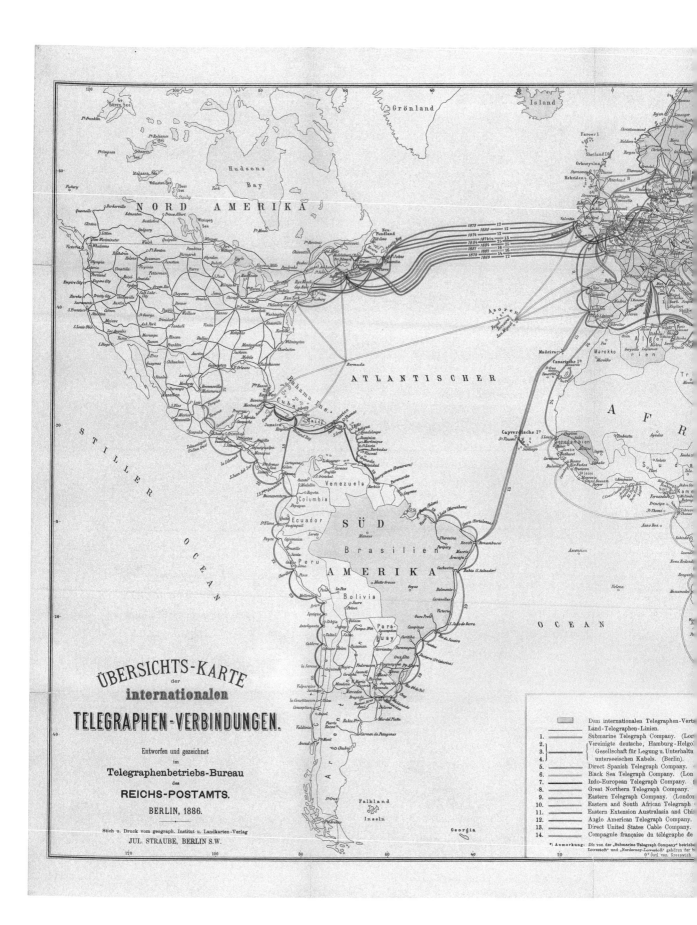

ÜBERSICHTS-KARTE
der
internationalen
TELEGRAPHEN-VERBINDUNGEN.

Entworfen und gezeichnet
im
Telegraphenbetriebs-Bureau
des
REICHS-POSTAMTS.

BERLIN, 1886.

Stich u. Druck vom geograph. Institut u. Landkarten-Verlag
JUL. STRAUBE, BERLIN S.W.

	Dem internationalen Telegraphen-Vert...
	Land-Telegraphen-Linien.
1.	Submarine Telegraph Company. (Lon...
2.	Vereinigte deutsche, Hamburg-Helgo...
3.	Gesellschaft für Legung u. Unterhaltu...
4.	unterseeischen Kabels. (Berlin).
5.	Direct Spanish Telegraph Company.
6.	Black Sea Telegraph Company. (Lon...
7.	Indo-European Telegraph Company. ...
8.	Great Northern Telegraph Company.
9.	Eastern Telegraph Company. (London...
10.	Eastern and South African Telegraph ...
11.	Eastern Extension Australasia and Chi...
12.	Anglo American Telegraph Company.
13.	Direct United States Cable Company.
14.	Compagnie française du télégraphe de ...

*) Anmerkung: Die von der „Submarine Telegraph Company" betrieb...
Lowestoft" und „Norderney-Lowestoft" gehören der b...
0° östl. von Greenwich.

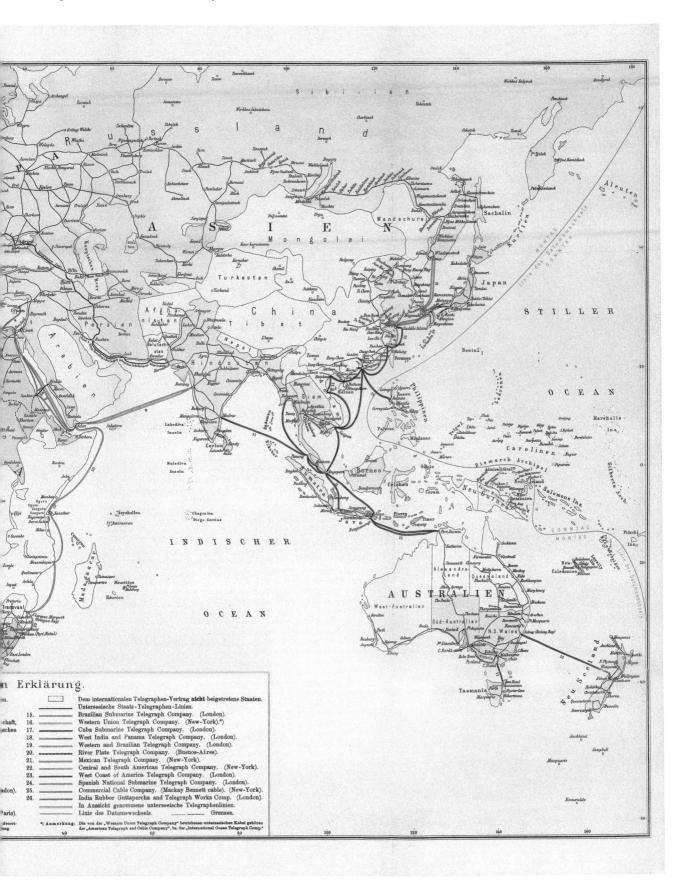

44–1 World map made by Deutsche Reichspost showing international telegraph connections in 1886 and a list of the nations that had already signed the International Telegraph treaty. The sea cabling used to establish this network was insulated with gutta-percha.

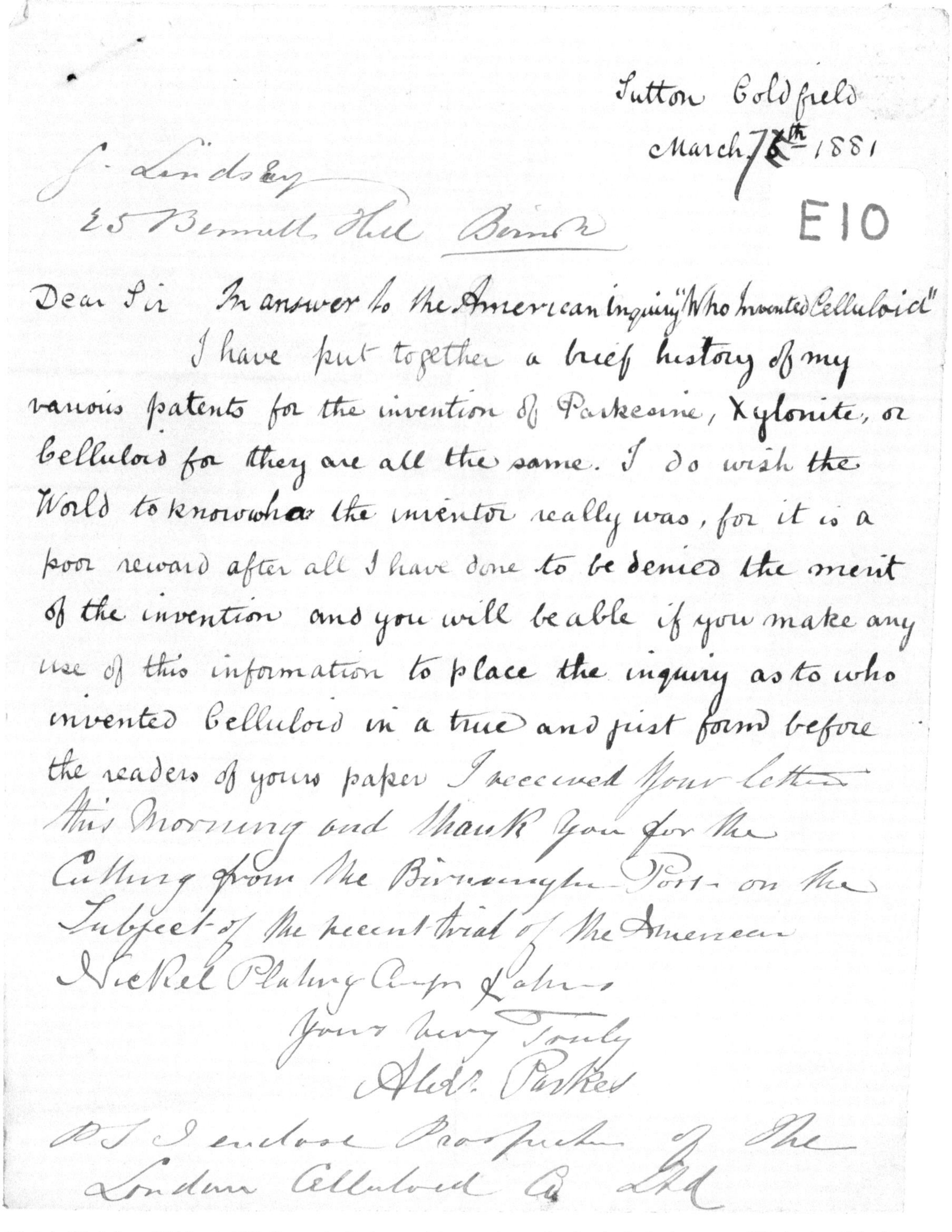

Sutton Coldfield

March 7th 1881

E10

J. Lindsay

25 Bennetts Hill Birm'r

Dear Sir   In answer to the American inquiry "Who Invented Celluloid"
       I have put together a brief history of my various patents for the invention of Parkesine, Xylonite, or Celluloid for they are all the same. I do wish the World to know who the inventor really was, for it is a poor reward after all I have done to be denied the merit of the invention and you will be able if you make any use of this information to place the inquiry as to who invented Celluloid in a true and just form before the readers of your paper I received your letter this Morning and thank you for the Cutting from the Birmingham Post on the Subject of the recent trial of the American Nickel Plating Comp & others

        Yours very Truly
        Alexr Parkes

PS I enclose Prospectus of the London Celluloid Co Ltd

46–1 In this letter of 7 March 1881, Alexander Parkes explains to a journalist that he is the inventor of "Parkesine, Xylonite, or Celluloid".

47–1 Daniel Spill's Ivoride Works in Homerton, London, c. 1870s. Lithograph by Daniel Greenaway. Alexander Parkes assigned his patents to Spill after his Parkesine company had been liquidated. Spill renamed the plastic Xylonite and Ivoride.

A Great Discovery in Photography.

The invention, announced Saturday morning, of a perfectly transparent and flexible support for photographic film by George Eastman of the Eastman dry plate and film company of Rochester, takes the first rank among scientific discoveries. The inventor, who is a brother of Almon R. Eastman of Waterville, is widely connected in Oneida county. The new support is a modification of celluloid and is four one-thousandths of an inch in thickness, and the film of sensitive gelatine upon it is one-thouandth of an inch in thickness. This product may be made in any proportion and wound upon rollers. It removes the greatest difficulty in the way of rapid and satisfactory outdoor work, in providing a perfect substitute for the glass plate. The problem was partially solved when the "stripping film," so called because the gelatine film was stripped from the paper upon which it was exposed and placed upon the glass plate, was invented by the Eastman company. The very difficult work of removing the film from the paper is rendered entirely unnecessary by the new invention. By means of it every operator will be able to develop and print his own negatives by the exercise only ordinary skill. Plans for the extensive manufacture of the support in America and Europe are being pushed.

48–1 Newspaper article of 1889 about a "great discovery in photography": George Eastman's invention of celluloid film, only "four one-thousandth of an inch in thickness" to carry an even thinner film of light-sensitive gelatine.

49–1 Two spools of celluloid with silver-notched margins for developing film, made by Louis Augustin Le Prince in 1888–89.

49–2 Clipping from an early film produced on celluloid, *Il piccolo venditore di ciclamini*, 1909.

50–1 Leo Baekeland's lab in Yonkers, New York, where he invented Bakelite in 1907. Photographed by his first employee Lawrence (Larry) C. Byck in the late 1930s.

50–2 Bakelite advertising leaflet, France, 1930s.

Images of Plastic 1850–Today

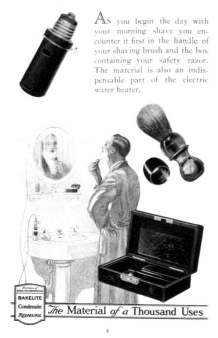

As you begin the day with your morning shave you encounter it first in the handle of your shaving brush and the box containing your safety razor. The material is also an indispensable part of the electric water heater.

The Material of a Thousand Uses

4

AT breakfast, your wife pours you a cup of coffee; the handle she takes hold of on the percolator is made of it. Also the button under the table she presses for service, and the twin-light plug from which are carried the wires to the toaster.

The Material of a Thousand Uses

5

You drive your wife downtown for a morning's shopping. Before leaving, she gives the baby a teething ring to keep him contented while she is away. Of course, it never occurs to her that this childhood necessity is of the same material as the automatic fire extinguisher which stands silent watch over her home.

The Material of a Thousand Uses

6

AFTER lighting a pipe made of it, or perhaps it's a cigarette or cigar holder, you step into your car and can find within reach thirty or more parts, either entirely or partly made of it, such as the radiator cap, timing gear, distributor head, gear shift ball, horn button, etc.

The morning is cold and as you speed along the windy stretches between your home and town you button your overcoat snugly about you. Doubtless you would be surprised to know that the buttons on the coat are also made of this material.

The Material of a Thousand Uses

7

51–1 Bakelite products in everyday life: from the morning shave to breakfast, from the drive to the butcher to the dentist and the office. *Bakelite: The Material of a Thousand Uses*, advertising brochure, 1923.

KUNSTSTOFFE

Zeitschrift für Erzeugung und Verwendung veredelter oder chemisch hergestellter Stoffe

mit besonderer Berücksichtigung von Kunstseide und anderen Kunstfasern, von vulkanisiertem, devulkanisiertem (wiedergewonnenem) und künstlichem Kautschuk, Guttapercha usw. sowie Ersatzstoffen, von Zellhorn (Zelluloid) und ähnlichen Zellstofferzeugnissen, von künstlichem Leder und Ledertuchen (Linoleum), von Kunstharzen, Kasein-Erzeugnissen usw.

mit Unterstützung von Dr. Paul Alexander (Berlin), Dr. Leo Baekeland (Yonkers), Professor Dr. M. Bamberger (Wien), Dr. Ludwig Berend (Wiesbaden), Dozent Dr. Ernst Berl (Tubize), Professor Max Bottler (Würzburg), Professor Dr. E. Bronnert (Dornach i. E.), Dr. Rudolf Ditmar (Graz), Dozent Dr. Karl Dieterich (Helfenberg-Dresden), Dr. Arthur Eichengrün (Berlin), Dr. H. Fuchs (Berlin), Dozent Reg.-Baumeister M. Gerstmeyer (Berlin), Geh. Reg.-Rat Professor Dr. Harries (Kiel), Professor Dr. Alois Herzog (Sorau), Professor Dr. F. W. Hinrichsen (Berlin), Direktor Julius Hübner (Manchester), Professor Dr. A. Junghahn (Berlin), Regierungsrat Dr. O. Kausch (Berlin), Dr. Arthur Klein (Pest), Arthur D. Little (Boston), Dr. J. Marcusson (Berlin), Professor Dr. W. Massot (Krefeld), Dr. Carl Piest (Hanau), Professor Dr. Carl G. Schwalbe (Darmstadt), Professor Dr. Wilhelm Suida (Wien), Regierungsrat Dr. Karl Süvern (Berlin), Dr. W. Vieweg (Hanau), Geh. Reg.-Rat Professor Dr. H. Wichelhaus (Berlin) und anderen Sonderfachleuten

herausgegeben von Dr. Richard Escales (München).

| 1. Januar 1911 | Die Zeitschrift Kunststoffe erscheint monatlich 2mal (am 1. und 15.) in Stärke von 16—20 Seiten. Bezugspreis jährlich M.16.—, fürs Ausland M.18.— ☐ Zusendungen werden für die Redaktion erbeten an Dr. Escales, München, Winthirstrasse 35; für den Bezug sowie für Anzeigen an J. F. Lehmanns Verlag, München, Paul Heyse-Str. 26. | 1. Jahrgang Nr. 1 |

Verfahren zur Herstellung von Kunstleder.

Nach der Patentliteratur bearbeitet von Dr. Oscar Kausch-Berlin.

Unter den in der Industrie ihrer für viele Zwecke vorzüglichen Eigenschaften wegen geschätzten Stoffen nimmt zweifellos das Leder einen hervorragenden Platz ein. Da aber dieser Stoff, dessen Verwendung besonders in der Schuhindustrie sehr erhebliche Mengen erfordert, verhältnismäßig teuer ist und sein Preis andauernd eine derartige Steigerung erfährt, daß das Naturleder für eine ganze Reihe von Verwendungsgebieten wohl kaum noch in Frage kommt, wie z. B. für die Herstellung billiger Lederartikel, Tapeten, Taschen u. dgl., so hat man schon seit Jahrzehnten versucht, diesen wertvollen von der Natur gelieferten Stoff durch billigere und ihm in seinen Eigenschaften ähnelnde Produkte zu ersetzen. Wie aus folgendem ersichtlich, ist die Anzahl der auf die Herstellung derartiger Produkte (Kunstleder) gerichteten Vorschläge ausserordentlich stattlich.

Unter den hier in Betracht kommenden Verfahren sind zunächst diejenigen zu nennen, die als Grundstoff die bei der Ver- und Bearbeitung des Leders sich ergebenden Lederabfälle verwenden.

Das älteste dieser Verfahren ist wohl dasjenige von B. John Bugg (britisches Patent Nr. 2519/1870). Darnach werden Lederabfälle zerkleinert und mit Wasser oder einer verdünnten Gelatinelösung zu einem Brei angerührt. Dieser Brei wird alsdann mit einer konzentrierteren Gelatinelösung gemischt und zwischen Filzen zu Blättern gepreßt, die nach hinreichender Pressung mit einer Gelatinelösung oder einer Mehlpaste behandelt und dann mit Leder oder Lederstücken bedeckt, einem wiederholten Preßdruck ausgesetzt werden.

Ferner will Sörensen (D. R. Patent Nr. 1694) künstliches Leder aus den in großen Massen aus der Lederindustrie herrührenden Lederabfällen in der Weise herstellen, daß er diese Abfälle von allen fremden Bestandteilen befreit, alsdann durch Zermahlen, Zerquetschen, Zerreissen, Schneiden, Raspeln oder Schleifen in eine gleichartig gefaserte Masse überführt, hierauf mit Ammoniakwasser mischt und endlich die so erhaltene gallertartige Masse in Formen preßt oder in Platten walzt und trocknet. Das auf diesem Wege erhältliche Produkt ist hart und steif und besitzt bedeutende Kohäsionskraft, ohne elastisch und wasserlöslich zu sein.

Um dem Produkt auch Elastizität zu verleihen, mengte der genannte Erfinder dem zu verwendenden Ammoniakwasser vor dem Mischen des letzteren mit dem feinzerteilten Leder eine Lösung von Kautschuk bei.

Als geeignete Gemische sind in der Patentschrift genannt für

Sohlen:	25	Teile	Kautschuk
	67	„	Ammoniak
	67	„	Leder
Absätze:	25	Teile	Kautschuk
	80	„	Ammoniak
	80	„	Leder
Einlegesohlen:	25	Teile	Kautschuk
	75	„	Ammoniak
	90	„	Leder.

Nach dem Kneten des Gemisches in einer dichtschließenden Knetmaschine bis zur Gleichmäßigkeit der Masse wird diese in Formen gepreßt oder in Längen ausgewalzt und darnach getrocknet. Während des Trocknens setzt man das Gut verschiedenem, immer waschsendem Preßdruck aus. Fertig gepreßt wird das Fabrikat entweder gefärbt oder lackiert, oder auf andere Weise aufgeputzt.

Ebenfalls Lederabfälle verarbeiten Hawthorn, Friend und Rabley (D. R. Patent Nr. 3128).

Diese behandeln die gereinigten Abfälle mit Natronlauge oder einer anderen alkalischen Lauge von einer Stärke, die sich nach der Dicke oder Natur des zu behandelnden Leders richtet. Ebenso richtet sich die Einwirkungsdauer der Alkalilösung nach der Natur des zu verarbeitenden Leders. Ist das Leder nun gallertartig geworden, so bringt man es nach Befreiung von allen chemischen Stoffen mit Wasser in einen Lumpenwolf, in dem es nach einigen Stunden in eine homogene, breiartige und faserige Masse umgewandelt wird. Der Brei wird in einen Behälter und aus diesem in gelochte Formen gefüllt, in denen er durch Druck oder durch Vakuum seines Feuchtigkeitsüberschusses beraubt wird. Die so erhaltenen einzelnen Blätter werden aus den Formen herausgenommen und zum Trocknen aufgehängt. Die annähernd trocknen Produkte werden, wenn nötig, von neuem in einer Kochsalz enthaltenden Gerbstofflösung gegerbt. Die von neuem aufgehängten und getrockneten Blätter werden zum Schluß zwischen schweren Walzen hindurchgeschickt. Das Kochsalz, von dem etwa 150 g auf 4 l Gerbstofflösung kommen, dient zum Ge-

52–1 Cover of the first issue of the German trade magazine *Kunststoffe*, founded by chemist Ernst Richard Escales, 1 January 1911. The magazine helped to establish the German term for "plastic".

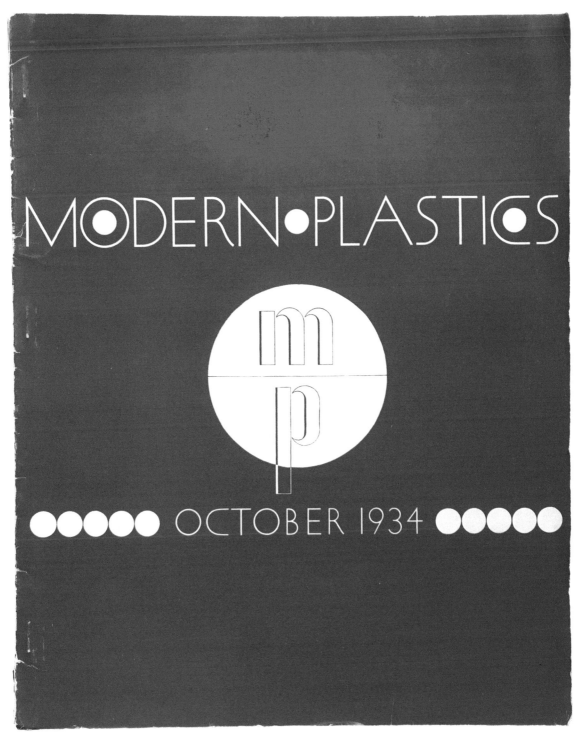

53–1 *Plastics* was the first North American trade journal, founded in 1925. After several name changes, in the fall of 1934 it was renamed *Modern Plastics*. With a restyle by designer Joseph Sinel, its focus was "to interpret to industry at large the growth of the plastic industry".

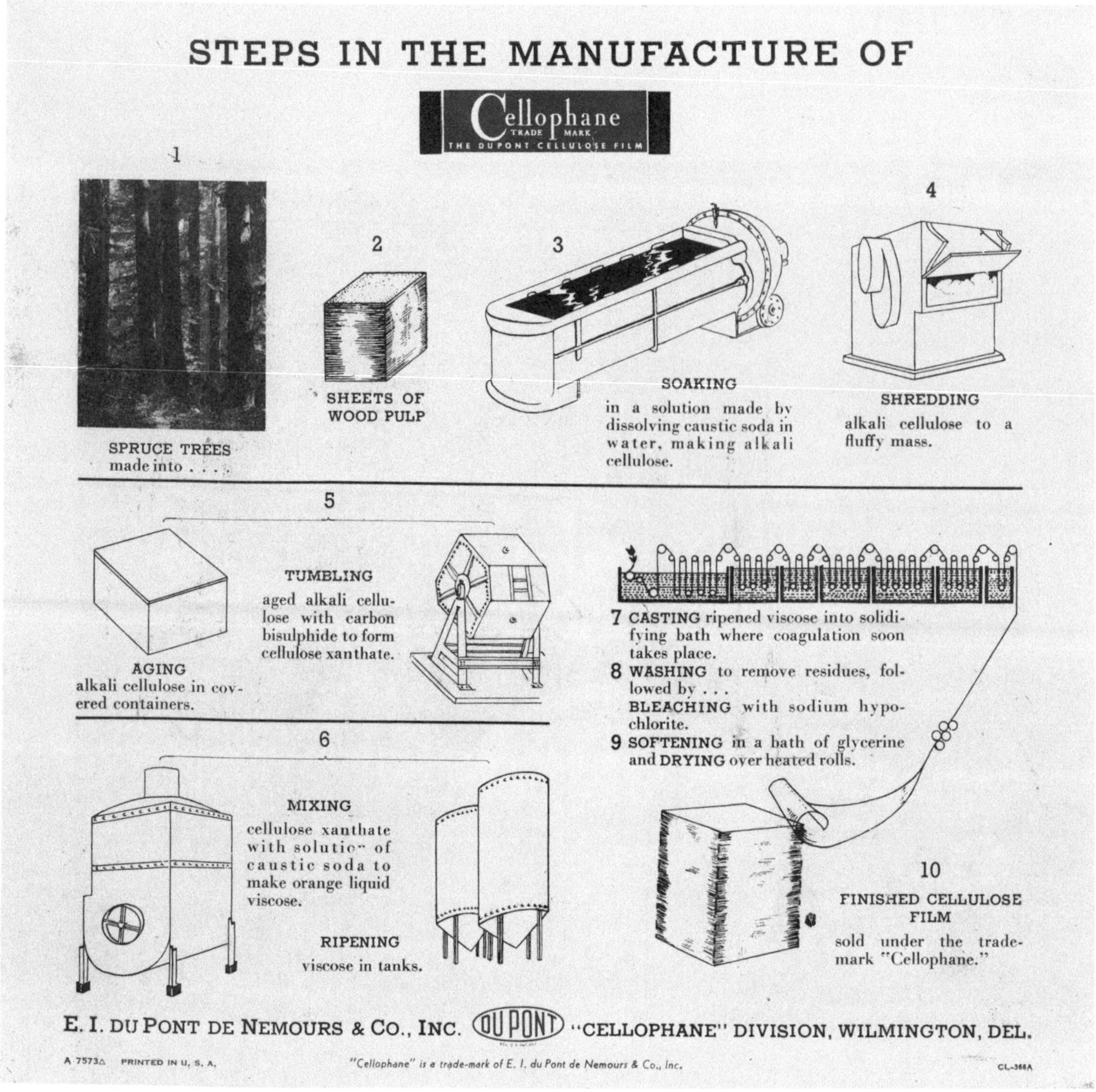

STEPS IN THE MANUFACTURE OF

Cellophane
TRADE MARK
THE DUPONT CELLULOSE FILM

1 SPRUCE TREES made into . . . .

2 SHEETS OF WOOD PULP

3 SOAKING in a solution made by dissolving caustic soda in water, making alkali cellulose.

4 SHREDDING alkali cellulose to a fluffy mass.

5 AGING alkali cellulose in covered containers.

TUMBLING aged alkali cellulose with carbon bisulphide to form cellulose xanthate.

6 MIXING cellulose xanthate with solution of caustic soda to make orange liquid viscose.

RIPENING viscose in tanks.

7 CASTING ripened viscose into solidifying bath where coagulation soon takes place.

8 WASHING to remove residues, followed by . . . BLEACHING with sodium hypochlorite.

9 SOFTENING in a bath of glycerine and DRYING over heated rolls.

10 FINISHED CELLULOSE FILM sold under the trademark "Cellophane."

E. I. DU PONT DE NEMOURS & CO., INC. **DUPONT** "CELLOPHANE" DIVISION, WILMINGTON, DEL.

A 7573△ PRINTED IN U.S.A. "Cellophane" is a trade-mark of E.I. du Pont de Nemours & Co., Inc. CL-366A

54–1 This DuPont advert from 1934 illustrates the manufacture of Cellophane from wood pulp. At DuPont, towards the end of the 1920s, chemist William Hale Charch succeeded in making the material—originally invented in 1912 in Switzerland—moisture-proof.

THROUGHOUT AMERICA many technicians in unrelated industries are busily engaged in independent research to determine the various applications of Dow Ethyl Cellulose to their own products.

Ethocel, to use its more familiar trade name, is a Dow development revealing such versatility that its ultimate possibilities beggar the imagination. There seems to be no end to the useful applications of this colorless, odorless, tasteless, non-toxic member of the cellulose family.

Already Ethocel is available in convenient granular form for producing a great variety of plastic products. Its dimensional stability, resistance to dilute acids and alkalies, to sunlight and to variations in humidity vastly increase its utility in this field.

From work now in progress it is evident that Ethocel will soon be giving new qualities to varnishes, lacquers and fast-dryers. It will shortly add lustre and finish to paper stocks, increase the flexibility and dielectric properties of wire insulation, provide desirable protective finish to textiles. There is scarcely an industry that will not find it offers advantages hitherto unobtainable.

And so the world seems destined soon to be all wrapped up in Ethocel—figuratively and almost literally, too. For, one of its most important developments is Ethocel film and Ethocel foil—materials for packaging and other purposes. Transparent, flexible, non-brittle, and available in various color tints, they offer exceptional strength. For example, Ethocel foil 0.001 inches in thickness tests 10,000 pounds per square inch.

When you find that Ethocel is soluble in a far wider range of solvents than is common with cellulose derivatives, is stable to heat, light and aging, imparts toughness and flexibility to surface coatings, possesses good electrical insulation properties and has low flammability—when these advantages and many others are known, you realize that Ethocel is perhaps the most promising and romantic product Dow has yet contributed to American industry.

THE DOW CHEMICAL COMPANY, MIDLAND, MICH.

Branch Sales Offices: 30 Rockefeller Plaza, New York City—Second and Madison Streets, St. Louis—Field Building, Chicago—1400 16th Street, San Francisco—2260 East 15th Street, Los Angeles

55–1 Advert for Ethocel (ethyl cellulose) by Dow, 1938.

56–1 Still from the 1936 science fiction film *Things to Come* by director William Cameron Menzies and based on a novel by H. G. Wells. The set design with furniture in acrylic glass was designed by László Moholy-Nagy.

56–2 Pontiac's Ghost Car—presented in the General Motors Pavilion at the 1939 New York World's Fair to celebrate the latest in automotive engineering—also demonstrated the possibilities of Plexiglass produced by Röhm & Haas.

Images of Plastic 1850–Today

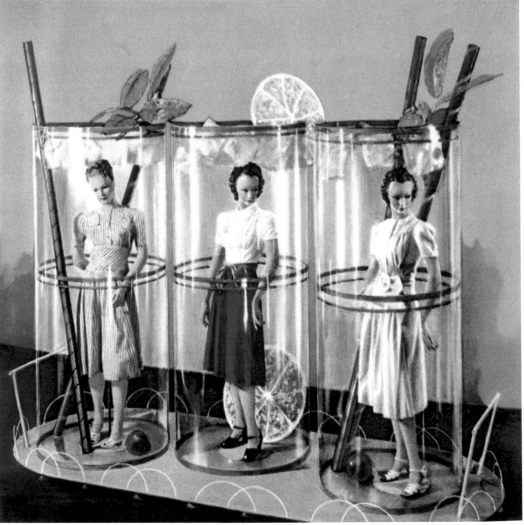

57–1 Page from *Popular Mechanics* magazine of May 1940 depicting Vue-Pak, a transparent plastic packaging material produced by Monsanto.

58–1 Henry Ford and Robert Boyer with the Ford soybean car—a car with a plastic body made from soybean fibre, 1941.

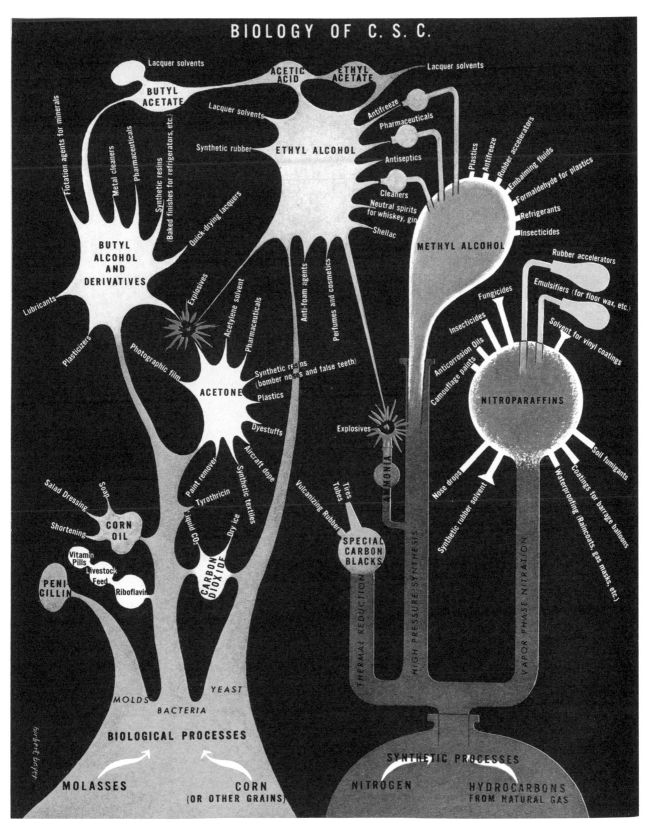

59–1 Diagram by Herbert Bayer illustrating how, at the Commercial Solvents Company, corn, molasses, and natural gases are converted by bacteriological action or chemical synthesis into a variety of chemicals, some of which are used in plastics production. From *Fortune* magazine, October 1944.

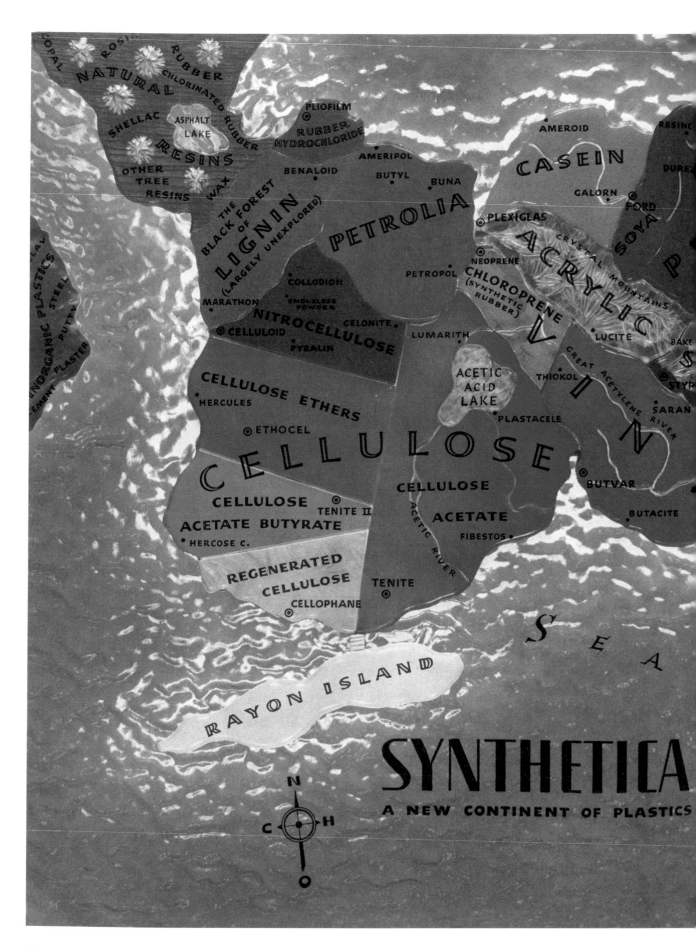

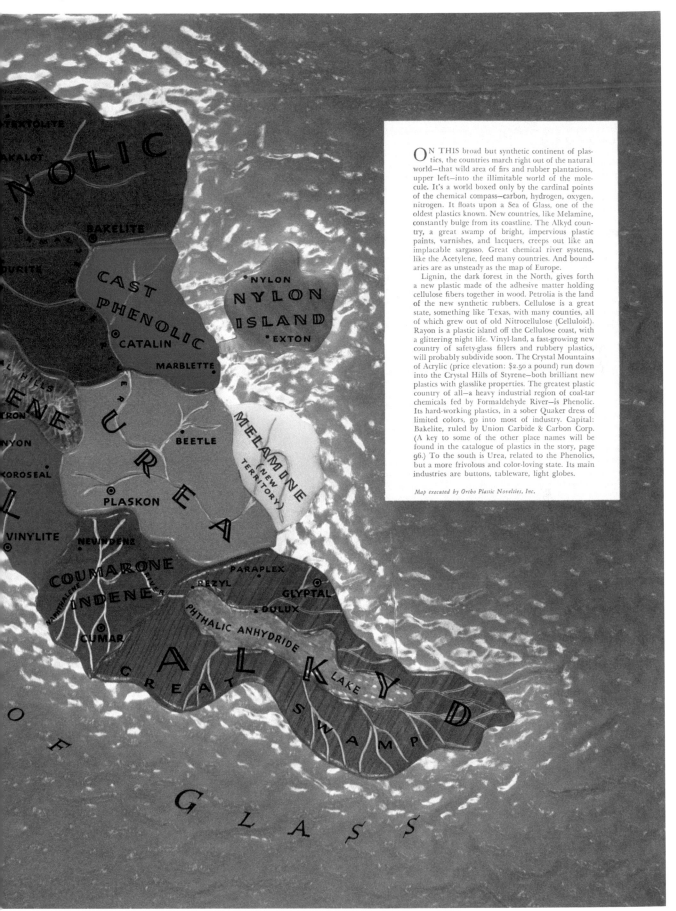

ON THIS broad but synthetic continent of plastics, the countries march right out of the natural world—that wild area of firs and rubber plantations, upper left—into the illimitable world of the molecule. It's a world boxed only by the cardinal points of the chemical compass—carbon, hydrogen, oxygen, nitrogen. It floats upon a Sea of Glass, one of the oldest plastics known. New countries, like Melamine, constantly bulge from its coastline. The Alkyd country, a great swamp of bright, impervious plastic paints, varnishes, and lacquers, creeps out like an implacable sargasso. Great chemical river systems, like the Acetylene, feed many countries. And boundaries are as unsteady as the map of Europe.

Lignin, the dark forest in the North, gives forth a new plastic made of the adhesive matter holding cellulose fibers together in wood. Petrolia is the land of the new synthetic rubbers. Cellulose is a great state, something like Texas, with many counties, all of which grew out of old Nitrocellulose (Celluloid). Rayon is a plastic island off the Cellulose coast, with a glittering night life. Vinyl-land, a fast-growing new country of safety-glass fillers and rubbery plastics, will probably subdivide soon. The Crystal Mountains of Acrylic (price elevation: $2.50 a pound) run down into the Crystal Hills of Styrene—both brilliant new plastics with glasslike properties. The greatest plastic country of all—a heavy industrial region of coal-tar chemicals fed by Formaldehyde River—is Phenolic. Its hard-working plastics, in a sober Quaker dress of limited colors, go into most of industry. Capital: Bakelite, ruled by Union Carbide & Carbon Corp. (A key to some of the other place names will be found in the catalogue of plastics in the story, page 96.) To the south is Urea, related to the Phenolics, but a more frivolous and color-loving state. Its main industries are buttons, tableware, light globes.

Map executed by Ortho Plastic Novelties, Inc.

We Borrowed Their "Nylons" to Make Tires for the Navy

A typical example of B. F. Goodrich leadership in tires

THINGS are happening in the rubber industry.

New ideas are being born which conserve rubber today—and will save you money tomorrow.

In the B. F. Goodrich laboratories they're trying out dozens and dozens of new methods of tire construction. For example, tires are being built with Nylon cord—as well as of cotton or rayon. Nylon has such great strength that it is possible to build tires with less rubber. Passenger car tires built with only two Nylon plies ran far longer than four-ply conventional type tires when tested for ply separation and overload!

And bruise resistance is so great in airplane tires made with Nylon cord that both the Army and Navy have placed orders for this new type tire that saves weight and makes landings safer. B. F. Goodrich was the first company to make and deliver such tires to the U. S. Navy.

So the Nylon your wife is *not* getting in the form of hose is going to war. Some of it is being used in experimental work that may save thousands of tons of rubber. Perhaps one day you may be able to buy B. F. Goodrich Silvertowns for trucks with eight plies instead of twelve, that with weight reduced considerably will run cooler at high speeds —all because of today's wartime developments. *Maybe*, we say. For there are still many problems to be solved:

We do know that when this war is over B. F. Goodrich will offer you far better tires than ever built before Pearl Harbor. Whether they are built with Nylon, rayon, or cotton cord, with crude or synthetic rubber, B. F. Goodrich will be *first* with the new mileage-saving, money-saving developments. In peace as in war, B. F. Goodrich will be "First in Rubber".

In war or peace
B.F.Goodrich
FIRST IN RUBBER

3

62–1 "We Borrowed Their 'Nylons' to Make Tires for the Navy", B. F. Goodrich advert, published in *Life* magazine, 3 May 1943.

63–1 A woman polishes a Plexiglass canopy for military aircraft. Press photo from Röhm & Haas, 1940s.

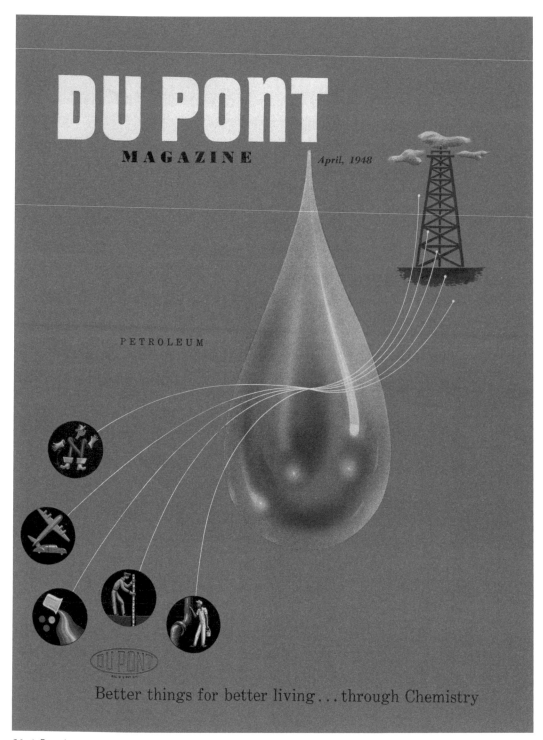

64–1 Petroleum as the basis for all types of plastic. Cover of *Du Pont Magazine*, April 1948.

65–1 With the lecture series and TV campaign *The Magic Barrel*, launched in 1953, DuPont promoted the possibilities of the petrochemicals industry and the production of plastics. *Du Pont Magazine*, October/November 1954.

65–2 "Esso Research works wonders with oil", Esso's advertising for synthetic fibres such as Dacron, 1955.

66–1 Poster for the exhibition *Kunststoffe. Synthetische Materialien und ihre Anwendung. Architektur, Haushalt, Technische Gebiete, Sport, Verkehr* (Plastics: Synthetic materials and their application in architecture, household, technical domains, sport, traffic), Gewerbemuseum Winterthur, 27 September–9 November 1958.

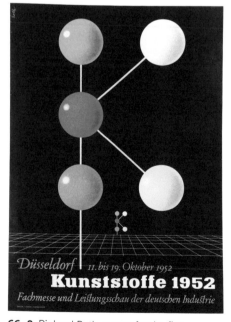

66–2 Richard Roth, poster for the first German plastics fair in Düsseldorf, 1952.

67–1 Cover of Italian magazine *Stile Industria*, no. 7, 1956, published in connection with the exhibition *Mostra internazionale estetica delle materie plastiche* (International exhibition of plastic materials), Milan, in April that year.

Mom says
I'm so fresh
and so clean
(*sometimes*)—
she ought to
wrap me in
Cellophane
to keep me
that way.

Everything's at its best in Cellophane

- Cellophane keeps things clean
- Cellophane keeps things fresh
- Cellophane lets you see what you buy

DU PONT
Cellophane

DUPONT
BETTER THINGS FOR BETTER LIVING
...THROUGH CHEMISTRY
Watch "Du Pont Cavalcade Theater" on Television

68–1 Advert for Cellophane, 1956.

69–1 Saran wrap tinsel on a Christmas tree. Press photo, 1964.

70–1 Photo by Peter Stackpole, staged to illustrate the article "Throwaway Living" about the use of disposable items as a way to cut down on household chores. *Life* magazine, August 1, 1955.

Images of Plastic 1850–Today

71–1 Squeezable bottles made from Polyethylene. Press photo of the British company Cascelloid Ltd, 1960s.

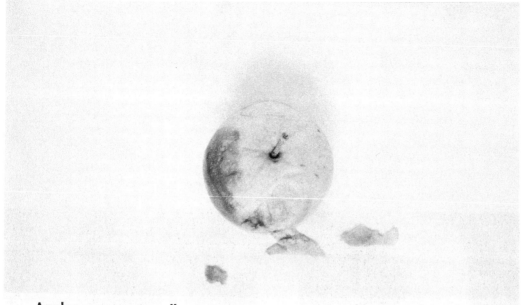

Apples are poor travellers.

So are most products, unless they are properly protected. Shell 'Styrocell' gives you the chance – as never before – to design protective packs that are strong, light, waterproof, colourful and cheap.

For co-operation on any aspect of design in plastics, contact your Shell Chemicals regional office or Plastics Advisory Service, Shell Chemicals U.K. Limited, Plastics & Rubbers Division, Shell Centre, Downstream Building, London SE1. It's all happening . . . in Shell plastics Below fruit tray vacuum-formed from 'Styrocell' expandable polystyrene.

72–1 "Apples are Poor Travellers", advert for Shell Chemicals' Styrocell packaging, published in *Design* magazine, no. 211, 1966.

73–1 Advertising poster for Coca-Cola "Easy-Goer", the first PET bottle introduced in 1975.

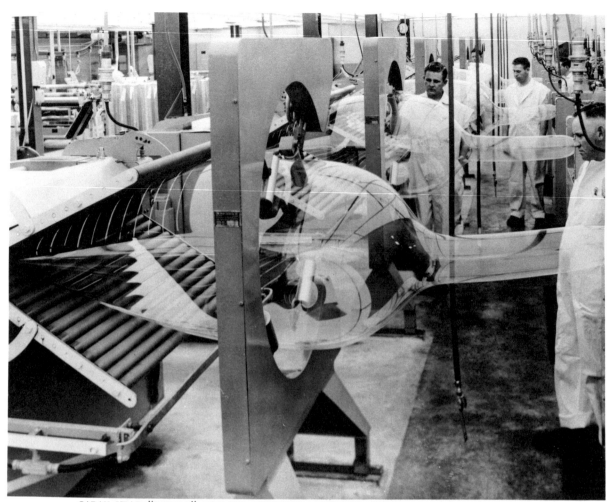

SARAN WRAP "BUBBLE" MIDLAND DIVISION, MIDLAND, MICH.

74-1 Extrusion of Saran wrap bubbles at Dow Chemical Company, 1957.

Images of Plastic 1850–Today

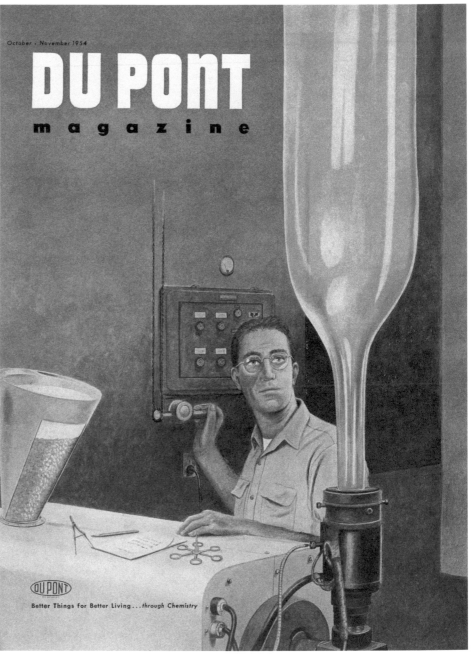

75–1 Cover of *Du Pont Magazine*, October/November 1954.

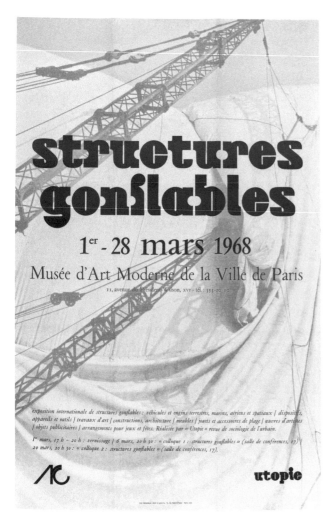

76–1 Poster for the exhibition *Structures gonflables* (Inflatable structures), Musée d'Art Moderne de la Ville de Paris, 1968.

76–2 Still from the film *L'écume des jours*, directed by Charles Belmont, 1968.

77–1 Coop Himmelb(l)au, *Restless Sphere*, Basel, 1971.

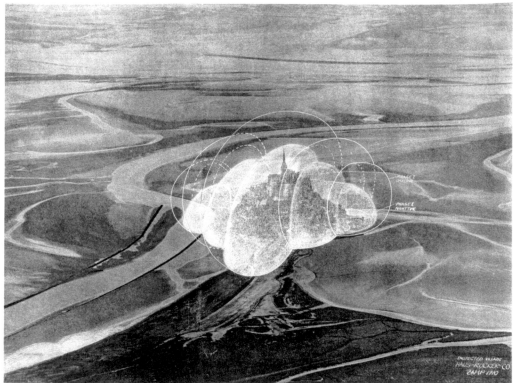

77–2 Haus-Rucker-Co, cover for *Survival in a Polluted Environment*, 1971.

*Wissen Sie
was das ist?*

*Die Geburtsstätte
des ersten
Vollkunststoffstuhles
aus
Duromer-Schaum*

78–1 "Do you know what this is? The birth of the first chair made of Duromer foam", a polyurethane foam made by the company Bayer. Announcement of the new Panton Chair, published in the Fehlbaum company newsletter, 1967.

Images of Plastic 1850–Today

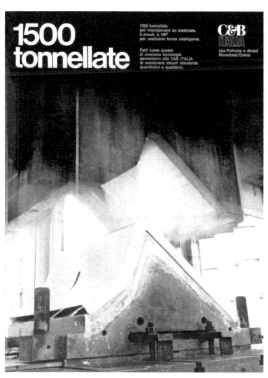

79–1 "1,500 tons to compress a material. Five minutes at 180° to give it back an intelligent form." C&B Italia advert published in the magazine *Domus*, June 1969.

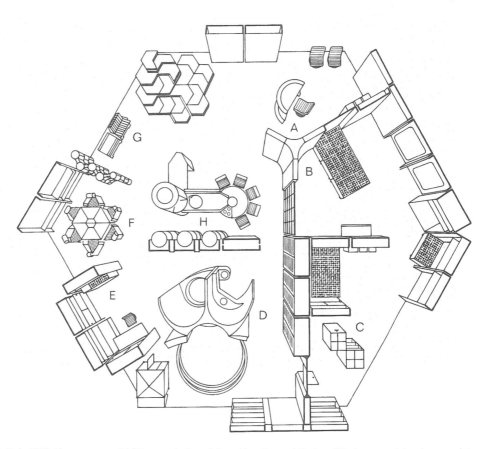

79–2 In 1969, the company BASF commissioned Arno Votteler and Herbert Hirche to each lead research teams to look into the question of housing in the future. The flexible, changeable "Wohneinheit 1980" (Dwelling unit 1980), consisting of modular plastic elements, was exhibited in Ludwigshafen in 1972.

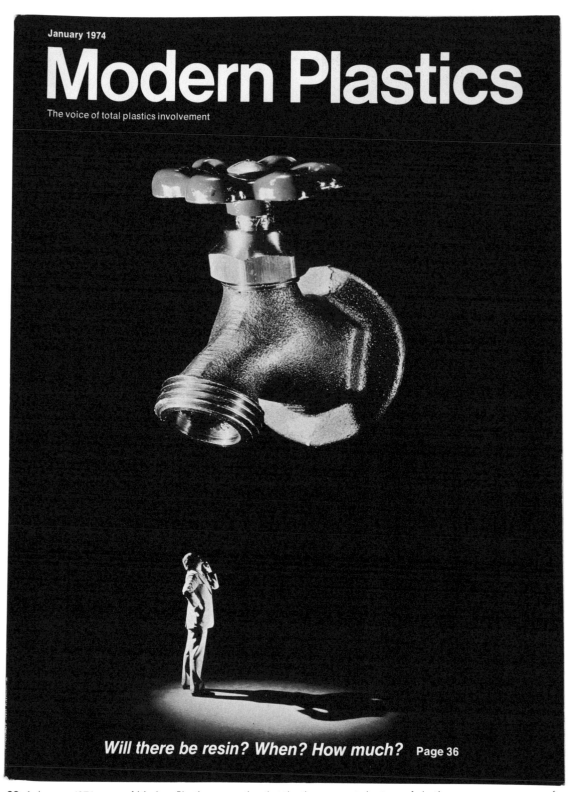

January 1974

Modern Plastics

The voice of total plastics involvement

Will there be resin? When? How much? Page 36

80–1 January 1974 cover of *Modern Plastics* suggesting that the then-current shortage of plastics was a consequence of the 1973 oil crisis.

81–1 Cover of *Modern Plastics*, January 1975.

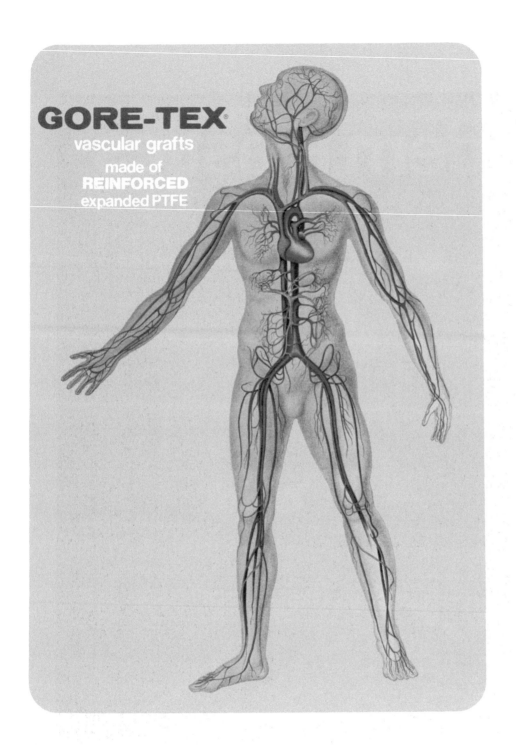

GORE-TEX®
vascular grafts
made of
REINFORCED
expanded PTFE

82–1 Gore-Tex starts producing plastic vascular grafts in 1975.

83–1 Alessi launched its Family Follows Fiction (F.F.F.) collection in 1993.

83–2 Advert of the Swiss watch manufacturer Swatch in 1983, the year the brand launched. In the decade that followed, more than 100 million Swatch watches were sold.

84–1 Charles Moore with a water sample from the North Pacific Gyre ("Great Pacific Garbage Patch"), 1999.

Images of Plastic 1850–Today

85–1 Chris Jordan, CF000313, from the series *Midway: Message from the Gyre*, 2009.

86–1 Mandy Barker, *EVERY ... Snowflake is Different*, 2011.

87–1 "Plastiglomerates", 2013. These found-object artworks stem from a scientific study by geologist Patricia Corcoran, oceanographer Charles Moore, and artist Kelly Jazvac.

06.2018

NATIONAL GEOGRAPHIC

PLANET OR PLASTIC?

18 billion pounds of plastic ends up in the ocean each year. And that's just the tip of the iceberg.

88–1 "Planet or Plastic?", June 2018, with a cover image by Jorge Gamboa, launches *National Geographic*'s long-running commitment to environmental protection.

89–1 Royal Dutch Shell "cracker plant" under construction in Ohio, 2019. In the plant, gas molecules are "cracked" into the chemical building blocks of plastic, to produce more than a million tons of tiny plastic pellets annually.

90–1 Digital advertising flyer (2021) by Break Free From Plastic, a global initiative committed to a plastic-free future.

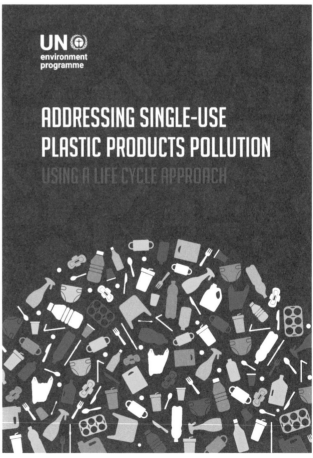

90–2 Cover of the report by the United Nations Environment Programme, *Addressing Single-Use Plastic Products Pollution Using a Life Cycle Approach*, 2021.

91–1 *iSphere* by Plastique Fantastique, 2020, in response to the Covid-19 pandemic.

Reprints

On The Properties Of Parkesine, And Its Application To The Arts And Manufactures

Alex. Parkes, Esq., Of Birmingham

In introducing to this meeting the subject of Parkesine, the author wishes to explain the reasons that led him to the production of this substance.

For more than 20 years the author entertained the idea that a new material might be introduced into the arts and manufactures, and in fact was much required; he succeeded in producing a substance partaking in a large degree of the properties of ivory, tortoiseshell, horn, hard wood, India rubber, gutta-percha, &c., and which will, he believes, to a considerable extent, replace such materials, being capable of being worked with the same facility as metals and wood. This material was first introduced, under the name of Parkesine (so called after its inventor), in the exhibition of 1862, in its rough state, and manufactured into a variety of articles in general use; it then excited the greatest attention, and received a prize medal, Class IV., 1112.

Parkesine is made from pyroxyline [pyroxylin] and oil, alone or in combination with other substances; the various degrees of hardness or flexibility are obtained in the easiest and most expeditious manner by varying the proportions of pyroxyline, oil, and other ingredients.

The pyroxyline used as the base in the manufacture can be made from any vegetable fibre, or fibre-producing grasses, starch, &c., but preferably of waste from cotton and flax mills, old rags, paper makers' half-stuff, or any fibrous waste material capable of being reduced into a soluble condition by the action of acids. To subdue the inflammable nature of this compound, the inventor has introduced several substances such as iodide of cadmium, tungstate of soda, gelatine, chloride of zinc, several carbonates, sulphates, phosphates, and other substances.

The oils employed are some of the vegetable and some of the animal kingdom; they may be used alone or combined, either in their normal condition, or changed by a solidifying agent, chloride of sulphur being preferred, which has the remarkable property of completely solidifying the oils almost instantaneously; but the chemical combination can be modified according to the percentages of the chloride of sulphur employed, which may be varied to meet the exigencies of commerce. These solidified oils, although unchanged by ordinary re-agents, are readily soluble in the author's solvents of pyroxyline, by which means the two ingredients are combined to form one of the descriptions of Parkesine.

Alexander Parkes, excerpted from: Alex. Parkes et al., "On the Properties of Parkesine, and its Application to the Arts and Manufactures", Journal of the Society of Arts, vol. 14, no. 683 (December 1865), pp. 81-84 ff.

The inventor, after much research, labour, and investigation, observed that the solid residue left on the evaporation of the solvent of photographic collodion produced a hard, horny, elastic, and waterproof substance. This led him to employ, in all his experiments, pyroxyline, xylodin, or some collateral matter, as his base for future operations. By the word pyroxyline the author wishes to be understood a less explosive preparation than the more highly converted compound "gun cotton", and his constant aim has been to apply to peaceful industrial purposes a material hitherto only used for military, blasting, and photographic purposes. The solutions of collodion known at the time of his first patent, in October, 1855, were practically unsuited to carry out the manufacture in solid masses and other large forms. This necessitated a new series of experiments, to discover a more economical mode of production, and he found that, by improving the manufacture of pyroxyline, and using different solvents, considerable success was attained [...].

The author commenced his investigations in face of the above-named difficulties, and endeavoured, by more economical methods of manufacturing the pyroxyline or other similar compounds, and by the use of improved and less costly solvents, to produce a new and cheap material; this, after many years of labour and thousands of experimental trials, he has succeeded in doing, and at the present time almost any quantity may be made per day (many tons—simply depending upon the apparatus), at a cost of less than 1s. per lb. and upwards, according to the quality required.

[...]

Having then satisfied himself as to the possibility of producing the material at such a price as would allow of its application in the arts, his next step was, by the combination of various substances, to counteract the inflammability of the material—to produce various colours—and to modify its hardness, toughness, and elasticity; and although from the above statements the object sought to be obtained may appear exceedingly simple, it nevertheless necessitated an enormous amount of application to arrive at the knowledge which has enabled him to produce the specimens which are now laid before you.

[...]

The author had long to contend against the adverse opinions of many, that his efforts to introduce such an article for the general purposes of manufacture, from such expensive materials, appeared hopeless; and even since specimens were shown at the Exhibition of 1862 much discouragement has been thrown in the way of the progress of the invention, by many who had conceived the idea that it would be impossible to produce the material at a price that would render it valuable for general application; the inventor feels proud that he has been enabled to surmount these obstacles in so far establishing a new manufacture which—by the intelligence of practical minds, which he trusts will be devoted to its further development—will, he ventures to hope, eventually become one of considerable commercial importance.

The innumerable trials and investigations required, involved no less than twelve years' labour and an expenditure of many thousand pounds, before the material could be proved to be really of commercial importance; and although this may appear a long time to pursue one object, the author wishes to explain that time has been itself of the utmost importance in developing this manufacture, as it has enabled him to test the effect of time on the material, and also of atmospheric changes, and many other influences; this has proved of great value in arriving at his present knowledge of the material. Although he has been much engaged in other important business he was determined not to relinquish the manufacture of Parkesine until the truth of what he stated at the Exhibition, in 1862—that the material could be produced in some of its qualities at 1s. per lb., was proved—and this he has satisfactorily established by twelve months' practical working. One of the means which enable him to produce Parkesine at a cheap rate, is the employment of waste cotton, in the shape of rags or otherwise, which are procurable at an exceedingly low price, and also the use of improved solvents, and the means of recovering them by special machinery; also the being able to dissolve the pyroxyline in a wet state, thus avoiding the time and great space and risk of drying, which was the practice until recent important improvements enabled him to accomplish this most important desideratum.

When it is necessary or desirable to increase the flexibility or elasticity of preparations of pyroxyline, the author combines therewith oils, solidified or partly solidified by the action of chloride of sulphur, a reaction discovered by him some 20 years ago, when engaged in investigations relative to the cold process of vulcanizing India rubber, patented by him about that time.

[...]

Another important improvement in the manufacture of Parkesine is the employment of camphor, which exercises an advantageous influence on the dissolved pyroxyline, and renders it possible to make sheets, &c., with greater facility and more uniform texture, as it controls the contractile properties of the dissolved pyroxyline; camphor is used in varying proportions according to requirement, from 2 per cent to 20 per cent. Another of the author's improvements for the like object consists in the use of gelatine dissolved in glacial acetic acid.

The author believes he was the first to employ colours in the dissolved pyroxyline. The solvents used in the manufacture of Parkesine are also good solvents of the aniline colours; this gives the great advantage of producing the most beautiful colours in a transparent substance, as well as in opaque or solid masses, as the specimens will show; and when these coloured articles are carved the most exquisite effects are produced, imitating amber, malachite, and many other natural substances; moreover, as the material can be moulded by pressure, the most beautiful works of art can be copied at a very small cost. For many large and cheap applications, as much as 60 per cent of pigments, sawdust or cork-dust, can be introduced with advantage, and thus is produced a beautiful and solid substance, very strong, which can be moulded and turned in a lathe or rolled into sheets, the cost, owing to these admixtures, being exceedingly low.

In all large manufactures the most important point to be considered is the production of raw material, which in many cases fails in quality and supply. The substances the author employs in the manufacture of Parkesine are procurable in any quantity, and having a perfect control in the manipulation of the materials used, he can always ensure a regularity in the various qualities required, thus placing at the command of the artisan a material to be had at all times of a uniform standard quality, which he conceives to be no slight boon to the manufacturer.

There is another important feature in the economy of this material; no loss in manufacture is experienced, every particle, scrap, or dust can be reworked, and the most beautiful effect produced. Specimens will show the effect of some of the waste scraps remanufactured, and it will be readily seen that by careful admixture of colours very pleasing results may be obtained. This is an important advantage over other materials, such as ivory, tortoiseshell, India rubber, vulcanite, gutta-percha, &c., with which this substance is calculated to compete.

The difficulties in manufacturing this material on a commercial scale were at first very great, as before explained, but by steadily persevering, the manufacture is now rendered very simple and rapid. From five to ten tons of Parkesine sheets can now be produced in less time than one ton of India rubber. Sheets of large size and of any thickness, solid blocks, tubing, or other forms, can be made in a few minutes, and from the cheapness and unlimited supply of the raw materials employed, the price of Parkesine will, it is believed, be much less than that of India rubber, ebonite, gutta-percha, ivory, tortoiseshell, and many other materials.

Many specimens on the table have been produced from materials made ten years ago, in which no change or decomposition has taken place; the substance is not affected by seawater, in which it has been immersed for a period of four years without the least deterioration, nor is it softened by heat—like gutta-percha, and, therefore, it is not likely to be affected by the heat of tropical climates.

It can be made transparent, or in any colours, variegated to imitate tortoiseshell, marble, malachite, hard or flexible; can be moulded, shaped, by dies or pressure, turned in a lathe, worked into screws, cut with a saw, planed, carved, engraved, rolled or pressed into sheets, as all the articles in the case before you will clearly show; it is very agreeable to the touch, and is susceptible of the highest polish; it can be inlaid with metals without any injurious effect upon them after years of exposure; it is also invaluable as a waterproofing agent, and can be used as a varnish for a variety of purposes, and as a non-oxidizing agent for the protection of iron ships, &c.

The various stages of manufacture are fully illustrated by the variety of specimens now before you, from the unprepared cotton waste to the ultimate conversion into the finished articles.

Perhaps one of the most interesting facts in connection with this new manufacture is the employment of nitrobenzole [nitrobenzene], or aniline, by which improvement very great facilities are obtained in dissolving pyroxyline, and as these materials are also solvents of India rubber and gutta-percha, a combination of these substances may be readily obtained which will be valuable for many purposes. A specimen of this combination is on the table.

The applications of this material to manufactures appear almost unlimited, for it will be available for spinners' rolls and bosses, for pressing rolls in dyeing and printing works, embossing rolls, knife handles, combs, brush backs, shoe soles, floorcloth, whips, walking sticks, umbrella and parasol handles, buttons, brooches, buckles, pierced and inlaid work, bookbinding, tubes, chemical taps and pipes, photographic baths, battery cells, philosophical instruments, waterproof fabrics, sheets, and other articles for surgical purposes, and for works of art in general.

There is one application of the Parkesine which, as far as experiments have gone, promises to be of great importance, viz., insulating telegraph wires. It will be at once evident, from the nature of the ingredients used, that by simple mechanical and chemical processes, perfect freedom from impurities or foreign ingredients can be attained; a most important property in a material which it is intended to employ for electrical and insulating purposes. The difficulty of producing a pure and homogeneous article, has, there is reason to believe, resulted in the total failure of some thousands of miles of submarine cables and underground wires. Parkesine is placed upon the wire by being forced through a die in successive coatings with the same facility as gutta-percha, and the author believes it to be far less liable to faults than India rubber.

A few specimens of the application of the material for electrical and telegraphic purposes are exhibited. It is, however, deemed advisable to state, that extensive experiments have been made under the direction of Mr. Owen Rowland (Electrician to the late Joint Committee of the Board of Trade and the Atlantic Telegraph Company, appointed to inquire into the construction of submarine telegraph cables, &c.), with a view of ascertaining to the fullest extent the electrical properties and applicability of the material for the above important purposes. The results of those experiments leave no reason to doubt that, on the completion of the necessary machinery, a most excellent and efficient insulator will be produced (and indeed it has already been produced, even by imperfect and inadequate machinery), possessing all the requirements of insulation.

Short specimens of insulated wire (made by hand) in this substance for underground and aerial lines are exhibited, the latter in the form of a multiple cable, according to the valuable patent of Professor Wheatstone, containing an insulated sustaining iron wire, and 79 insulated conducting copper wires, both insulation and protecting envelope being effected by Parkesine, which, possessing great strength and flexibility, and being a non-oxidizing material, is extremely well adapted for the latter purpose. This cable is believed to be capable of bearing its own weight in air for a distance of upwards of one mile.

In its hard and solid form, by virtue of its high insulating and non-oxidizing properties, this material is peculiarly well adapted for electrical instruments, terminal boards, testing boxes, batteries, insulators for poles, and many other philosophical purposes, and the advantages to be derived from the employment of a material which remains free from oxidation under all conditions, will be duly appreciated by electricians and experimentalists in their daily operations and investigations. Its tensile strength is considerably above that of either gutta-percha, India rubber, or any other insulating material. Joints can be made with the greatest facility and perfection.

[…]

It is satisfactorily proved that the more perfect the means adopted for rendering the material free from impurities, the more its efficiency for insulating purposes increases.

This is a reprint of a lecture given by Alexander Parkes to the Royal Society for the Encouragement of Arts, Manufactures and Commerce (Royal Society for Arts, RSA for short) in London on 20 December 1865. The text has been thoughtfully shortened and adapted to modern spelling.

Plastic

Roland Barthes

Despite having names of Greek shepherds (Polystyrene, Polyvinyl, Polyethylene), plastic, the products of which have just been gathered in an exhibition, is in essence the stuff of alchemy. At the entrance of the stand, the public waits in a long queue in order to witness the accomplishment of the magical operation par excellence: the transmutation of matter. An ideally-shaped machine, tabulated and oblong (a shape well suited to suggest the secret of an itinerary) effortlessly draws, out of a heap of greenish crystals, shiny and fluted dressing-room tidies. At one end, raw, telluric matter, at the other, the finished, human object; and between these two extremes, nothing; nothing but a transit, hardly watched over by an attendant in a cloth cap, half-god, half robot. So, more than a substance, plastic is the very idea of its infinite transformation; as its everyday name indicates, it is ubiquity made visible. And it is this, in fact, which makes it a miraculous substance: a miracle is always a sudden transformation of nature. Plastic remains impregnated throughout with this wonder: it is less a thing than the trace of a movement. And as the movement here is almost infinite, transforming the original crystals into a multitude of more and more startling objects, plastic is, all told, a spectacle to be deciphered: the very spectacle of its end products. At the sight of each terminal form (suitcase, brush, car-body, toy, fabric, tube, basin or paper), the mind does not cease from considering the original matter as an enigma. This is because the quick-change artistry of plastic is absolute: it can become buckets as well as jewels. Hence a perpetual amazement, the reverie of man at the sight of the proliferating forms of matter, and the connections he detects between the singular of the origin and the plural of the effects. And this amazement is a pleasurable one, since the scope of the transformations gives man the measure of his power, and since the very itinerary of plastic gives him the euphoria of prestigious free-wheeling through Nature.

But the price to be paid for this success is that plastic, sublimated as movement, hardly exists as substance. Its reality is a negative one: neither hard nor deep, it must be content with a "substantial" attribute which is neutral in spite of its utilitarian advantages: resistance, a state which merely means an absence of yielding. In the hierarchy of the major poetic substances, it figures as a disgraced material, lost between the effusiveness of rubber and the flat hardness of metal; it embodies none of the genuine produce of the mineral world: foam, fibres, strata. It is a "shaped" substance: whatever its final state, plastic keeps a flocculent appearance, something opaque, creamy and curdled, something powerless ever to achieve the triumphant smoothness of Nature. But what best reveals it for what it is is the sound it gives, at once hollow and flat; its noise is its undoing, as are its colours, for it seems capable of retaining only the most chemical-looking ones. Of yellow, red and green, it keeps only the aggressive quality, and uses them as mere names, being able to display only concepts of colour. The fashion for plastic highlights an evolution in the myth of "imitation" materials. It is well known that their use is historically bourgeois in origin (the first vestimentary postiches date back to the rise of capitalism). But until now imitation materials have always indicated pretension, they belonged to the world of appearances, not to that of actual use; they aimed at reproducing cheaply the rarest substances, diamonds, silk, feathers, furs, silver, all the luxurious brilliance of the world. Plastic has climbed down, it is a household material. It is the first magical substance which consents to be prosaic. But it is precisely because this prosaic character is a triumphant reason for its existence: for the first time, artifice aims at something common, not rare. And as an immediate consequence, the age-old function of nature is modified: it is no longer the Idea, the pure Substance to be regained or imitated: an artificial Matter, more bountiful than all the natural deposits, is about to replace her, and to determine the very invention of forms. A luxurious object is still of this earth, it still recalls, albeit in a precious mode, its mineral or animal origin, the natural theme of which it is but one actualization. Plastic is wholly swallowed up in the fact of being used: ultimately, objects will be invented for the sole pleasure of using them. The hierarchy of substances is abolished: a single one replaces them all: the whole world can be plasticized, and even life itself since, we are told, they are beginning to make plastic aortas.

Plastics on the Sargasso Sea Surface

Edward J. Carpenter and K. L. Smith Jr.

While sampling the pelagic *Sargassum* community in the western Sargasso Sea, we encountered plastic particles in our neuston (surface) nets. The occurrence of these particles on the sea surface has not yet been noted in the literature. (We also collected petroleum lumps, which have received attention.)[1] The plastics were collected with a neuston net,[2] one metre in diameter with 0.33-millimetre meshes, towed at two knots (one knot is equal to 1.85 kilometres per hour) on cruise 62 of the *Atlantis II* (27 September–18 October 1971). The particles of plastic were manually sorted from the contents of the neuston tows; they were counted and their weights were determined on shore with a Mettler H-15 balance. Plastics were present in all eleven neuston tows. Their occurrence was widespread, since the distance from the southernmost to the northernmost tow was 1,300 kilometres.

There were, on the average, about 3,500 plastic particles per square kilometre (the range was from 50 to 12,000). This density gives a mean of one particle per 280 square metres and a maximum of one particle per 80 square metres. The weight per square kilometre was from one to 1,800 grams and averaged about 290 grams. The lowest concentrations were observed at stations 10 and 11, as we began to enter the Gulf Stream.

Most of the pieces were hard, white cylindrical pellets, about 0.25 to 0.5 centimetres in diameter, with rounded ends. Chemical weathering and wave action may have produced the pellet shape. Many pieces were brittle, which suggests that the plasticizers had been lost by weathering. Some had sharp edges, which indicates either recent introduction into the sea or the recent breaking up of larger pieces. A few particles (6 per cent by number) were coloured green, blue, or red, and there were also a small number of clear sheet plastics. Several larger pieces could be identified as a syringe needle shield, a cigar holder, jewellery, and a button snap. From the variety of identifiable objects, it was evident that many types of plastics were present. Solvent assays and burning properties of some of the white pellets indicated that they were not polystyrenes, acrylics, or polyvinyl chlorides. Most plastics had populations of hydroids and diatoms attached to their surfaces. We noted the hydroids *Clytia cylindrica* and *Gonothyraea hyalina* and the diatoms *Mastogloia angulata*, *M. pusilla*, *M. hulburti*, *Cyclotella meneghiniana*, and *Pleurosigma* sp. With the exception of the last, these species have previously been observed on pelagic *Sargassum*.[3] Hydroids and diatoms have not been reported on petroleum lumps, whereas goose barnacles *(Lepas)* and isopods *(Idotea)* have.[4]

Originally published in *Science*, vol. 175, no. 4027 (17 March 1972), pp. 1240–41.

1. See Michael H. Horn, John M. Teal, and Richard H. Backus, "Petroleum Lumps on the Surface of the Sea", *Science*, vol. 168 (1970), pp. 245–46, here p. 246; see also B. F. Morris, "Petroleum: Tar Quantities Floating in the Northwestern Atlantic Taken with a New Quantitative Neuston Net", *Science*, vol. 173 (1971), pp. 430–32, here p. 432.

2. Martin R. Bartlett and Richard L. Haedrich, "Neuston Nets and South Atlantic Larval Blue Marlin *(Makaira nigricans)*", *Copeia*, vol. 3 (1968), pp. 469–74.

3. Øjvind Winge, "The Sargasso Sea, its Boundaries and Vegetation", *Report of the Danish Oceanographical Expedition 1910*, vol. 3, no. 34, (1923), pp. 3–24; Edward J. Carpenter, "Diatoms Attached to Floating *Sargassum* in the Western Sargasso Sea", *Phycologia*, vol. 9, nos 3/4 (1970), pp. 269–274, here p. 274.

4. Horn et al., "Petroleum Lumps on the Surface of the Sea", p. 246.

5. George R. Harvey, Vaughan T. Bowen, Richard H. Backus, George D. Grice, "The Changing Chemistry of the Oceans" (forthcoming) [published in]: David Dyrssen and Daniel Jagner, *The Changing Chemistry of the Oceans: Proceedings of the Twentieth Nobel Symposium Held 16–20th August, 1971 at Aspenäsgården, Lerum and Göteborg*. Stockholm: Almqvist & Wiksell, 1972.

The source of the particles may have been the dumping of waste from cities or by cargo and passenger ships. However, no metropolitan dumping occurs in the areas sampled, although some of the southernmost sample areas are within major shipping lanes from Europe to Central America and the Panama Canal. The station closest to land, station 6, was 240 kilometres northeast of Bermuda. Stations 10 and 11, the closest to the continent, were about 900 kilometres southeast of New York City. Plastics have been produced in large quantities only since the end of World War II. The increasing production of plastics, combined with present waste disposal practices, will probably lead to greater concentrations on the sea surface. At present, the only known biological effect of these particles is that they act as a surface for the growth of hydroids, diatoms, and probably bacteria. Many plastics contain considerable concentrations of polychlorinated biphenyls (PCBs) as plasticizers. If the plasticizers have been lost to seawater, as suggested above, the incorporation of PCBs by marine organisms is possible. Polychlorinated biphenyls have recently been observed in pelagic *Sargassum* and oceanic animals.[5]

How Plastic Is a Function of Colonialism

Max Liboiron

Nain is the most northern Inuit community in Nunatsiavut, Canada. It was one of the first places in Newfoundland and Labrador to ban plastic grocery bags in 2009 after villagers saw hundreds of plastic bags snagged on rocks underwater when they went out to fish. The bag ban has appeared to reduce the number of grocery bags in the water, but many other types of plastic bags, as well as food packaging, ropes, building insulation, and tiny unidentifiable fragments, line the shores and waters of the area.

None of these plastics are created in Nain. But since plastics have been found in the Arctic, government and scientific projects are looking to find ways to reduce plastic pollution coming from Arctic communities with initiatives like recycling and treating sewage. But these solutions look at the end of the pipeline—the point after plastics have already arrived, thousands of miles from their point of production, to the Arctic. These types of solutions assume that plastics can and will continue to be produced and imported to the North, and Northerners are supposed to deal with this import of pollution.

Colonialism refers to a system of domination that grants a colonizer access to land for the colonizer's goals. This does not always mean property for settlement or water for extraction. It can also mean access to land-based cultural designs and culturally appropriated symbols for fashion. It can mean access to Indigenous land for scientific research. It can also mean using land as a resource, which may generate pollution through pipelines, landfills, and recycling plants.

Lloyd Stouffer, editor of *Modern Packaging* magazine, declared in 1956 that "The future of plastics is in the trash can." This call for the "plastics industry to stop thinking about 'reuse' packages and concentrate on single use" came at the start of a new era of mass consumption of plastics in the form of packaging, which now accounts for the largest category of plastic products produced worldwide. He saw that disposables were a way to create new markets for the fledgling plastics industry.

This idea assumes access to land. It assumes that household waste will be picked up and taken to landfills or recycling plants that allow plastic disposables to go "away". Without this infrastructure and access to land, Indigenous land, there is no disposability.

Nain does not have an "away". Neither do many other places whose lands are colonized as places to ship disposables or are used for landfills. Nor do many extractive zones that provide the oil and gas feedstock for producing plastics. They're in the Far North, Southeast Asia, and western Africa, among many other places. Some of these same places serve as an "away" for wealthier regions who export their waste. In fact, the term "waste colonialism" was coined in 1989 at the United Nations Environmental Programme Basel Convention when several African nations articulated concerns about the disposal of hazardous wastes by wealthy countries into their territories.

This article by Max Liboiron, an assistant professor at Memorial University and fellow at Science for the People, was originally published in *Teen Vogue* on 21 December 2018 as part of the "Plastic Planet" series of articles about the global plastics crisis.

China has been the place where nearly half the world's plastic waste has been sent to go "away". This ended in January 2018 when China banned the import of scrap plastics and other materials, which will leave an estimated 111 million metric tons of plastic waste displaced. Recycling programmes in the United States and around the world that depend on using other countries' land for waste have slowed down, shut down, or are stockpiling plastics as new solutions are sought. Currently, this next round of waste colonization is headed for Southeast Asia.

Perhaps you've heard that the top five countries responsible for most marine plastics are China, Indonesia, the Philippines, Vietnam, and Sri Lanka. Some of these countries are also the ones receiving a disproportionate amount of plastic waste from other regions. They also happen to be places where waste systems do not mimic American curb-to-landfill systems. These regions are framed in scientific articles, the media, and policy papers as "mismanaging" their waste. This is a perpetuation of colonialist mindset, discourses that have long associated some uses of land as civilized and moral and other uses as savage and deficient. As Cole Harris writes in his book *Making Native Space: Colonialism, Resistance, and Reserves in British Columbia* [2002], historically, when local people were not using land "properly", colonizers would come and take it away to use it "better". In 1876 a white Indian reserve commissioner on Vancouver Island in the region currently known as Canada addressed members of "a Native audience" (Nation unspecified) who were being moved to reserves that were a fraction of the size of their previous land bases. He explained, "The Land was of no value to you. The trees were of no value to you. The Coal was of no value to you. The white man came [and] he improved the land, you can follow his example." Similar mindsets still exist today.

In September 2015, an American-based environmental NGO called the Ocean Conservancy released a report looking for solutions to marine plastic pollution. One of the core recommendations was for countries in Southeast Asia to work with foreign-funded industries to build incinerators to burn plastic waste. This recommendation follows a long line of colonial acts from various entities, from access to Indigenous land to extract oil and gas to make plastics, to the production of disposable plastics that requires land to store and contain them, to pointing the finger at local and Indigenous peoples for "mismanaging" imported waste, and then gaining access to land to solve their uncivilized approach to waste management.

The Philippines arm of the Global Alliance for Incinerator Alternatives (GAIA), a grassroots environmental-justice coalition, rejected the Ocean Conservancy recommendation for incineration. They argued against the health and environmental impacts of burning waste, particularly in countries that struggle with air pollution, such as in China, where increasing protests against waste-to-energy incinerators occur in a context where 69 per cent of current incinerators have records of violating environmental air pollution standards. They talked about the costs of building and maintaining this infrastructure and what it means for debt to foreign bodies. They wrote about how burning waste and plastic perpetuates climate-changing fossil fuel extraction. In short, they argued against the entire system that assumes access to land for come-from-away industry and environmentalists. GAIA's efforts have been uneven. They've helped to successfully block some incinerators, such as one that was planned in Wellington, South Africa, and continue to battle on other fronts.

Disposability is not the result of the bad behaviour of some individuals choosing to buy some things and not others. Consumer choice as a concept makes no sense in many places. In Nain, there is one store. There is one kind of ketchup you can buy. There is one type of lettuce. Both are in plastic packaging because the producers assume that there is a place for that packaging to go. It goes into the dump, where it is usually burned so bears aren't attracted to town, and then the scraps blow into the water. There is no way to behave differently. Bag bans don't eliminate the problem. Degradable plastics made of corn would move the problem onto someone else's land. Shipping Nain's plastics to a recycling plant in Vietnam or even elsewhere in Canada produces pollution and plastic leakage on other lands still. Disposable plastics are simply not possible without colonizer access to land. The end of colonialism will result in the end of plastic disposability.

A Giant Factory Rises to Make a Product Filling Up the World: Plastic

Michael Corkery

The 386-acre property looks like a giant Lego set rising from the banks of the Ohio River. It is one of the largest active construction projects in the United States, employing more than 5,000 people. When completed, the facility will be fed by pipelines stretching hundreds of miles across Appalachia. It will have its own rail system with 3,300 freight cars. And it will produce more than a million tons each year of something that many people argue the world needs less of: plastic.

As concern grows about plastic debris in the oceans and recycling continues to falter in the United States, the production of new plastic is booming. The plant that Royal Dutch Shell is building about 25 miles northwest of Pittsburgh will create tiny pellets that can be turned into items like phone cases, auto parts and food packaging, all of which will be around long after they have served their purpose. The plant is one of more than a dozen that are being built or have been proposed around the world by petrochemical companies like Exxon Mobil and Dow, including several in nearby Ohio and West Virginia and on the Gulf Coast. And after decades of seeing American industrial jobs head overseas, the rise of the petrochemical sector is creating excitement. On Tuesday, President Trump is scheduled to tour the Shell plant.

The boom is driven partly by plastic's popularity as a versatile and inexpensive material that keeps potato chips fresh and makes cars lighter. But in parts of the Appalachian region, the increase is also being fueled by an overabundance of natural gas. It has been about 15 years since hydraulic fracturing, or fracking, took hold in Pennsylvania, which sits atop the huge gas reserve of the Marcellus Shale. But natural gas prices have collapsed and profit must be found elsewhere, namely the natural gas byproduct ethane, which is unleashed during fracking and can be made into polyethylene, a common form of plastic.

This is a place where, right now, plastic makes sense to many people. To the labor union gaining new members. To the world's third-largest company struggling with low oil prices. And to the former government officials who, in seeking to create jobs, offered Shell one of the largest tax breaks in state history. Shell says much of the plastic from the plant can be used to create fuel-efficient cars and medical devices. But the industry acknowledges that some of the world's waste management systems are unable to keep up with other forms of plastic like water bottles, grocery bags and food containers being discarded by consumers on the move.

Studies have detected plastic fibers everywhere — in the stomachs of sperm whales, in tap water and in table salt. A researcher in Britain says plastic may help define the most recent layer of the earth's crust because it takes so long to break down and there is so much of it. "Plastic really doesn't go away," said Roland Geyer, a professor of industrial ecology at the University of California, Santa Barbara. "It just accumulates and ends up in the wrong places. And we just don't know the long-term implications of having all this plastic everywhere in the natural environment. It is like this giant global experiment and we can't just pull the plug if it goes wrong."

The roots of Shell's sleek, ultramodern plant date back hundreds of millions of years, when the area was occupied by a wide inland sea. Over time, the earth shifted and the sea was covered by rock, which compressed all of the dead organisms and sediment that had settled on its watery bottom into rich layers of hydrocarbons, including those that make up natural gas.

Hilary Mercer has spent 32 years traveling the world for Shell — in southern Iraq and in eastern Russia — helping turn those hydrocarbons deep within the earth into energy. These days, Ms. Mercer, an English-born, Oxford-educated engineer, works out of a red brick building in Beaver, Pa.

The plant Ms. Mercer has come here to build is "as big as you get," she said. When finished, Shell's cracker plant — named for the chemical reaction of "cracking" gas molecules into the building blocks of plastic — will consume vast quantities of ethane pumped from wells across Pennsylvania into an enormous furnace. The superheated gas is then cooled, forming solid pellets about the size of arborio rice. The process takes about 20 hours. In Ms. Mercer's view, this is a positive development for the environment. Creating more plastic, she says, helps to reduce carbon emissions by creating lighter and more efficient cars and airplanes. "You have plastic in wind turbines. You have plastic in solar panels." She added: "The ability to do those renewable things relies to some extent on the plastics we produce and the chemicals that we produce. I don't see a contradiction. I see it as part of a journey."

Shell's journey into plastics was driven by a need to generate profits at a time its primary business — oil and gas production — struggles with persistently low prices. It is also a way for the energy industry to hedge against declining gasoline consumption as cars become more efficient or powered by electricity. A big demand for plastic comes from auto manufacturers and for consumer packaging like the ones displayed in a mock grocery store in the lobby of Shell's Pennsylvania offices: plastic cups, diapers and paper towel rolls wrapped in plastic. There's also a stack of brochures in the lobby titled the Shell Polymers "Constitution" that reads: "We are called to Beaver Valley by the desire to be part of something larger than ourselves — to leave a legacy of care, innovation and success for future generations."

Ms. Mercer said the problem with plastic is not its production, but when it is improperly disposed. "We passionately believe in recycling." she said.

Shell is involved in a broad industry effort to clean up the world's largest sources of plastic waste. And in Beaver County, Shell recently donated money to extend the hours of the local recycling center and it supports other initiatives that the company believes will contribute to a "circular economy."

But a circular economy has not yet taken hold in Beaver. Like many areas around the country, the county has had to limit the type of plastic packaging it can accept for recycling because there are relatively few buyers who want to repurpose it. "We are looking for long-term solutions right now," a spokeswoman for the recycling center said.

It was a golden autumn afternoon in Pittsburgh, sunny and mild. The Steelers were in town playing at Heinz Field, and Gov. Tom Corbett got two box-seat tickets to the game. The governor's guest at the game in October 2012 was a Shell executive, who was helping to decide where the company would locate its giant cracker plant. Mr. Corbett took the executive down to the field to meet some of the players. Then the governor walked him out to midfield to stand on the Steelers' yellow and black logo.

"I told him, 'This is where you want to be,'" Mr. Corbett recalled. Shell agreed, and was offered a tax break that was projected to save the company an estimated $1.6 billion.

Mr. Corbett, a Republican, said the plastics plant would bolster communities in an area devastated by the collapse of the steel industry in the 1980s, when the unemployment rate hit 28 percent. "Did you know there is a Steelers bar in Rome?" Mr. Corbett asked in a phone interview. "The reason the Steelers travel so well is because when steel died many people moved away." Mr. Corbett said he believed the Shell plant was only the beginning of the state's plastics boom. He envisions manufacturers coming to Beaver County to be closer to the source of the raw plastic. His successor, Tom Wolf, a Democrat, has been courting more petrochemical development.

Plastics is also solving a challenge for the state's fracking industry. The western part of the Marcellus Shale produces not just methane gas that is used for heating homes and cooking, but also so-called wet gases like ethane. Ethane has a higher energy level, measured in British thermal units, or B.T.U.s, than methane. There are regulatory limits on how many B.T.U.s can be safely used in homes and businesses. So, much of the ethane is stripped out of the gas before the methane is shipped. Plastic production is one of the few viable uses for the ethane, and without it some fracking executives say they would not be able to operate many of their wells.

"What became apparent to me and the governor is that there needed to be an outlet for the ethane," said Patrick Henderson, Mr. Corbett's top energy adviser. He helped persuade the legislature to approve the tax credit, which will benefit Shell and any other petrochemical company that agrees to buy locally produced ethane and create a certain number of jobs. Mr. Henderson now works on the government affairs team at the Marcellus Shale Coalition, which represents the state's fracking industry.

When burned, natural gas emits less carbon than oil and coal, but some people worry that it is preventing the widespread adoption of renewable energy sources and that gas production will only be increased.

The cracker plant itself is allowed by the state to emit 2.2 million tons of carbon dioxide each year, which is the equivalent of about 480,000 cars. Shell says the plant is likely to emit less than that. "Will you eventually see everything renewable? Probably in 100 years," Mr. Corbett said. "But right now natural gas is giving a future to your grandchildren."

Around Beaver County, the cracker plant is creating opportunities for some and deep concerns for others. Kristin Stanzak is the owner of Don's Deli in downtown Beaver, which she opened with her husband in 2016, just before construction of the Shell plant took off. On many afternoons, Ms. Stanzak runs out of sub rolls largely because of the orders from Shell — as many as 100 orders a day. When that happens, she posts a picture of herself on Instagram dressed as Little Orphan Annie that reassures: "The subs will be back tomorrow! Betchyer bottom dollar that tomorrow ... we'll have suuuubsss."

At the local union hall of the International Brotherhood of Electrical Workers, Larry Nelson oversees about 380 electricians working on the plant, including many who have relocated from 28 states. After decades of decline, union membership is growing again. "The guys are tickled pink to be working on this thing," Mr. Nelson said. But there will be only about 600 permanent jobs at the plant, about 12 percent of the construction workers at the site now. A company spokesman said the plant was expected to open "in the early 2020s."

Some residents say their worries about the cracker plant and fracking over the long term are already coming to bear. The impact of climate change, for example, can be seen around Beaver County, and at the plastics plant in particular.

This spring, the huge furnace that will heat the ethane was being shipped on the Mississippi River, but had difficulty fitting under some bridges because the water was so high from flooding. At the construction site, Shell has installed giant tarps to keep the workers dry in the frequent rain, which hit a record last year in Pittsburgh. Some residents see other signs of trouble. At a community meeting Shell held in late June, Barbara Goblick quizzed a company representative about the safety of its pipelines that will feed ethane to the plant. Ms. Goblick explained that she lives in a neighborhood, about two miles from the plant, where a pipeline exploded in September. The fire incinerated a nearby house, and the blast cracked walls and ceilings in Ms. Goblick's home. A landslide, partly caused by heavy rains, is believed to have set off the explosion. The damaged pipeline was not operated by Shell, but a new ethane pipeline is being installed about 800 feet from her house. "I worry it could happen again," she said.

Amanda Miller never paid much attention to the cracker plant rising 16 miles from her home in Franklin Park, an affluent suburb. What made her speak out at a municipal meeting in January was a proposal by a fracking company to drill under a local park with hiking trails and playing fields.

"That was going too far," said Ms. Miller, an occupational therapist at a children's hospital in Pittsburgh. The company's proposal was rebuffed. But it has leases on private land in the area that is rich in ethane. The morning after the meeting, Ms. Miller woke up early to feed her 14-month-old daughter. Her other three children were still asleep. They had just celebrated her husband's grandmother's 99th birthday. In that quiet moment, alone with her daughter, Ms. Miller thought of the plastics plant and the fracking that was increasing around her.

"That's when it hit me," she said. "I looked at her and wondered what is life going to be like when she is 99. And for the first time I wasn't hopeful. I actually started to cry."

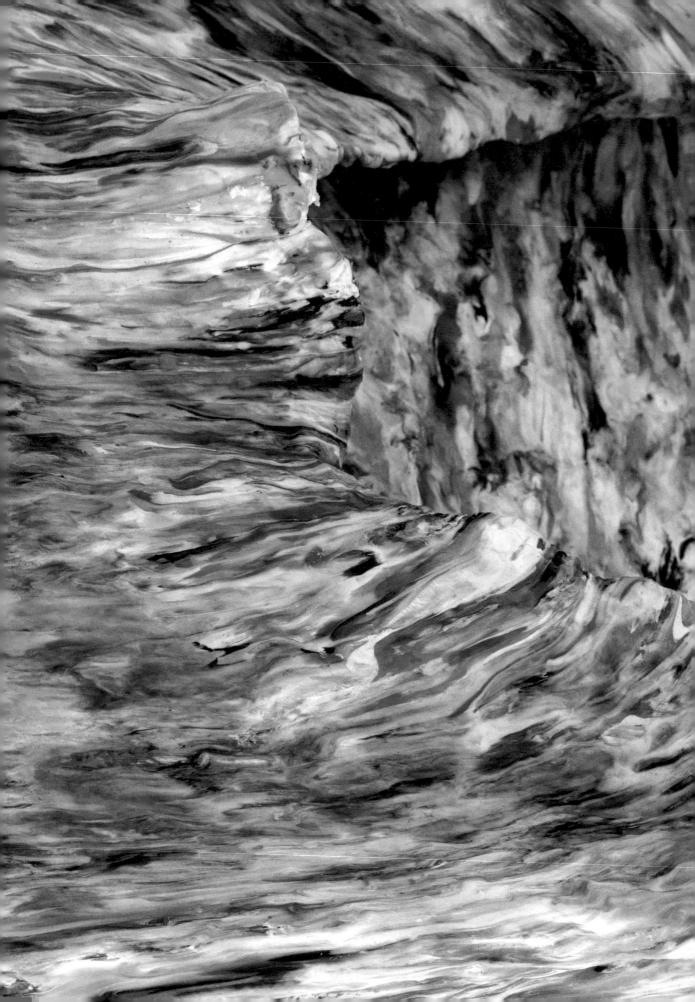

Objects

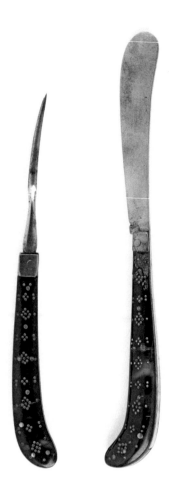

114–1

"Plastic" from Nature

Travel knife and fork, early eighteenth century
Silver and tortoiseshell
14.4 × 1.7 cm (fork), 17 × 2.2 cm (knife)
Victoria and Albert Museum, London. Given by
C. R. Beard

This fine travel knife and fork set, in silver and decorated tortoiseshell, folds at the top of the haft to fit into a leather pouch. Sheets of tortoiseshell featuring delicate piqué work encase the handles. Originally developed in France, piqué work involves inlaying small gold or silver pins into tortoiseshell or similar materials to create a decorative surface design. In eighteenth-century Europe, this type of fine cutlery was often decorated with imported organic plastics such as ivory and tortoiseshell.

Tortoiseshell is a protein-based keratinous material derived from the scales of marine turtles, most commonly the hawksbill (*Eretmochelys imbricata*) as well as the loggerhead (*Caretta caretta*) and green turtle (*Chelonia mydas*). The variegated patterns in warm browns and ambers, as well as the brilliant shine when polished and translucent qualities, have made tortoiseshell a much sought after material for making and decorating luxury objects. Tortoiseshell's thermoplastic properties means that it can be softened either by the application of direct heat or by boiling in salt water. It can then be manipulated, shaped, or impressed. At room temperature, it regains its rigidity. The naturally thin scales of tortoiseshell make it ideal as an inlay or veneer.

Perennially expensive and out of reach to the average consumer, manufacturers often sought to imitate tortoise-shell by staining horn with the characteristic mottled colouring. When man-made plastics were first developed, again, manufacturers sought to mimic tortoiseshell with it. The trade in tortoiseshell was banned worldwide under the Convention on International Trade in Endangered Species (CITES) in 1973, although the hawksbill turtle is still classed as a critically endangered species by the International Union for Conservation of Nature today. CKB

Shaped by Hand

Horn production-process samples, c. 1900
Horn
Each: 7.5 × 4.4 × 0.4 cm
The Worshipful Company of Horners,
Museum of Design in Plastics

Horn is an animal product that comes mainly from cows or sheep in Europe as a by-product of the meat and leather industry. Five samples show the different stages to a finished horn comb, which has been cut into shape, ground down, teeth cut, scouted, and polished. Rivalling plastic as a wonder material, horn is strong and easily malleable and also a good insulator. It can be carved and engraved. In sheet form it is translucent, which meant that for centuries it was used for lantern windows; the word lantern is thought to derive from the late medieval word *lanthorn*.

To work raw horn to a finished object, the horn layer is separated from its bony centre, usually by leaving the core to rot away in water. The horn can then be used in its natural form, such as for drinking vessels, or the natural form can be cut apart, heated, and forced into flat sheets to be worked into objects such as buttons, combs, and cutlery. Finally, the horn is finished and polished.

In the nineteenth century, horn processing was industrialized to meet the rising demand for decorative household items. In Europe, companies like the Aberdeen Combworks imported horn from around the world to produce millions of combs annually.[1] The ready availability of horn and its resemblance to tortoiseshell made it very popular with manufacturers and consumers.

By the mid-1900s, the proliferation of cheaper plastics such as casein and celluloid drastically reduced demand for hornware.[2] Only a few horn companies adapted to working with plastics. Recently, the demand for horn-rimmed spectacles, as consumers look for alternatives to man-made plastics, has enlivened the market again.[3] HP

1. See the Aberdeen Combworks Co. Ltd website, https://www.aberdeencombworks.co.uk/, accessed 19 November 2021.
2. Ibid.
3. Matt Granfield, *HipsterMattic*. London: Allen & Unwin, 2011, p. 150.

115–1

1. *The Electrical World,* vol. 21, no. 8 (25 February 1853), p. 140.
2. John Tully, "A Victorian Disaster: Imperialism, the Telegraph, and Gutta-Percha", *Journal of World History*, vol. 20, no. 4 (2009), pp. 559–79, here p. 569.
3. Siemens website: https://new.siemens.com/global/en/company/about/history/stories/transatlantic-cable.html, accessed 25 November. 2021.
4. Tully, "A Victorian Disaster", p. 568.
5. Ibid., pp. 572–79.
6. H. Thurn, "Guttapercha, ihre Gewinnung und Verwendung in der Seekabelfabrikation", *Kunststoffe*, no. 1 (January 1911), p. 7.

116–1

Gutta-Percha for a Global Network

Boxed examples of five submarine cables
for Direct United States Cable Company's
transatlantic cable England-US, 1874
Siemens Brothers & Co.
Wood, glass, metals, gutta-percha, textiles
12 × 32 × 16.5 cm
Museumsstiftung Post und Telekommunikation /
Museum für Kommunikation Frankfurt

In the late 1840s, engineer Werner von Siemens discovered that the natural plastic gutta-percha could be used to insulate electrical telegraph cables.[1] The first submarine cable was laid between France and England in the early 1850s, consisting of seven copper wires, each wrapped in three layers of gutta-percha. Braided and covered in tarred hemp, these were then protected with iron wire.[2] US entrepreneur Cyrus W. Field succeeded in establishing the first transatlantic cable connection between Ireland and Newfoundland in 1858. In order to connect England and the US directly, the Siemens brothers founded the Direct United States Cable Company in 1873, improving the cables for this purpose.[3] By 1907, around 200,000 nautical miles of submarine cables had been laid by

various companies.[4] The resulting submarine cable network facilitated the world's first ever global telecommunications network.

For colonial powers like Great Britain and the Netherlands, high-speed telecommunications were an essential part of their administrative infrastructure. The tropical rainforests of Southeast Asia were heavily exploited to harvest the gutta-percha required for cabling: in 1875 alone, England imported around one million kilograms of gutta-percha, felling millions of trees for this purpose, and driving them to the brink of extinction in some regions.[5]

Thus, the first issue of the German magazine *Kunststoffe* (*Plastics*), published in 1911, already discussed possible alternatives: "[...] the increase in consumption [has] been so steep in relation to production that the great demand can hardly be met, not even through the most ruthless overexploitation or the fortuitous development of new regions. The gutta-percha issue has developed in such a way that one [...] has to consider [...] under certain circumstances to produce substitutes in the form of artificial products [...]."[6] Nevertheless, gutta-percha was still used for submarine cables up until the 1930s. JE

Plastic Made from Animal Blood

Bell pull in bois durci, 1898
Société du Bois Durci, A. Latry & Cie., Paris, France
6 × 6 × 12 cm
Amsterdam Bakelite Collection

This bell pull was used for attracting the attention of house staff and is typical of bois durci moulded objects. Small with intricate decoration, it had a practical application in the wealthy homes of Europeans in the late nineteenth century. Other objects regularly made from this material at the time included inkwells, pipes, portrait medallions, and decorative plaques.

Bois durci, or hardened wood, is composed of sawdust mixed with an animal protein, such as egg or blood albumen. The substance is heated to the correct consistency before then being poured into a hot mould and left to cure under heat and pressure to create the hard, glossy surface that typifies these objects.

Bois durci was invented by Charles François Lepage in Paris in 1856. In the British patent application of the same year, the material was described as "a new composition if materials which may be employed as a substitute for wood, leather, bone, metal and other hard or plastic substances".[1]

The Société du Bois Durci was set up to produce household items in bois durci, including this late nineteenth-century bell pull. The bell pull handle is decorated with the face of a young woman wearing a fashionable hairstyle—potentially pointing to the aspirations of the person who would have used it. Bois durci was soon superseded by more easily mass-manufactured materials such as Bakelite. JAR

1. Susan Mossman, *Early Plastics: Perspectives 1850–1950*. Leicester: Leicester University Press, 1997, p. 21.

117–1

1. Anon, "Wie eine Schellackplatte hergestellt wird", *Willkommen auf Grammophon-Platten.de*, online: https://grammophon-platten.de/page.php?275, accessed 5 January 2021.
2. Anon, "The History of 78 RPM Recordings", Yale University Library, Irving S. Gilmore Music Library, online: https://web.library.yale.edu/cataloging/music/historyof78rpms; see also Anon, "V-Disc: The Story of the American Military Record Label During WWII", *Save the Vinyl*, online: https://www.savethevinyl.org/v-disc-the-story-of-the-american-military-record-label-during-wwii.html, accessed 5 January 2021.

118–1

Groove by Groove

Record, 1901
E. Berliner's Gramophone Record
Shellac, stone dust, Vinsol, fillers
Diameter: 17.7 cm
Private Collection

The gramophone record was invented by German émigré Emil Berliner in Washington, DC, and registered for patent in 1887. Initially, Berliner used hard rubber for his records, but they quickly showed wear and tear. When he established his company Berliner Gramophone in Philadelphia in 1895, he switched to using shellac instead, a resinous substance secreted by lac beetles *(Kerria lacca)*, native to Southeast Asia. Meanwhile, Berliner's brothers Joseph and Jakob, who had remained in Germany, founded the Deutsche Grammophon company in 1898 in Berlin.

For the recordings, produced mechanically up until 1925, a horn was used to capture the sound and transmitted through air vibrations to a cutting stylus which carved a spiral groove in the record's thick wax layer. Responding to variances in audio frequency, the needle in Emil Berliner's invention would move slightly from left to right. The wax record was then immersed in an electrolytic bath and thus given a copper coating. The resulting metal record, called the "father", was a negative copy with elevated sound grooves instead of engraved ones. A positive metal matrix was then made, called the "mother", so that the sound recording could be played back for the first time. Finally, the so-called "son" negative, copied in turn from the mother, was the stamper matrix used in producing the actual shellac records.

Shellac records only consisted of about 15 per cent shellac. In production, shellac was used as a binding agent for various other materials that were finely ground, heated, and rolled together: stone dust, Vinsol—an early thermosoft plastic—other fillers such as cotton fibre, animal hair, or ground glass, and carbon black, which gave the records their black colour.[1]

While today's long-play (LP) records rotate at 33 revolutions per minute and singles at 45 RPM, shellac records rotated much faster. In 1925, in the early days of electronic sound recording via microphone and amplifier, the standard for shellac records was set at 78 RPM. Due to the shortage of shellac during World War II, the V-Disc label that produced records for the US troops began pressing vinyl records.[2] In the post-war period, vinyl records became increasingly popular due to cheaper production costs and improved sound quality, thus shellac records were quickly replaced with vinyl. JE

An Explosive Start to Early Plastics

Boxed set of Crystalate Billiard Balls, 1920s
Crystalate
Diameter each: 4.7 cm
Vitra Design Museum

Pool became popular with Americans in the 1860s and democratized a game typically reserved for the European aristocracy.[1] But the scarcity in ivory, the natural material used to make billiard balls, presented a problem.

In 1863, games-table makers Phelan & Collender offered 10,000 dollars for the invention of a non-ivory pool ball.[2] Printer John Wesley Hyatt explored countless materials that might replace ivory before landing on a mixture of nitrocellulose and camphor oil, more commonly known as celluloid, in 1868. The material—easily moulded, coloured, and shaped, whilst maintaining many of the material properties of ivory—is considered one of the earliest plastic composites after Parkesine.

Hyatt's lack of chemistry training meant his material choices were unorthodox: nitrocellulose is a combustible compound, which meant on occasion that the billiard would produce a mild explosion on contact, like a gun cap. Hyatt received a memorable letter from a billiard saloon proprietor in Colorado, stating how "instantly every man in the room pulled a gun" when the billiards made their distinctive sound.[3]

Hyatt's process was refined to prevent this problem, and he created the Albany Dental Plate Company selling a wide variety of celluloid-based products. In the 1920s, a variation of Hyatt's original plastic Bonzoline was produced in Britain and marketed as Crystalate. It became the standard for billiard balls by the Billiards Association and Control Council in 1926.[4] LB

1. Mike Shamos, *A Brief History of the Noble Game of Billiards: The Billiard Congress of America* (1995), online: https://bca-pool.com/page/39, accessed 5 September 2021.

2. Kat Eschner, "Once Upon a Time, Exploding Billiard Balls Were An Everyday Thing", *Smithsonian Magazine* (6 April 2017), online: https://www.smithsonianmag.com/smart-news/ once-upon-time-exploding-billiard-balls-were-everyday-thing-180962751/, accessed 1 December 2021.

3. Ibid.

4. Clive Everton, *The Story of Billiards and Snooker*. London: Cassell, 1979, p. 53.

119–1

1. Elizabeth Brayer, *George Eastman: A Biography*. Baltimore, MD: Johns Hopkins University Press, 1995, p. 35.
2. Andy Boyd, "No. 3084: Leo Baekeland and Bakelite", *Engines Our Ingenuity* (podcast broadcast 8 September 2016), online: https:// www.uh.edu/engines/ epi3084.htm, accessed 1 October 2021.
3. "Kodak Box Brownie Camera", *The Franklin Institute* (2003), online: https:// www. fi.edu/history-resources/kodak-brownie-camera, accessed 1 October 2021.
4. James E. Paster, "Advertising Immortality by Kodak", *History of Photography*, vol. 16, no. 2 (1992), pp. 135–39.

120–1

"You press the button, we do the rest."

No. 1A Autographic Kodak Special, 1916
Eastman Kodak Company Ltd
Metal, leather, glass, Bakelite
17.5 × 9 × 15.5 cm
Amsterdam Bakelite Collection

The Eastman Kodak Company was founded in 1892 in New Jersey, USA. Embracing innovations in new plastic materials to produce affordable film cameras and accessories for the mass-market, the company launched a craze for taking "snap shots" and is seen by many as the driving force in popularizing "amateur" photography.[1] A business deal with Leo Baekeland helped Eastman Kodak in the early days: Baekeland eventually sold the rights to Velox—one of the first monochrome printing papers able to be processed under artificial light, which he'd invented—to Kodak.[2]

While the popular 1900 Brownie series camera cost a dollar and catered to those seeking the cheap "snap shot", the slightly larger, more durably encased

Autographic series of 1914 appealed to the more "statement"-oriented type of photographer, which enabled the company to shift into the mid-range market.[3]

This 1916 No. 1A Autographic Kodak Special with its calf-leather-covered body, bellows, and Bakelite side panels was designed to make an impression. Adding to its appeal, photographers could also autograph the space between each photo to document the time or place it was taken.

Kodak dominated the mass photographic market until the turn of the twenty-first century. With innovations such as Kodachrome colour film in 1935 and the Bayer pattern colour filter array for digital cameras introduced in 1976, their well-known slogan—"You press the button, we do the rest"—is synonymous with the photographic age. Many people still refer to family portraits as a "Kodak moment".[4] LB

Furniture Setting the Tone for the Future

Smoker's Cabinet, 1916
Charles Rennie Mackintosh
Ebonized wood, lined with cedar and inlaid with casein
59 × 33 × 58.4 cm
Victoria and Albert Museum, London

The striking colour contrast of this cabinet is achieved using inlaid plastic. Designed in 1916 by Charles Rennie Mackintosh, it is one of the earliest known examples of plastic inlay in furniture. It was created for Mackintosh's final major commission—the remodelling of 78 Derngate in Northampton, home of businessman W. J. Bassett-Lowke. Mackintosh's unifying decorative colour scheme in black and yellow for the hallway of 78 Derngate had a repeating geometric motif of yellow triangles and diamond shapes. It was used for the stained glass, wall-paper, lighting, and on other pieces of furniture.

The top and legs of this small cabinet are inlaid with Erinoid,[1] the trade name for casein plastic, which was produced in Britain from 1912. Casein's tendency to shrink limited its potential applications in furniture design,[2] but this cabinet is nevertheless a predecessor to later examples of furniture that marries wood and plastic. The laminates of brands such as Formica and Micarta were invented in the 1910s, but weren't widely used in furniture until later in the twentieth century. In the 1930s, an advert for Micarta reads: "In sheet form, plastic laminated material is readily applied as veneer on wood, metal, and other materials. Its durability and permanency of finish make it particularly suitable on surfaces that are subjected to severe usage or require repeated cleaning." In this regard, Mackintosh's Smoker's Cabinet is well before its time. JW

121–1

1. Roger Billcliffe, *Charles Rennie Mackintosh: The Complete Furniture, Furniture Drawings & Interior Designs*. Moffat: Cameron & Hollis, 1986, p. 278.
2. John Morgan, "From Milk to Manicure Sets: The Casein Process", *Journal of the Plastics Historical Society*, no. 1 (Winter 1988), p. 12.

122–1

Small-Scale Style in Abundance

Card of buttons, c. 1937
John Templeton (Buttons) Ltd
Acetate, casein, and acrylic on card
30.4 × 20.2 × 2.3 cm
Victoria and Albert Museum, London, Selwyn Slater
Collection. Given by Mr and Mrs John Innell

The small scale and relative simplicity of buttons made them an ideal product for trialling innovative materials. From the late nineteenth century onwards, button manufacturers adopted many of the novel man-made plastics emerging on the market. Styles were divided into those mimicking traditional materials such as tortoiseshell, and those experimenting with the diverse design possibilities of new materials. This sample card showcased the imaginative range of buttons manufactured by John Templeton Ltd. It includes samples in an assortment of man-made plastics—casein, acetate, and acrylic—that have been turned, carved, fret cut, or moulded. Much of the finishing was done by hand until automatic button-making machinery was introduced in the firm's factory in the 1970s.

Buttons are often designed to be decorative as well as functional. In the 1930s, leading Parisian fashion designers such as Elsa Schiaparelli sought to make a feature of fastenings, creating a range of sculptural buttons in brilliant hues and imaginative shapes which were worn decoratively across the body on clothes' designs. A range of materials and techniques to achieve novel button designs accelerated at both ends of the market. At that time, casein's versatility—offering a wide range of colours and patterned effects, and capable of being cut, carved, drilled, embossed, inlaid, textured, bonded, or laminated—made it particularly popular for both haute couture and ready-to-wear fashions. CKB

Milk as Plastic?

Lactoid: The Casein Plastic, brochure issued by British
Xylonite Co. Ltd., 1938
Maurice V. Bennett for Percy Lund, Humphries & Co. Ltd
Paper, printed, metal spiral binding
21.7 × 22 × 0.7 cm
Victoria and Albert Museum, London

Maurice V. Bennett designed this brochure about Lactoid in 1938 for the British Xylonite Co., which had begun manufacturing casein-formaldehyde plastic in 1922. Bennett's spiral-bound design celebrates the style and technologies of graphic modernism—a dramatic mix of photomontage, line illustration, and asymmetric layout.

The first use of casein in solid plastics is attributed to Wilhelm Krische and Adolf Spitteler in the late nineteenth century. It was widely reported to have been caused by Spitteler's cat knocking over a formaldehyde bottle that dripped into its saucer of milk. The following day, Spitteler discovered the milk had curdled into a horn-like substance. The two subsequently founded Vereinigte Gummiwarenfabriken, the first company to mass-produce casein plastic, patented as Galalith in 1899[1] and presented at the 1900 Paris Exposition Universelle.

Casein is produced by drying out the curds of skimmed milk to produce a granular powder, to which water is added. It is then heated and pressed into sheets, blocks, or extruded rods and placed into formalin "hardening baths" for stabilization.[2] In Britain, it was manufactured in 1914 under the trade name Erinoid and exhibited at the British Industries Fair (1915), where a captivated Queen Mary ordered several pieces of Erinoid jewellery.[3]

Art and Industry (1938) hailed it "a most amazing material", drawing attention to its chameleonic qualities. Able to imitate rare materials, such as tortoiseshell and ivory, it could be moulded, polished, drilled, stamped, and printed upon, suitable for the mass production of fountain pens and spectacle frames, dressing table ware, lipstick holders, decorative buttons, and knitting needles.[4] This innovative plastic democratized consumer goods and culture, making these desirable products affordable. SJ

123–1

1. Kat Arney, "A Cat Turned Milk into Popular Plastic", *Chemistry World* (28 June 2018), online: https://www.scientificamerican.com/article/a-cat-turned-milk-into-popular-plastic/, accessed 5 November 2021.
2. Dr. Harry Barron, "Milk as a Plastic", *Art and Industry*, vol. 25, no. 148 (1938), pp. 148–49.
3. British Plastics Federation, "A History of Plastics. 1900–1929 – Early Synthetics, Casein, Bakelite, Ureas", online: https://www.bpf.co.uk/plastipedia/plastics_history/default.aspx, accessed 5 November 2021.
4. Barron, "Milk as a Plastic", p. 148.

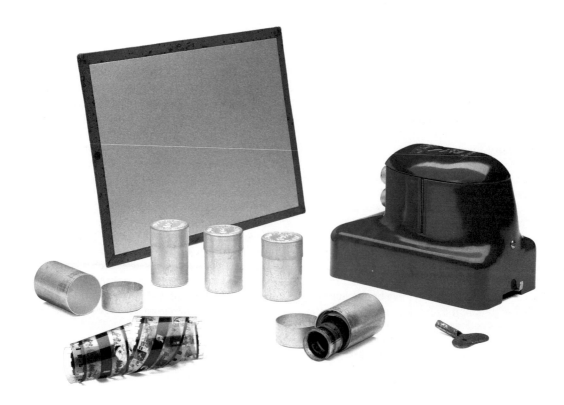

124–1

Promoting Plastics through Child's Play

Dux Kino film projector, 1935–39
Markes GmbH & Co
Compression-moulded phenol-formaldehyde resin
(Bakelite), metal, cellulose acetate, aluminium, cardboard
Projector: 12 × 9 × 7 cm; Screen: 14 × 20.4 cm
Victoria and Albert Museum, London. Given by
Mrs P. F. D. Wallis

This child's tabletop film projector is operated manually
via an internal clockwork mechanism. The 35-mm film
rolls are fed through a narrow slot on the projector's left
side, which is lit up by a battery-powered light. The film
carries two horizontal rows of pictures that are projected
alternately on the accompanying screen by an oscillating
shutter which moves between the two projection lenses.

The streamlined projector housing is moulded in dark-red
Bakelite, while the film rolls are made from a recent innovation—cellulose acetate film. This new plastic material,
invented by Henry and Camille Dreyfus in Basel in the
1910s, became known for its non-flammability (in contrast
to cellulose nitrate film).

Dating from the 1930s, the Dux Kino came with a small
screen, making it possible for children to play at recrea-
ting a cinema, and reflecting a time when cinema-going
was fast becoming the most popular form of entertain-
ment; audiences were flocking in droves to the newly
built film theatres. As a product, this German-made film
projector is an early example of the way innovations in
plastics targeted children's play to build both acceptance
and a new market for plastic products. JAR

A Rival for Silk Stockings: Synthetic's Debut

Stockings, late 1940s
Polyamide (knitted)
99 × 17.4 cm
Victoria and Albert Museum, London. Given by
Ms J Easton

Nylon stockings mark the beginning of the fully synthetic revolution in fashion and textiles. The production of synthetic fibres has grown exponentially in this vein since the late 1930s, and now accounts for around 63 per cent of all textiles produced today.[1]

Nylon, a generic name for a type of polyamide thermoplastic, was the first synthetic fibre engineered in a laboratory from petroleum and coal derivatives. The chemical process for "nylon 6/6" (the "6/6" relating to the number of carbon atoms in its structure) was first patented by chemist Wallace Carothers (1896–1937) at the US firm DuPont in 1935. After refinement over several years, it was launched publicly with great fanfare in October 1938. US news reports described the fibre as "strong as steel, yet fine as a spider's web".[2] Following DuPont's release, in 1939 chemist Paul Schlack (1897–1987) at IG Farben in Germany developed "nylon 6", known commercially as Perlon. It reproduced (in some aspects improving upon) the properties of DuPont's nylon 6/6 without violating the patent.[3]

Initially, its uses included toothbrush bristles, fishing line, and suture thread, but its most notable commercial use was in the form of stockings. The thermoplastic properties of nylon meant that stockings could be permanently moulded to a desired shape, which would not be impacted by wear or washing. As one reporter put it: "what more could one wish for in a stocking?"[4]

Nylon production was diverted for military use during World War II (see entry p. 129). In Britain, limited production and a focus on exports meant that nylon stockings remained difficult to obtain until at least 1948.

This prized pair of stockings, featuring delicate diamante ankle decorations, undoubtedly would have been highly sought after for formal evening wear. The reinforced welt, toes, and heels promised longevity. CKB

125–1

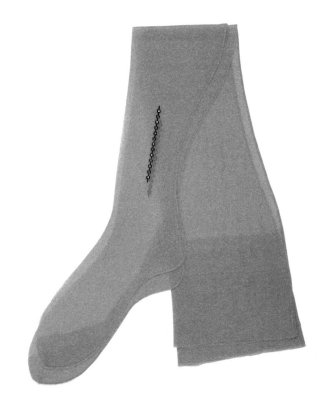

1. Sophia Opperskalski et al., *Textile Exchange Preferred Fiber & Materials Market Report 2020*, online: https://textileexchange.org/wp-content/uploads/2020/06/Textile-Exchange_Preferred-Fiber-Material-Market-Report_2020.pdf, accessed 24 October 2021.
2. Paul Jobling, *Advertising Menswear: Masculinity and Fashion in the British Media since 1945*. London: Bloomsbury, 2014, p. 120.
3. Susannah Handley, *Nylon: The Story of a Fashion Revolution—A Celebration of Design from Art Silk to Nylon and Thinking Fibres*. Baltimore, MD: Johns Hopkins University Press, 1999, p. 33; Donald Coleman, "Man-Made Fibres before 1954", in David Jenkins (ed.), *Cambridge History of Western Textiles*. Cambridge: Cambridge University Press, 2002, pp. 933–47, here p. 945.
4. E.W.T., "Wanted: More Nylon Stockings", *Hampshire Telegraph*, 2 September 1949.

GRAPHITE IMPREGNATED
DO NOT PAINT

126–1

Streamlined Reception

Radio compass loop antenna housing, c. 1940–45
Bakelite, graphite, aluminium
37 × 63 × 25 cm
Amsterdam Bakelite Collection

The 1930s were the decade of streamline design in the United States. The aerodynamic streamline shape represented a powerful push towards a new age of technological progress and quickly became a paragon of industrial design. The new streamline design language extended beyond automobiles and trains to household items such as refrigerators, telephones, even pencil sharpeners. The reasons for the success of the streamline shape were many-faceted, but the emergence of plastics, whose malleability not only facilitated rounded shapes but practically necessitated them in production, played an important role. Liquid plastic mass could be spread more easily and evenly in rounded moulds than in those with pointed corners and sharp edges. And when cured, rounded plastic parts were also easier to remove from the mould and were less prone to breakage.[1]

Nowhere do aerodynamic qualities make more sense than in aircraft construction. This housing for an aircraft radio antenna, as used for navigation in World War II, looks like the epitome of a streamlined form. The circular antennas, protected by cases such as these, originally lacked a casing and were installed above or below the fuselage of military aircraft. However, the turbulence that resulted had an unfavourable effect on flight behaviour.[2] While metal antenna housings could be shaped similarly, they, in turn, impaired reception.[3] So ultimately the plastic Bakelite, which had already been used earlier in the automotive and aircraft industries, was an obvious choice. It was lightweight, resistant to heat and cold, and permeable to radio waves. JE

1. Jeffrey L. Meikle, *American Plastic: A Cultural History*. New Brunswick, NJ: Rutgers University Press, 1995, pp. 115 f; C. W. Blount, "Do Designers Know Why Molding Costs Are High?", *Modern Plastics* (May 1935), pp. 17–21, 57, 58.
2. Anon, "A Loop Antenna: One of the Many Ways Flyers Navigated in WWII", *Commemorative Air Force Minnesota Wing* (uploaded 16 November 2019), online: https://www.cafmn.org/news/a-loop-antenna-one-of-the-many-ways-flyers-navigated-in-wwii, accessed 21 December 2012.
3. Cooper Hewitt Collection, "Radio compass loop antenna housing", *Cooper Hewitt*, online: https://collection.cooperhewitt.org/users/russelldavies/visits/tx5s/3288759/, accessed 21 December 2012.

Floating in a Plastic Bubble

Hawker Sea Fury cockpit canopy, 1945–55
Sir Sydney Camm
Hawker Aircraft
Metal, clear acrylic
45 × 147 × 65.5 cm
Museum of Design in Plastics

During World War II, "bubble canopies"—made of lightweight acrylic sheets—were deployed on a number of aircraft. These revolutionary canopies provided pilots with 360-degree vision without the need for windshield metal bracing, whilst also reducing the weight of the aircraft.[1] The most notable of these was the "Malcolm" hood, designed by R Malcolm & Co in 1934, and fitted in the Supermarine Spitfire commissioned by the RAF and used by other Allied countries.[2]

The Hawker Fury was developed towards the end of the war in 1943, and the Sea carrier version of the plane, the Sea Fury, finalized in 1945. This was one of the first fighter planes fitted with vacuum-formed canopies made from polymethyl methacrylate. Discovered in the early 1930s by British chemists Rowland Hill and John Crawford, this pliable material—the first British-made "safety glass" of its kind—was marketed as Perspex by the company they worked for, Imperial Chemical Industries (ICI).[3] German company Röhm & Haas also launched their own Plexiglass, alongside American company DuPont's Lucite, all made from the same acrylic sheeting.

The enclosed canopy was key to the design of modern fighter jets, providing increased visibility in adverse weather conditions. Unlike glass, the bubble hood did not look cloudy when the material was bent to curve and was more effective at reducing temperature flux inside the cockpit. Acrylic is 20 times more effective than standard glass at maintaining an ambient temperature in an enclosed space.[4] The shatterproof nature of acrylic also aided pilots' escape and reduced the likelihood of injury from broken glass shards. LB

1. Tony Bingelis, "What You Should Know About Canopies", *EAA Sport Aviation Magazine* (October 1992), online: https://www.eaa.org/eaa/aircraft-building/builderresources/while-youre-building/building-articles/canopies-and-windshields/what-you-should-know-about-canopies, accessed 20 January 2022.
2. John Sweetman, *Sydney Camm: Hurricane and Harrier Designer Saviour of Britain*. Barnsley: Pen & Sword Books, 2019, p. 15.
3. Ibid., p. 30.
4. Simply Plastics, "What Are the Benefits of Acrylic/Perspex Compared to Glass?" (18 September 2018), online: https://www.simplyplastics.com/blog/what-are-the-benefits-of-acrylicperspex-compared-to-glass/, accessed 20 January 2022.

127–1

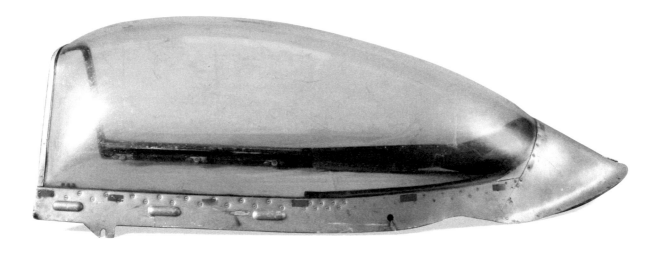

1. Robert Hawes, *Radio Art*. London: Greenwood, 1991, p. 14.
2. Council of Industrial Design, *Britain Can Make It*, exhib. cat. Victoria and Albert Museum, London, 1946, p. 101.

128–1

Radios in the Round

EKCO A22 Radio, 1946
Wells Coates for E. K. Cole Limited
Compression-moulded Bakelite, acrylic, fabric, chromium
35.7 × 33.5 × 20.5 cm
Victoria and Albert Museum, London

The circular design of the A22 radio is a far cry from earlier radios, which were housed in large hand-built, wooden cabinets.[1] Using Bakelite instead of wood for radio casings allowed for the creation of radically new forms that appealed to consumers of this relatively new technology.

The British radio manufacturer EKCO, founded by Eric Kirkham Cole in 1926, invested in plastic moulding presses in its Southend factory in the early 1930s and began using Bakelite as its main encasing material. The presses revolutionized the company's radio designs, with well-known architects such as Wells Coates and Serge Chermayeff making EKCO radios synonymous with British modernism.

The A22 launched in 1946 and was displayed in the *Britain Can Make It* exhibition of the same year.[2] It is a relatively late design for Wells Coates, who had presented his first round radio for EKCO, the A65, over a decade earlier in 1934. However, while the styling of the A65 is a little more traditional—with a semicircular tuning dial and a stylized grill in front of the central speaker—the A22 is pared back and minimal.

To emphasize the design's underlying functionalism, Coates made the unadorned speaker the focal point of the design, encircling it with a 360-degree tuning dial. Despite its minimalism, it was out of step with the post-war mood. The fashion was increasingly for smaller, portable models, a trend that Coates himself recognized in his other designs for EKCO. JW

From Flight to Fashion

Fabric sample, 1946
Lída Ascher for Ascher (London) Limited
Polyamide (woven, screen-printed)
169 × 92 cm
Victora and Albert Museum, London. Given by
Zika Ascher

The lively design and bold colours of this dress fabric are characteristic of the celebrated London-based textile firm Ascher Ltd, founded by Zika and Lída Ascher in 1942. The floral design obscures the original purpose of the fabric: parachutes.

During and for some time after World War II, Britain's textile industry was focused on the war effort, leaving the domestic market in short supply. As Japan produced most of the world's silk fibre, most of the Allied nations experienced shortages. Supplies in Britain were limited to the extent that silk was withdrawn from civilian production in October 1940. Globally, governments sought an alternative fabric suitable for much-needed military parachutes that required up to eight metres of high-performance fabric.[1] The lightweight, superhydrophobic characteristics of nylon (see p. 125), combined with its superior strength and durability, made it ideal for the purpose.

Clothes rationing didn't fully end in Britain until 1949. The British government released surplus stock originally manufactured for military purposes to boost the textile and fashion industries immediately after the war. Ascher was one of the first textile companies to transform the translucent, finely woven parachute nylon into fashionable dresswear. The non-porous nylon fibres resisted most traditional dyes, but after numerous experiments Zika Ascher (1910–92) created a formula (probably based on acid dyes) for maintaining the painterly, vivid colours characteristic of the firm's fabric designs. A trio of black, green, and red warp threads along the selvedge are the only hint of the fabric's provenance. Ascher made a feature of the fabric's redeployment from military to civilian use at a trade event titled *Transformation of a Fabric* at London's Dorchester Hotel in February 1946.[2] CKB

129–1

1. Frank Illingworth, "Every Small Parachute Has Enough Silk to Dress 30 Women", *Belfast Telegraph*, 28 September 1942, p. 2.
2. Konstantina Hlavackova, *The Mad Silkman. Zika & Lida Escher: Textiles and Fashion*. Prague: Museum of Decorative Arts/Slovart Publishing, 2019, p. 165.

1. Mehmet Demirors, "The History of Polyethylene", in E. Thomas Strom and Seth C. Rasmussen (eds), *100+ Years of Plastics: Leo Baekeland and Beyond*. Washington, DC: American Chemical Society, 2014, pp. 115–45.
2. Alison J. Clarke, *Tupperware: The Promise of Plastic in 1950's America*. Washington, DC: Smithsonian Institution Press, 1999, p. 21.
3. Ibid., p .51.
4. Ibid. p. 13.
5. Tupperware Corporation, *Tupperware: The Nicest Thing That Could Happen to Your Kitchen*, product cat. Orlando, FL: Tupperware Home Parties Inc, 1956.
6. Jon Kelly, "Did Tupperware parties change the lives of women?", *BBC News Magazine* (10 May 2011), online: https://www.bbc.co.uk/news/magazine-13331830, accessed 5 November 2021.

130–1

"Modern families use Tupperware … everywhere!"

Tupperware food storage containers, 1950–60
Earl Tupper, Tupperware Plastics Company
Moulded polyethylene
Largest container top left: 17.1 × 12.9 × 12.9 cm
Victoria and Albert Museum, London

Plastic Tupperware containers launched in the US in the late 1940s. Although now synonymous with post-war homemaking and the "Party Plan" promotion strategy, the origins of Tupperware link closely to the development of polyethylene and wartime innovations.

Polyethylene—first developed and produced by ICI in the UK in 1939 on the basis of the experiments of German chemist Hans von Pechmann in 1898—was used for cable insulation and radar sets during World War II.[1] Seeking new, peacetime uses, the DuPont and Bakelite corporations started large-scale production of polyethylene under license from ICI in 1944.

Originally employed by a DuPont-owned plastics factory,[2] inventor and designer Earl Tupper set up The Tupperware Plastics Company to explore uses for polyethylene—or "Poly-T, material of the future", as DuPont advertised it—introducing its first Tupperware range in 1945. But despite favourable reviews and a broad distribution network, it was only after adopting the "Party Plan" as its sole sales tool that the "Tupperization of the American home" started in earnest.[3]

The plan developed based on the success of Brownie Wise—a single parent from Detroit—who started selling Tupperware door to door via social events.[4] By 1951, the homes of American women had become the perfect stages for demonstrating the qualities of Tupperware, with the host providing plenty of refreshments. As one Tupperware advertising leaflet states: "Food keeps longer, leftovers become planovers. Less dishwashing, too! Prepare, serve and store in same dish."[5]

As well as modernizing food storage, the Tupperware sales model was an opportunity for some women to earn a living while juggling home and family duties: "Tupperware parties were about women helping other women and enabling them. It wasn't discussed as work, it was an extension of socialising. It was the antithesis of male corporate culture. It was the opposite of Mad Men."[6] JAR

Atomic Inspiration: Designing with Science

"Helmsley" furnishing fabric, 1951
Marianne Straub for Warner & Sons
Cotton
175 cm × 115 cm
Victoria and Albert Museum, London. Given by
Warner & Sons Ltd

"Polythene 8.59c" dress fabric, 1951
Mildred Taylor for Dobroyd Ltd
Wool
102 cm × 141 cm
Victoria and Albert Museum, London. Given by
the Council of Industrial Design

The patterns on these fabrics depict the molecular structures of polythene and nylon, two synthetic polymers derived from petroleum hydrocarbons. The fabrics were designed for the 1951 Festival of Britain's displays, which attracted a record 8.5 million visitors. The "Crystal Designs", as they became known, featured patterns and motifs inspired by X-ray crystallography-derived diagrams of various organic and man-made materials.

Sir William Henry Bragg and his son William Lawrence Bragg's development of X-ray crystallography in around 1912 won them the Nobel Prize for Physics in 1915. The technique enabled scientists to calculate, for the first time, the relationships between atoms and create diagrams detailing the molecular structure of a material.[1]

Applying the often beautiful, repeating structural diagrams to designed objects was an idea put forward by Dr. Helen Megaw, a crystallographer at Birkbeck College, London. Inspired by her idea, in 1949 Mark Hartland Thomas from the Council of Industrial Design brought together a group of manufacturers, subsequently known as the Festival Pattern Group, to apply the crystallography X-rays to a range of domestic goods and fabrics. The resulting designs were showcased in the Festival of Britain "Regatta Restaurant" interior, the South Bank pavilion, and in the *Exhibition of Science* backdrops.

The representation of molecular structures on these textiles of wool and cotton does not correspond to their constitutive fibres. The simple, repetitive, and modern look of the nylon and polythene structures seems to have appealed to the designers of these two fabrics, Mildred Taylor of the company Dobroyd and Marianne Straub of Warner & Sons.

Megaw was keen that the designs kept their "proper" names to maintain their connection with science. Straub, however, christened this design "Helmsley". The "Helmsley" pattern was produced in five colourways and at two different scales. It went into further production after the festival, suggesting it remained popular—perhaps prized for the modern aesthetic given by the "atom and spike" design. CKB

1. Lesley Jackson, From *Atoms to Patterns: Crystal structure designs from the 1951 Festival of Britain*. Yeovil: Richard Dennis, 2008.

131–1

131–2

132–1

1. George Nelson, "Peak Experiences and the Creative Act", in George Nelson, *On Design*. New York: Whitney Library of Design, 1979, p. 20. Architect Paul Rudolph had already used Cocoon in the late 1940s for his Healy Cocoon House in Siesta Key, Florida. In order to create the house's arching ceiling, the spray was applied to a lattice of steel flat bars. See Timothy M. Rohan, *The Architecture of Paul Rudolph*. New Haven, CT: Yale University Press, 2014, pp. 19–20.
2. Barbara Fitton Hauss, "Consumer Products for a 'Kleenex Culture': Home Accessories by George Nelson", in Jochen Eisenbrand and Alexander von Vegesack (eds), *George Nelson: Architect, Writer, Designer, Teacher,* exhib. cat. Vitra Design Museum, Weil am Rhein, 2008, pp. 110–35.

From Battleship to Living Room

Bubble Lamp, 1952
George Nelson for Howard Miller
Polyvinyl chloride (PVC), steel wire
40.7 × 48.3 cm
Vitra Design Museum

At the international design conference in Aspen, Colorado in 1977, designer George Nelson recalled what had prompted him to design a new product in the late 1940s. While searching in vain for simple and affordable ceiling lamps that would evenly illuminate a room, a picture from the *New York Times* suddenly appeared in his mind's eye: battleships "mothballed" in port, with a plastic-spray layer to protect them from rust.[1] From this idea, Nelson developed the series of Bubble Lamps, produced by Michigan-based company Howard Miller from 1952. The plastic spray in question was called Cocoon, a product of the R. N. Hollingshead Corporation, developed initially for the US military as dust protection, packaging, and sealing material.

For the Bubble Lamps, William Renwick, a designer in Nelson's office, developed a wire frame consisting of two perforated retaining rings into which bent wire rods were inserted to form a globe of sorts. Welding was not necessary. The wire frame was then placed on a turntable and sprayed with resin varnish as a carrier material, after which the Cocoon plastic layer was applied with a spray gun. The slight shrinkage of the plastic skin helped stabilize the construct and accentuate the silhouette.[2] And just like that, the Bubble Lamp was finished—a highly efficient production technique, albeit one which required a large amount of solvents. JE

"Squeeze Me!"

Hax and Flip squeeze bottles, c. 1950–70
Produced by Cascelloid for Edward Hack, London
Polyethylene
Height: between 5.5 and 8 cm
Museum of Design in Plastics

Unbreakable and lightweight, their contents are easily measured out with a light squeeze: The first soft polyethylene squeeze bottles came onto the market in the late 1940s and quickly began replacing glass containers. In 1947, chemical scientist Jules Montenier designed the very first squeeze bottle in the United States for deodorant brand Stopette and would go on to develop them further with the North American company Plax Corporation.[1] Collaborating with renowned designers such as Egmont Arens and Donald Deskey on their shapes, the industry leader advertised the squeeze bottles in 1960 as "safe in the home, soft to the touch, unbreakable and attractive".[2]

In the late 1940s, British plastics manufacturer Cascelloid imported its first machine for blow-moulding plastic bottles such as these from the US.[3] Bill Pugh, who was Cascelloid's chief plastics designer from 1947 to 1965, designed a lemon-shape squeeze bottle for lemon juice in the early 1950s.[4] The clever, intuitive design quickly made its way around the world—also owing to numerous copies being made—and is still in production today. London-based entrepreneur Edward Hack began selling the lemon bottle in 1954 under the brand name Hax, a homonym, possibly inspired by Plax, and Flip.[5] Spurred on by its success as well as by pressure from his competitors, he patented further squeeze containers in the USA and Canada in 1957 and 1958:[6] a banana, a strawberry, and a pineapple for different types of fruit syrup to flavour milk and a sausage shape for hot dog mustard. The bottle thus became a signifier without any real need for further elaboration or labels. JE

1. Jeffrey L. Meikle, *American Plastic: A Cultural History*. New Brunswick, NJ: Rutgers University Press, 1997, p. 190. See also "Stopette", *Cosmetics and Skin* (updated 22 January 2022), online: https://www.cosmeticsandskin.com/ded/stopette.php, accessed 10 November 2021.
2. Advert in *Fortune* magazine, May 1960.
3. In blow-moulding, a so-called plastic preform is heated and blown-up using a tool whose inner contours define the final shape.
4. Valerie Moore, "Obituary: Bill Pugh", *Independent* (29 June 1994), online: https://www.independent.co.uk/news/people/obituary-bill-pugh-1426051.html, accessed 10 November 2021.
5. "Packaged (past tense): The HAX plastic lemon pack", *BEACH Branding & Package Design* (23 July 2015), online: https://beachpackagingdesign.com/boxvox/packaged-past-tense-the-hax-plastic-lemon-pack, accessed 10 November 2021.
6. "AX Packs: More fruit-shaped plastic bottles ...", *BEACH Branding & Package Design* (24 July 2015), online: https://beachpackagingdesign.com/boxvox/hax-packs-more-fruit-shaped-plastic-bottles, accessed 10 November 2021.

133–1

134–1

1. Emily Stevens et al., "A History of Infant Feeding", *Journal of Perinatal Education*, vol. 18, no. 2 (2009), pp. 32–39.
2. "Microplastics in drinking-water", in *WHO-HSD Brochure*. Geneva: World Health Organization, 2019, pp. 16–24. Licence: CC BY-NC-SA 3.0 IGO (flipping book), online: http://www.emro.who.int/hsd/files/basic-html/page16.html, accessed 2 December 2021.
3. Damian Carrington, "Bottle-fed babies swallow millions of microplastics a day study finds", the *Guardian* (19 October 2000), online: https://www.theguardian.com/environment/2020/oct/19/bottle-fed-babies-swallow-millions-microplastics-day-study, accessed 26 October 2021.

First Encounters

Freflo Feeding Bottle, c. 1954
Polyethelene [probably]
15 cm × 5.4 cm
Victoria and Albert Museum, London. Given by Mary Jane-Ansell

Glass was used for feeding bottles from the mid-nineteenth century, but infant mortality from dirty bottles was a prime concern and prompted practical, open-ended feeding bottle designs which were popular into the 1950s.[1] The development of heat-resistant, moulded glass, particularly Pyrex, brought about the straight-sided feeding bottle. Materials such as Bakelite were used for the rings of bottles after World War II and from the 1960s onwards, bottles were made from polypropylene, a cheaper, easier to clean, shatterproof alternative to glass.

Convenient and time-saving baby-feeding solutions were essential within the context of the women's liberation movement and the lack of flexibility imposed by traditional working patterns. This UK-manufactured Freflo bottle represents an early example of a light, unbreakable, and low-cost plastic bottle that offered a sanitary and convenient method of feeding.

Today, the WHO estimates adults consume 300–600 microplastic particles daily from food, water, and the air, with other sources including plastic water bottles, cups, and cutlery.[2] Whilst the impact of microplastics on the health of infants is unknown, the safety of plastic feeding bottles is under scrutiny.[3] This—combined with rising awareness of plastic pollution—has seen a return to glass and stainless-steel feeding bottles. CH

The Doll that Shaped a Generation

Barbie and Ken, 1960/61
Mattel Inc.
Polyvinyl chloride (PVC)
Barbie: c. 29.2 × 7 × 5 cm;
Ken: c. 30 × 7.5 × 5 cm
Vitra Design Museum

With 100 dolls sold every minute and a total of 58 million sold annually,[1] the Barbie doll is one of the most successful toys of all time. The American entrepreneur, Ruth Handler, who co-founded the toy company Mattel[2] together with her husband Elliot Handler, identified a gap in the market when observing her daughter play with cut-out "female model" paper dolls. Up until this point, the majority of lifelike dolls available in the US were infant types designed for girls to play at mothering; according to Handler, no mass-produced adult dolls for children, particularly girls, featured different female role models.

Handler came across a curvy doll with a blond ponytail called the Bild-Lilli during a trip to Switzerland and returned home with her. Inspired by this doll, which was based on a cartoon strip aimed at male readers of the German tabloid *Bild*, she had a version produced in Japan and launched the first Barbie in 1959 at the New York Toy Fair. She named the teenage fashion model[3] Barbie, after her daughter Barbara, while her male counterpart Ken, introduced in 1961, was named after her son Kenneth. For her debut, Barbie wore a black-and-white striped swimsuit, high-heels, and earrings. Although the doll became an immediate success, the majority of revenue was created through sales of accessories, offering a plethora of clothes, houses, and friends for Barbie.

While the Barbie doll has been criticized for perpetuating an unrealistic body image, for objectifying women and for a lack of diversity, her cultural impact is still unparalleled. Ruth Handler wrote in her 1994 autobiography: "My whole philosophy of Barbie was that through the doll, the little girl could be anything she wanted to be. Barbie always represented the fact that a woman has choices."[4] In her lifetime, Barbie has had over 200 different careers including that of US President, she even explored space four years before Neil Armstrong landed on the Moon.[5] Moreover, Barbie has shaped the aesthetic perception of a whole generation: As the Danish pop band Aqua sarcastically put it in their 1997 hit song "Barbie Girl", "life in plastic it's fantastic". MH

135–1

1. Global Markets, "Barbie, Fast Facts" (2009–16), online: http://www.barbie-media.com/about-barbie/fast-facts.html, accessed 23 December 2021.
2. The company originally produced picture frames and doll's house furniture.
3. Mattel catalogue, quoted from Valerie Steele, "Barbie Fashion", in *Art Design, and Barbie: The Evolution of a Cultural Icon*. Leuven: Exhibitions International, 1995, p. 17.
4. Sarah Kershaw, "Ruth Handler, Whose Barbie Gave Dolls Curves, Dies at 85", *New York Times* (29 April 2002), online: https://www.nytimes.com/2002/04/29/arts/ruth-handler-whose-barbie-gave-dolls-curves-dies-at-85.html, accessed 23 December 2021.
5. Global Markets, "Barbie, Fast Facts".

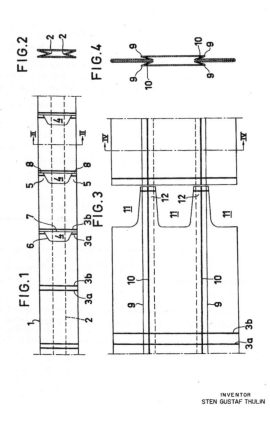

April 27, 1965   S. G. THULIN   3,180,557

BAG WITH HANDLE OF WELDABLE PLASTIC MATERIAL

Filed July 10, 1962

INVENTOR
STEN GUSTAF THULIN

136–1

1. Sarah Laskow, "How the Plastic Bag Became So Popular", the *Atlantic* (10 October 2014), https://www.theatlantic.com/technology/archive/2014/10/how-the-plastic-bag-became-so-popular/381065/, accessed 28 October 2021.
2. Susan Freinkel, *Plastic: A Toxic Love Story*. Melbourne, VIC: Text Publishing Company, 2011, pp. 143–45.
3. Anon (Reuters), "From Birth to Ban: A History of the Plastic Shopping Bag", *UN Environment Programme* (25 April 2018), https://www.unep.org/news-and-stories/story/birth-ban-history-plastic-shopping-bag, accessed 11 November 2021.
4. Anon, "How many plastic bags are used per year" The World Counts https://www.theworldcounts.com/challenges/planet-earth/waste/plastic-bags-used-per-year/story, accessed 7 January 2022.
5. Matt Wilkins, "More Recycling Won't Solve Plastic Pollution", *Scientific American* (6 July 2018), https://blogs.scientificamerican.com/observations/more-recycling-wont-solve-plastic-pollution/, accessed 2 November 2021.
6. Laura Parker "Plastic Bag Bans are Spreading. But are they Truly Effective?", *National Geographic* (April 17 2019), https://www.nationalgeographic.com/environment/article/plastic-bag-bans-kenya-to-us-reduce-pollution, accessed 4 November 2021.

The Immortal Plastic Bag

Bag with handle of weldable plastic material,
patent filed 1962, obtained 1965
Sten Gustaf Thulin

Able to carry up to a thousand times their own weight, they are cheap, waterproof, light, and convenient—no wonder the world is addicted to plastic bags.

Paradoxically, the "T-shirt bag", as it was originally called, was invented in the 1960s by engineer Sten Thulin and colleagues as a sustainable alternative to the handle-less paper bag while working at the Swedish plastics manufacturer Celloplast. To modify the design, Thulin cut into the top of the prototype plastic tube to create handles. Celloplast patented the design in 1965 and the ubiquitous "T-shirt bag"—so named because it resembled the shape of a T-shirt—was born.[1]

Leading polyethylene manufacturers were eager to find new uses for this material that had been core to the war effort[2] and this, along with a post-war culture of consumption, convenience, and advertising, ultimately led to the success of the plastic bag. Celloplast's patent was lifted in 1977, and by the 1980s plastic accounted for 80 per cent of Europe's bag market with the US fast behind.[3]

Approximately 5 trillion plastic bags are used worldwide annually.[4] On average, a plastic bag is used for 12 minutes but can take 500 years to degrade.[5] Plastic bag bans, charges, and taxes have been rolled out worldwide, starting with Bangladesh in 2002. The African continent now leads the world in bag regulations.[6] Numerous reusable alternatives have surfaced, including bags for life, cloth totes, and home compostable bags, but these so-called solutions bring their own problems—not least biodegradability and a reliance on resources like cotton and water. CH

Pallo is Finnish for "Ball"

Pallo / Ball Chair, 1963
Eero Aarnio for Asko
Glass fibre-reinforced polyester, lacquered steel,
foam-rubber padding, fabric covering
125 × 108.5 × 108 cm
Vitra Design Museum

The spherical, swivelling lounge chair is made from fibre-glass-reinforced polyester. A cosy private retreat upholstered in red leather, the Pallo Chair was originally fitted with a red Ericsson telephone—today's version can connect to the Internet.

In the 1960s, plastic opened up opportunities for furniture makers to experiment with bold colours and new forms and production methods, which a young generation in pursuit of leisure and easy living enthusiastically embraced. A ball to sit in, the Pallo Chair by Finnish designer Eero Aarnio was one of the most iconic and symbolic innovations of the era.[1]

Envisaging a "big chair with a bold new look", Aarnio built the first prototype at home in 1962–63: "I didn't have a clear idea in my mind when I started sketching […] I kept simplifying the shape until I stumbled on the idea of making it a perfect sphere." Finishing the first full-scale sketch—Aarnio only works in 1:1 scale—he pinned it to the wall, sat on a spinning stool in front of it, and pretended he was sitting in the chair. His wife marked key positions to determine the heights, and "From there on, the proportions fell into place spontaneously."[2]

An immediate success at the International Furniture Fair Cologne in 1965, the Finnish tabloid *Ilta-Sanomat* dubbed it the "sensation of Cologne".[3] The Pallo was later featured in films, showrooms, and on numerous magazine covers, with politicians, pop stars, and fashion models all photographed in it. The chair became one of the most visible pieces of furniture of the 1960s.[4]

The Pallo pays tribute to the designs of Eero Saarinen. Like the Tulip Chair, Aarnio's design is perched on a single, swivelling central leg, lacquered to match the colour of the seat. Thus, the Pallo appears to hover above the ground while being able to rotate 360 degrees.

Aarnio later pushed lounge seating further with the transparent, ceiling-mounted Bubble Chair (1969) and the drop-like Pastilli (1968). Made possible thanks to the mouldability of plastic, they all embody Aarnio's philosophy that "A chair must be comfortable for sitting, and after that everything is free."[5] AK

137–1

1. Anniina Koivu, "Pallo", in Mateo Kries et al. (eds), *Atlas of Furniture Design*. Weil am Rhein: Vitra Design Museum, 2019, pp. 472–73.
2. Eero Aarnio, "Birth of the Ball Chair", in *Assume a Round Chair: Eero Aarnio and the 60s*. Helsinki: University of Art and Design, 2003, pp. 108–11.
3. Ibid.
4. Florencia Colombo and Ville Kokkonen (eds), *A = 4πr2 – Eero Aarnio*. Helsinki: Design Forum Finland, 2014.
5. "Eero Aarnio: One of the great innovators of modern furniture design", *Artek* (n. d.), online: https://www.artek.fi/en/company/designers/eero-aarnio, accessed 12 December 2021.

138–1

1. Rachel Newar, "Celebrating 80 Years of LEGO", *Smithsonian Magazine* (10 August 2012), online: https://www.smithsonianmag.com/smart-news/celebrating-80-years-of-lego-20358245/, accessed 1 September 2021.
2. Category "Kiddicraft", *Brighton Toy Museum*, online: https://www.brightontoymuseum.co.uk/index/Category:Kiddicraft, accessed 1 September 2021.
3. Erin Blakemore, "The Disastrous Backstory Behind the Invention of Lego Bricks" (21 September 2017; updated 29 August 2018), *History* online: https://www.history.com/news/the-disastrous-backstory-behind-the-invention-of-lego-bricks, accessed 1 September 2021.
4. Category Lego System, *Brighton Toy Museum*, online: https://www.brightontoymuseum.co.uk/index/Category:Lego_System, accessed 1 September 2021.
5. Ibid.
6. Adam Augustyn, "LEGO", *Encyclopaedia Britannica* (19 November 2018), online: https://www.britannica.com/topic/LEGO, accessed 27 October 2021.
7. Courtney Crowder, "New book gives insight into the world of adult Lego fans", *Chicago Tribune*, (22 June 2010), online: https://www.chicagotribune.com/entertainment/ct-xpm-2010-06-22-sc-ent-0623-lego-author-20100622-story.html, accessed 14 December 2021.

Another Brick in the Wall

Lego Town Plan (Set 810), 1959–62
Lego Company Ltd
Injection-moulded acrylonitrile-butadiene-styrene copolymer, cardboard, metal
52 × 42.3 × 7.7 cm
Vitra Design Museum

Named after the Danish "Leg Godt" (Play well), the Lego company began as a small-scale wooden toy manufacturer.[1] In 1946, a visiting UK plastics sales rep changed this by demonstrating an early injection-moulding process and the work of Hilary Page at Kiddicraft, who'd already begun manufacturing plastic building bricks. This inspired Lego company founder Ole Kirk Christiansen to replicate and adapt Page's block-building system and enter the plastic-toy manufacturing market, becoming the first Danish company to own an injection-moulding machine.[2]

After two years of refinement, Lego entered the market with their own "Automatic Binding Bricks"—modified versions of Page's designs, but not yet having the tubular locking system for which Lego is now renowned.[3] Initially, the product floundered—the early 1950s proving a limited market for plastic toys. Further adaptations in 1958, combining the studs with tubes for locking security, along with "systems" of building bricks, roof bricks, windows, and instructional manuals, improved the company's success.

The initial "Lego System in Play" comprised 28 sets and eight vehicles, marketed in the US with the help of a bright and colourful campaign and a production and distribution deal with luggage manufacturers Samsonite.[4] Post-war American optimism, and a focus on educational and universal toys, made the bricks attractive, with the Town Plan (set 810) and Railway (set 080) becoming bestsellers.[5] In 1968, Lego sales reached over 18 million units. Named "Toy of the Century" in 2000, the company was among the inaugural inductees to the U.S. National Toy Hall of Fame in 1998,[6] Lego mini figures now outnumber humans—62 units for every one person.[7] LB

Suited up for Space

Dress and coat, 1966
John Bates for Jean Varon
Cotton, polyester, polyvinyl chloride (PVC)
83.5 × 37 cm
Victoria and Albert Museum, London

The striking, structured silver PVC collar that crowns this otherwise simple ensemble reflects the public's obsession with space exploration in the 1960s. The imaginations of designers within many disciplines mimicked the aerodynamics of space rockets or the metal- and plastic-clad interiors of high-tech aircraft. The textile industry played a direct role in the space race, working with agencies to develop materials suited to putting a man on the Moon. The 1969 Moon landing gave the US chemical giant DuPont the opportunity to boast that 20 of the materials used in the 21-layer Apollo spacesuits originated with the firm.[1] The materials used included nylon, Lycra, Neoprene, Mylar, and Teflon.

The fashion world expressed these space-age influences by adopting synthetic materials and plastics and using them in novel ways. Many leading couture designers—in particular, Andre Courrèges, Paco Rabanne, and Pierre Cardin—experimented with hard plastics, technical textiles, and unfamiliar construction techniques to create garments fit for the world's next space explorer. The hard, shining surfaces offered by PVC (polyvinyl-chloride) proved popular for adding an on-trend futuristic touch.

In London, fashion designer John Bates pioneered a certain futuristic look from the early 1960s, incorporating unconventional plastic materials. He established his high-end womenswear label under the name of Jean Varon in 1959. In 1965, Bates gained notoriety for designing the racy costumes worn by Diana Rigg's character in the British TV series *The Avengers*. Bates designed this bespoke ensemble especially for fashion journalist Marit Allen's wedding in June 1966. The streamlined silhouette and elements such as silver buttons and PVC bands at each wrist evoked the imaginative and otherworldly costumes of characters from the many sci-fi films from the decade. CKB

139–1

1. Susannah Handley, *Nylon: The Manmade Fashion Revolution*. London: Bloomsbury, 1999, p. 88.

SAVESAVEᴿᴿᴿᴿPLANET!PLANET
SAVESAVEOOOOPLANET!PLANET

save our cities

140–1

1. Mark Wigley, *Buckminster Full Inc.: Architecture in the Age of Radio*. Zurich: Lars Müller Publishers, 2015, p. 150.
2. Ibid., pp. 226–32.
3. Ibid., p. 225. In the 1950s and '60s, plastics manufacturers such as British Xylonite promoted polyethylene for building greenhouses and for use as mulch film. See caption "Greenhouse lining", *Museum of Design in Plastics*, online: https://www.modip.ac.uk/artefact/bxl-07321, accessed 22 December 2021.

Manhattan as a Greenhouse

Poster "Save Our Planet, Save Our Cities", 1971
R. Buckminster Fuller
Half-tone and screen print
69.2 × 74.5 cm
Victoria and Albert Museum, London. Given by
Olivetti Ltd

Probably no other architect's work embodies the utopian potential of plastic in the mid-twentieth century better than R. Buckminster Fuller's. From a dome structure with a pneumatic membrane, which Fuller built together with students at Black Mountain College in 1949, to the spherical American pavilion at the 1967 World's Fair in Montreal, which he built using transparent Perspex panels produced by Rohm & Haas: the self-supporting geodesic domes with which Fuller aimed to revolutionize architecture would be inconceivable without the use of plastic as a building membrane.[1]

Fuller's vision of a dome spanning half of Manhattan was first shown at the Museum of Modern Art in 1959—initially as a drawing of a spherical structure composed of triangular elements, which he superimposed onto the orthogonal street grid. In the following year, the project

was presented at MoMA in the exhibition *Visionary Architecture*, which travelled to different destinations over the next eight years. Fuller used the image shown here, in which the dome hangs over the peninsula like a water drop, during a lecture in London in 1962. The supporting triangular metal web is invisible—practically dissolved—at this distance; what remains is the plastic membrane.[2]

This iconic poster was part of a series on the subject "Save our Planet", conceived in 1970–71 by the Pace Gallery in New York. Many other well-known names besides Fuller contributed images to the series, among them Roy Lichtenstein, Georgia O'Keefe, Edward Streichen, Ernest Trova, and Alexander Calder. Sponsored by the Olivetti Underwood Corporation, the proceeds from the sale of the posters went to a UNESCO campaign for the environment.

Fuller's vision was that of a gigantic greenhouse with the urban landscape of Manhattan as a symbolic field to be cultivated, on which the existing vegetation had to perish and be ploughed over to promote new growth. For Fuller, saving the cities and the planet meant reinventing both—using plastic as a catalyst.[3] JE

Space-age Design and the Sound of the Future

Panasonic Toot-a-Loop R-72S, 1969–72
Panasonic, Japan
Acrylonitrile butadiene styrene (ABS), metal
15.5 × 15.9 × 7.9 cm (closed)
Vitra Design Museum

The Panasonic R-72S transistor radio, more commonly known as the "Toot-a-Loop", is one of the most iconic of portable consumer electronics—dubbed "Poppies"[1]—from the early 1970s. The small doughnut-shaped radio can be worn on the wrist or twisted open into an "S" to reveal a tuning dial on one end. Its bright and joyful pop-colour choices—red, blue, green, white, and yellow—and versatility made it particularly popular among the youth.

The radio's plastic encasing consists of four moulded half-circles that insulate its electronic core and keep it lightweight and flexible—the perfect portable companion. It has a headphone jack for private listening and an exterior volume control for use when closed.

Like many objects from the late 1960s and early '70s, the radio's round, organic silhouette illustrates the significant design impact of space travel and the Moon landing. When open, the quirky device itself even resembles a small alien-like creature. Thanks to plastic's infinite mouldability, space-age design as such became a celebration of the material's expressive potential. In 1972, the radio was presented in Germany at the Hannover Fair, where it won over the jury with its modern playfulness. It even made it onto the cover of *Form* magazine.[2]

The Toot-a-Loop further indicated a trend towards a more personal relationship with our technical devices, which continued through to the Sony Walkman in 1979 and to the first Apple iPod in 2001. The history of consumer electronics is closely intertwined with that of plastic, as it allowed for the ever-cheaper manufacturing, smaller size, customization, and original design of everyday gadgets. Where technological appliances previously resided in the home or office environment, they could now transform into personal accessories and, as such, into an extension of the body. MH

141–1

1. Other examples in a Panasonic advertisement of 1974 include the Panapet R-70 and the R-63.
2. *Form,* design magazine, no. 58 (February, 1972).

1. Henrike Büscher and Peter Dunas, "Untitled/Multipl's", in Mateo Kries et al. (eds), *Atlas of Furniture Design*. Weil am Rhein: Vitra Design Museum, 2019, pp. 180–81.
2. Matthias Remmele, "BA1171/ Bofinger Chair", in ibid., pp. 480–81.
3. Jens Thiel, "Fauteuil 300", in ibid., pp. 520–21.
4. Alice Rawsthorn, "Celebrating the Everychair of Chairs, in Cheap Plastic", in Arnd Friedrichs and Kerstin Finger (eds), *The Infamous Chair: 220°C Virus Monobloc*. Berlin: Gestalten Verlag, 2010, pp. 14–15.

142–1

Monobloc: The Ideal Chair for All, Or Environmental Nightmare?

Fauteuil 300 / Monobloc, 1972
Henry Massonnet
STAMP (Société de Transformation de Matières Plastiques)
Polypropylene
72.5 × 53.4 × 59 cm
Vitra Design Museum

A white, all-plastic chair. Lightweight, stackable, and cheap, it is the most widely used piece of furniture in the world. Produced by the billion, the Monobloc was made possible thanks to the injection-moulding process that revolutionized furniture production and the entire plastics industry from the end of World War II. This one-step process fuelled designers' dreams of creating the ultimate mass-produced, single-material chair.

The origins of the Monobloc can be traced to the 1920s, when engineer Joseph Mathieu experimented with the legs of a sheet-steel chair, making them concave and tapered at the feet for greater stability. This leg shape became a typical characteristic of the Monobloc.[1]

A number of attempts were made in the 1960s to design an all-plastic chair. Helmut Bätzner's Bofinger Chair from 1964—considered the first chair made entirely of plastic—was closely followed by designs such as Universale by Joe Colombo (1967), Selene by Vico Magistretti (1967/68), and Verner Panton's cantilever chair (1967).[2]

The first Monobloc chair can be credited to Henry Massonnet, a French engineer, designer and owner of STAMP. Massonnet had the knowledge and experience necessary to solve many of his predecessors' stability challenges, choosing to use polypropylene, which was both substantially cheaper than other commonly used plastics and allowed for a very fast production time—less than two minutes for each Fauteuil 300 chair.[3]

With its global popularity, the Monobloc chair has come to embody both the best and worst of consumer society. Symbolically democratic in its universal accessibility and affordability, but, at the same time, exemplifying the global mass consumption of unsustainable plastic products that are almost impossible to repair and inevitably end up in landfill.[4] AK

Bottled Up and Shipped Out

"Easy-Goer" plastic bottle, 1975
The Coca-Cola Company
Acrylonitrile and polyethylene terephthalate
27 × 7.5 × 7.5 cm
Vitra Design Museum

Around a million plastic bottles are purchased worldwide every minute; they make up most of the litter washed up on beaches.[1]

In 1973, DuPont engineer Nathaniel Wyeth patented the first plastic bottle.[2] Wyeth's polyethylene terephthalate (PET) container solved a problem that soft-drink companies had grappled with before: a bottle to withstand the pressure of carbonated liquids.

While Pepsi relied on the Wyeth-patented PET bottle, the Coca-Cola company partnered with the chemical company Monsanto, which allegedly used a more durable blend of acrylonitrile and polyethylene terephthalate.[3] Coca-Cola praised the advantages of the new "Easy-Goer"

disposable bottle over glass vessels as a more resistant and lighter alternative to glass, and therefore cheaper to transport; the energy required in manufacture was lower than refilling or recycling.[4]

However, the American Food and Drug Administration pulled this bottle from sale in early 1977 due to concerns about a chemical reaction between the contents and the container. This incident, believed to be the first to raise awareness of the contamination of liquids by plastic, led to the closure of Coca-Cola's Monsanto bottling plant.[5]

These concerns did not curb consumption of plastic bottles: in 1979, Coca-Cola returned to the market with its own PET bottle. PET continued to be seen as the recyclable one-way alternative until plastic waste was discovered in the ocean currents in the 1990s; this exacerbated by the trend for bottled drinking water in the late 1970s and early '80s. Currently, according to the Plastics Industry Association, 75 per cent of all plastic containers in the US that end up as waste are bottles.[6] LB

143–1

1. "The Facts", *Plastic Oceans* (2021), online: https://plasticoceans.org/the-facts/, accessed 1 September 2021.
2. Gene Smith, "Coca-Cola Trying the Plastic Bottle", *New York Times* (4 June 1975), online: https://www.nytimes.com/1975/06/04/archives/cocacola-trying-a-plastic-bottle-pepsicola-contends-it-will.html, accessed 1 September 2021.
3. Bill Bregar, "Monsanto Saw the Potential of Michael Gigliotti", *Plastic News* (22 June 2003), https://www.plasticsnews.com/article/20030622/NEWS/306229996/monsanto-saw-potential-of-michael-gigliotti, accessed 1 September 2021.
4. Smith, "Coca-Cola Trying the Plastic Bottle".
5. Bregar, "Monsanto Saw the Potential of Michael Gigliotti".
6. Laura Parker, "How the Plastic Bottle Went from Convenience to Curse", *National Geographic* (27 August 2019), online: https://www.nationalgeographic.co.uk/environment-and-conservation/2019/08/how-plastic-bottle-went-miracle-container-despised-villain, accessed 1 September 2021.

1. Sarah D. Coffin et al., *Feeding Desire: Design and the Tools of the Table, 1500-2005*. New York: Assouline Publishing with Cooper Hewitt, Smithsonian Institute, 2006, pp. 216-26.
2. Habits of Waste, "Plastic Straws and Cutlery", https://habitsofwaste.org/call-to-action/plastic-straws-cutlery/, accessed 14 December 2021.
3. Shubhangi Goel, "India will ban single-use plastics next year to cut pollution", *CNBC* (10 October 2021), https://www.cnbc.com/2021/10/11/india-to-ban-single-use-plastics-but-experts-say-more-must-be-done-to.html, accessed 11 December 2021.
4. European Commission, "Single-use plastics" (2 July 2019), https://ec.europa.eu/environment/topics/plastics/single-use-plastics_en, accessed 12 December 2021.
5. Habits of Waste, "#cutoutcutlery campaign", https://habitsofwaste.org/campaigns/cutoutcutlery/, accessed 14 December 2021.

144–1

Dining on the Move: Playful or Wasteful?

"Plack" picnic ware, c. 1977
Jean-Pierre Vitrac for Alfaplac
Polystyrene
20 × 28 × 5.5 cm
Museum of Design in Plastics

"Plack", designed by Jean-Pierre Vitrac in 1977 and produced in France, is a polystyrene, injection-moulded picnic platter, comprising cup, plate, knife, fork, and spoon, made to be snapped apart for use and then disposed of. The ultimate in convenience, the units can be stacked and stored easily, with each picnic-goer having a ready-made place setting. The bright colours make for a playful take on informal dining with none of the work.

So-called "disposable" plastic cutlery was introduced in the 1940s, although it wasn't mass-produced until the 1950s and '60s when car, train, and air travel helped cement a culture of dining on the move. Suburban living gave way to a proliferation of fast-food restaurants and picnics, accompanied by single-use plastic cutlery and plates.[1]

Today, approximately 40 billion plastic forks, spoons, and knives are thrown away each year.[2] Globally, countries are fast moving towards a ban on single-use plastic, including India in 2022.[3] The EU banned ten plastic products, including disposable tableware, in 2021.[4] Campaigners in the US have forced change in the takeaway industry to ensure customers have to "opt in" to plastic cutlery.[5] Bio-based, compostable, and even edible cutlery alternatives are growing in popularity. Zero-waste campaigners now argue for the return of a practice popular until the seventeenth century—personal portable cutlery sets, similar to the growing habit of carrying a refillable water bottle. CH

Once Is Not Enough

Poster "Once is Not Enough", 1990
Richard Browning for The Body Shop Ltd
Lithographic print on recycled paper
99.9 × 66.7 cm
Victoria and Albert Museum, London

Anita Roddick founded The Body Shop cosmetics company in 1976 in Brighton, England, initially selling 25 products in returnable packaging, partly to minimize costs.[1] The focus on sustainability reflected the values of both the Roddick family and city of the company's founding.[2] The Body Shop became known for attracting increasingly environmentally aware consumers in the late 1980s.[3]

Attention-grabbing advertising campaigns and a recognizable logo fed into British consumers' debates on ethical values. Focusing on acts of protest, global women's rights, fair trade, and ecological issues, the company's environmentally conscious branding became a mainstay of the British high street. This poster, produced in 1990, advertised the company's refillable containers to reduce plastic waste. Richard Browning's design focuses on the well-known logo and iconic green-bottle shape, in which most of the products were sold; the poster was printed on recycled paper.[4]

In 2006, The Body Shop was sold to cosmetics firm L'Oreal, which previously Roddick had criticized for animal cruelty and wasteful practices. A more ecologically aware cosmetics company, Natura, bought The Body Shop in 2017 and reverted to the reusable containers in 2019.[5] LB

145–1

1. Anna Chesters, "A Brief History of The Body Shop", the *Guardian* (21 November 2011), online: https://www.theguardian.com/fashion/fashion-blog/2011/nov/21/brief-history-of-body-shop, accessed 21 November 2021.
2. Ibid.
3. "About Us", *The Body Shop* (updated 2021), website: https://www.thebody-shop.com/en-gb/about-us/a/a00001, accessed 1 September 2021.
4. Victoria and Albert Museum "Search the Collections", Once is Not Enough poster (record created 11 October 2006), online: https://collections.vam.ac.uk/item/O128498/once-is-not-enough-poster-browning-richard/, accessed 1 December 2021.
5. Imogen Watson, "The Body Shop Goes Back to Its Roots Preaching Self-Love Like Founder Anita Roddick", the *Drum* (6 July 2021), online: https://www.thedrum.com/news/2021/07/26/what-anita-did-the-body-shop-s-self-love-journey-going-back-its-roots, accessed 1 September 2021.

146–1

"The conscience of design"

Ecolo, 1995
Enzo Mari for Alessi
Wood, Polyvinyl chloride, polyethylene terephthalate, cardboard
Wooden case with four vases (limited edition)
11.0 × 50.6 × 29.5 cm
Zurich University of the Arts / Museum für Gestaltung Zurich / Design Collection

These decorative vases, made from discarded plastic household cleaning product bottles, were designed by the artist, furniture designer, educator, and theorist Enzo Mari for the Italian design brand Alessi. The playful and provocative designs of Ecolo are typical of Mari's work.

This boxed set was produced by Alessi as a limited edition, but as a consumer product Ecolo could be accessed in two ways: as a DIY manual with an Alessi sticker to "certify" the design or, as a ready cut and labelled vase signed by Mari.[1] As a meditation on the value of labour, consumption, and provenance, the products connected entirely with Mari's approach as a designer.

Often referred to as the embodiment of "the conscience of design",[2] Mari passionately advocated for ethical and sustainable practice and spoke out against the short-termism of the design world. Incorporating ideas of the arts and crafts movement as an essential part of his design philosophy and practice, Enzo Mari believed that good design should be accessible to everyone. This is perhaps best illustrated by his project, Autoprogettazione (1974) meaning "self-design", a manual for building simple-to-assemble furniture, and an attempt to empower people to self-build furniture using sheets of timber and nails.

Ecolo is in this exact same vein, using the detritus of consumer society as its building material. SJ

1. Tim Parsons, *Thinking, Objects: Contemporary Approaches to Product Design*. Lausanne: AVA Academia, 2009, p. 137.
2. Interview with Tommaso Trini, "Enzo Mari, the conscience of design", *Domus* (25 December 2016), online: https://www.domusweb.it/en/from-the-archive/2016/12/19/digging_the_archive_2.html, accessed 29 December 2021.

Reconstructed with Plastic: Synthetic Bodies

Surgical implant, 2004
Richard Browning for Ellis Developments Ltd
Polyester
14.2 × 14.2 cm
Victoria and Albert Museum, London. Given by Julian Ellis

A surgical implant made from machine-embroidered polyester thread developed in collaboration with textile engineers and physicians. Technical textile specialists Ellis Developments, in conjunction with medical materials manufacturer Pearsalls Ltd and medical professionals at Nottingham City Hospital in the UK, developed the use of surgical implants like this one using embroidered synthetic fibres to mimic the tough, elastic qualities of ligaments.

Designed for reconstruction of a patient's shoulder after removal of a tumour, this bespoke device has multiple attachment points to facilitate the use of all available tissue, giving it the appearance of a snowflake. The flexibility and strength of the embroidered polyester ensures the joint retains full movement.

The fibre used for surgical suture thread varies depending on the specific purpose. Synthetic fibres including polyamide, polyester, polyethylene, and polypropylene are commonly used in orthopaedic and cardiac surgery. For this type of implant, conventional polyester suture thread provided the strength and resilience required for a permanent internal implant. The blue used for certain elements within the design ensures that it remains visible during surgery.

Each embroidered implant blueprint is custom-designed on computer-aided design (CAD) software. The implant is manufactured on a standard lockstitch sewing machine—to ensure high-security stitching—and sewn onto a soluble base cloth that, once dissolved, leaves only the embroidered polyester threads. This same technique has long been used to manufacture some types of machine-made lace. The implant is sterilized by gamma irradiation before insertion.

With plastics increasingly used for medical implants, calls for greater testing and regulation are growing. Today's manufacturers of medical implants are continually developing high-performance polymers configured to provide strength and longevity and guard against breakdown of the material in the body over a long period. CKB

147–1

148–1

Returning to the Origins of Man-made Plastics

Botanica vessels, 2011
Formafantasma
Wood, egg albumen, shellac
34 × 20 × 20 cm
Shellac, sycamor wood, leather
41 × 21 × 21 cm
Victoria and Albert Museum, London

It is difficult to establish what material these vessels are made from initially: some of them look as though they are made from organic matter, while others look fragile and close to breaking. Made for the Botanica project by the Italian design studio Formafantasma,[1] these vessels are part of Andrea Trimarchi and Simone Farresin's exploration of plastic and its perception in the early twenty-first century. The project was commissioned by Plart, an Italian organization focused on scientific research and technological innovation in the conservation of artworks made from plastic.

Contemporary consumer society has become increasingly familiar with the sleek, impeccable surfaces of mass-produced plastic born out of petrochemical compounds. Botanica's focus is on plastics from the pre-Bakelite period (before 1907) instead, with the intention to understand what can be learnt from early man-made or semi-synthetic plastics in which organic and animal matter, as opposed to oil, were fundamental material elements.

As experiments with natural polymers extracted from plants and animals, these vessels question modern society's over-reliance on chemically produced plastics and the overconsumption of plastic materials. With this project, Formafantasma seeks to encourage a more considered attitude to plastic; to once again see plastics as awe-inspiring and something to admire for how they ape and copy the qualities of naturally occurring materials. JAR

1. See the Formafantasma website: https://formafantasma.com/studio, accessed 11 January 2022.

Plastic Protection

Three-ply face mask, 2022
Polypropylene
9.5 × 17.5 cm

Face masks have become everyday objects, produced and worn in their billions since the advent of the Covid-19 pandemic in early 2020.[1] This medical-grade mask is one of the most common types and is made up of three layers of breathable, melt-blown non-woven fabrics. It is disposable and designed to be used only once.

Melt-blown fabrics are made by extruding molten polypropylene polymers through small nozzles into a stream of heated air. As the fibres pass through the air, they become even finer and are deposited randomly to form a non-woven fabric sheet. This network of microfilaments and its inherent electrostatic charge makes it highly effective at blocking viruses and bacteria.

Face masks and other personal protective equipment (PPE) made from melt-blown fabrics are essential tools in the fight against Covid-19. Yet fit only for single use, they have forced a re-evaluation of our dependence on plastic in the medical sector. They reduce transmission and keep us safe, but once used, they add vastly to the problem of plastic waste—and therefore pose a significant threat to human and planetary health. Thrown-away masks are already polluting our waterways and have been found washed up on beaches across the globe.[2] CG

1. Nsikak U. Benson et al., "Covid Pollution: Impact of Covid-19 Pandemic on Global Plastic Waste Footprint", *Heliyon*, vol. 7, no. 2 (2021), online: https://pubmed.ncbi.nlm.nih.gov/33655084/, accessed 11 January 2022.
2. Yiming Peng et al., "Plastic Waste Release Caused by Covid-19 and its Fate in the Global Ocean", *Proceedings of the National Academy of Sciences of the United States of America* (23 November 2021), online: https://www.pnas.org/content/118/47/e2111530118, accessed 11 January 2022.

149–1

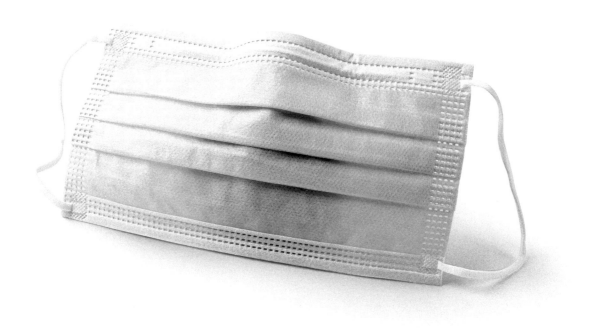

Conversations

Our job is to develop

Peter Ghyczy in conversation with Jochen Eisenbrand

When did you start working with plastics as a designer?

I was already designing objects made of fibre-glass-reinforced polyester (GRP)—a telephone booth, for example, followed by chairs for a kindergarten—back when I was studying architecture at the RWTH Aachen. That was in the late 1960s.

Did your studies cover plastics as part of the curriculum?

No, they didn't. At the time, the most important source of information about plastics for me was the Italian magazine *Domus*, which our university library stocked. I really enjoyed that, and even took an Italian course to better understand what I was reading.

152–1 Peter Ghyczy, polyurethane nursery furniture, c. 1970.

Did you have any ties to the Institute for Plastics Processing that was established at Aachen university in the 1950s?

I was a frequent visitor there, because I was interested in the whole topic; it was fascinating. But the Institute's focus was more on foils and pipes for sewer systems. They had an extrusion machine, which would push out these plastic worms whenever it was turned off due to its internal pressure decreasing—bizarre pieces of waste, but very artistic in their forms. I used to collect them and put them on pedestals. That was my art—instant art.

You graduated with an architecture degree in 1967, and then in 1968 you were invited by the entrepreneur and inventor Gottfried Reuter to work for him and his company, Elastogran. How did the two of you meet?

Through lucky coincidence, really. The spouse of one of my friends knew Reuter's daughter; they had both attended the School of Applied Arts in Hanover. When she saw that I had an interest in plastics, she told me that the father of one of her friends was working on something very interesting—polyurethane [PU]—and told me to get in touch with him. I went to visit him, and he made me an offer: to design products using his plastics, as application examples and display pieces. Reuter said, "Any idiot can produce, our job is to develop." That's also how the Senftenberg Egg or Garden Egg [lounge chair] came about.

Were you the first designer to work for Gottfried Reuter?

Yes, I was the first. You must understand that polyurethane was still in development back then. When I started working at Elastogran, they didn't even have any load-bearing structural elements yet. Those were only developed over the course of the four years that I was there. My first Garden Egg, for example, had a wall thickness of six or seven centimetres for structural stability. With the second prototype, the wall was already thinner—around three centimetres—and the third prototype looked like the final product that we know today, with two-centimetre walls. That's because the polyurethane became stronger with time. Polyurethane is a two-component resin and a reactive plastic, not a thermoplast. It foams and becomes lighter through this process. Depending on how finely poured the foam is or how much pressure is applied, it changes its firmness. We

used temporary forms for my designs. They didn't keep for long, just long enough to be able to experiment.

So your job at Elastogran mainly revolved around developing prototypes that potential customers could adopt for serial production?

Reuter basically gifted my designs to the manufacturers. A while ago, I found the old guestbook from the Elastogran Design Center. There are a lot of names of renowned furniture manufacturers in there, including Interlübke and Willi Fehlbaum from Vitra. Vitra also produced two of my designs for a while—the Spring Chair and the Endless Sofa. It was a kind of trade off: Take these designs, and in exchange you buy the raw material for their production from me.

Did Elastogran only supply the furniture industry, or other industries, such as the car industry, as well?

Elastogran's success came from their ability to produce elastic polyurethane—as the company name already indicates. In the car industry, elastic polyurethane became a substitute for rubber parts, for example used in the springs of shock absorbers. Whilst rubber ages, dries out, and becomes brittle, that doesn't happen with polyurethane. I'd estimate that 80 per cent of Elastogran's production output went to the car and installation industry. And likewise, polyurethane foam replaced natural foam rubber, because, for one, natural rubber has a slightly sulfuric smell, and secondly, it's heavier and more expensive.

These applications were arguably less visible to the public. The furniture you designed for Elastogran probably received much more attention.

Indeed—they were something of a display window for Reuter. He showed my furniture at fairs, and all visitors were shown around the Design Center in Lemförde.

And you also designed the building for the Design Center.

Yes, that was another one of my application examples. I made the roof and walls in the shape of barrels; the construction consisted of two-and-a-half-metre-width sandwich panels mounted on parallel steel girders. That was pioneering work. I put aluminium panels into moulds and poured

154–1 Elastogran Design Center, Lemförde, West Germany, designed by Peter Ghyczy in 1969, opened in 1970.

154–2 Interior view of the Elastogran Design Center.

154–3 Elastogran's advertising for Peter Ghyczy's Garden Egg, c. 1970.

„Flexi-Traction" heißt der Dreisitzer, dessen Karosserie und Chassis fast nur aus Kunststoff bestehen. Wegen seiner großen Steigfähigkeit und Wendigkeit soll sich das Gefährt besonders gut für die Forst- und Landwirtschaft eignen. Das von einer Lemförder Firma entwickelte Gefährt soll auf der Hannover-Messe ausgestellt werden.

154–4 Experimental plastic vehicle "Flexi-Traction", designed by Ulm-based Delta Design for Elastogran, c. 1970.

154–5 Production of an armchair prototype at Elastogran for the manufacturer Fehlbaum Collection, 1970. Wooden blocks were used for the mould so that the contours could be easily corrected by sanding.

PU foam onto them. The advantage of this was that you could then use them straight from the mould. They were both the roof and wall structures and served as insulation at the same time. The PU foam we applied was five centimetres thick—in those days, that was an exemplary level of insulation.

You must have had to build gigantic moulds for those sandwich panels?

The pressure in foaming isn't as high as with a compression-moulded thermoplastic. The forms were wood-beam lattices with a concave curvature covered by several layers of multiplex. They were rather primitive, but sufficiently covered the whole building in a short amount of time. We built it over the course of three months. Unfortunately, it was torn down later, because they needed the space.

And what did you think of the spatial quality?

It was beautiful, also due to the height of the space. There was a two-storey entrance foyer with a longitudinal gallery. I installed white Perspex elements where the walls met the ceiling, so that you'd have scattered light shining into the space from above—a great working atmosphere.

I've heard that Gottfried Reuter also planned a collaboration with the designer Luigi Colani at one point?

Colani was a genius in selling himself. He made an offer to Reuter to design a car for him and wanted a budget of 10,000 Deutschmarks a month to work on it with a whole team. After half a year had passed, I said to Reuter that we should probably check how the project was progressing. I visited Colani, and he showed me a large egg-shaped plaster model of a car, formed like a used bar of soap—Colani was obsessed with streamlined forms. A few months later, he presented an even larger model. I asked him where the detailing was, and he said, "That's up to your engineer pigs to sort out."

He once visited the Design Center in Lemförde in his Lamborghini Miura. As soon as he had peeled himself from the car, he lit a long cigar. After I showed him around, and before he got back into his Lamborghini, he handed me the cigar and said that, sadly, there wasn't any space for it in the Lamborghini—that's the kind of person he was.

The 1950s and '60s saw the development of quite a number of cars with plastic bodywork. Was that something you were working on as well?

We considered developing a plastic car. The problem was that the market already had quite enough fibreglass-reinforced plastic cars. Fibreglass-reinforced plastic is like sheet metal in that it only needs to be five-millimetres thick at most. Polyurethane, on the other hand, would have to be two centimetres thick to withstand that kind of stress. The cardan tunnel used to be located next to the gas pedals, and then on the side were the wheel cases, so another wall and then the outer wall of the wheel case. This meant you'd have to subtract six times two centimetres from the external dimensions—twelve centimetres—and that was a problem.

You worked for Elastogran from 1968 until 1972. Gottfried Reuter then sold Elastogran to the BASF [chemical company], and you became an independent designer. Was your work after this influenced by the 1973 oil crisis?

I mainly worked with glass, metal, and wood after parting ways with Reuter in 1972 and becoming self-employed. One of the reasons was the sudden tripling of the price of plastics, another was that I simply couldn't afford working with plastics without having an industry partner who would invest in the forms. So I focused on building my own collection for manufacture instead. Gottfried Reuter and I actually also spoke about the fact that polyurethane was non-recyclable. You couldn't simply melt it down like polypropylene, polyethylene, or ABS [acrylonitrile butadiene styrene]. You could, however, shred it. Reuter and his wife were breeding orchids on a large scale, and they used shredded polyurethane as substrate for some of them. He might have wanted to test if the roots of the orchids could break down the material. Perhaps, even back then, we were trying to appease our conscience.

We need to reduce our dependency on plastics

Jane Atfield in conversation with Johanna Agerman Ross

156—1 Jane Atfield, recycled plastic furniture, 1995.

157–1 Jane Atfield in her London Studio, 1995.

At what point did you decide to pursue a career in design?

As a young teenager, I moved from Pembrokeshire to Bristol and lived with my grandparents for a year. My grandpa, Ralph Brentnall, was a retired architect who had helped redesign some of the university buildings that had been bombed in the war. He was my inspiration to study architecture when I later moved to London. After completing a mostly theoretical degree, I realized I needed to learn more about materials and hands-on construction, so I studied at the London College of Furniture and then applied to do an MA in Furniture Design at the Royal College of Art in 1990. I loved working at this smaller scale and decided to focus on the furniture and product world. I felt that I had found my niche.

Did any of the issues around the use of plastics ever make it into your education in the late 1980s and early '90s? Despite increased environmental awareness, it seems that the use of virgin plastics within the design industry was still on the rise.

I don't recall learning about environmental issues or the ethics of design as part of the teaching programme. And it was not always easy, pre-Internet, to uncover information; the study of materials seemed to be a do-it-yourself course. Plastics were still being celebrated as a wonder material within the institutions and by furniture manufacturers in the early '90s, and design interest in the wider social or environmental context was limited. Instead, there was a cult of elevated designers, such as Philippe Starck who seemed to design by force of personality—designers as pop stars with endless performances.

Despite this, you started developing the idea for what would become Made of Waste. What made you look in the direction of recycling and reuse?

I felt alienated from the status- and style-driven designer furniture world. I was searching for another direction, casting a wider net. Luckily, during my second year at the RCA, I came across a book by Victor Papanek in the library—reading his *Design for the Real World* was a complete revelation. I loved the work of the radical and egalitarian Italian designers Enzo Mari and Bruno Munari too.

During that second year, I also came across an interestingly speckled, blue material sample on the desk of a fellow student studying sculpture. They had brought it back from a New York trade fair, but the manufacturer's name wasn't on it. Using material resource books, I eventually found out it was made by Yemm & Hart, a company in rural Missouri that recycled post-consumer

158–1 Detail of the RCP2 (1992–96) chair by Jane Atfield.

plastics such as shampoo and detergent bottles into sheet construction materials. I got in touch with them and was so excited by their approach. They were connecting new materials with a wider societal context, namely the problems of plastic waste, and using waste as a resource. I saw the potential for making furniture and everyday objects from it, and they shipped over some sheets for me to explore with.

Do you remember having a specific concern with throwaway culture and plastic waste in particular?

When I'd lived by the sea in Pembrokeshire as a child in the 1970s, I had seen plastic pollution on the beaches. Growing up in a family that had left the city for a rural, "alternative" lifestyle, I had not been seduced by consumer culture. Instead, there was an emphasis on experiences over possessions. Later at college, I remember hearing about the plastic-bottle tax in New York, which was introduced to combat rising waste levels in the 1970s, only to be defeated by industry lobbying and the US Supreme Court. I realized then that waste and plastics were political. Also, I had

read Rachel Carson's *Silent Spring*, with her devastating account of the ways humans were destroying the environment.

What was the reaction at the time from fellow students and teachers at the RCA?

My fellow students, especially the fine art and textile students whom I spent time with, were encouraging and curious. However, eco-design was marginalized at the time and often seen as an eccentricity or a leftover from the hippy movement. I loved being at the RCA, but the teaching staff had quite entrenched ideas of how things should be done. It was suggested that the work I made from recycled plastic be left out of my end-of-year show in 1992.

But you continued pursuing it...

Stumbling on the recycled plastic was a really exciting opportunity and effectively led to a decade-long research project that I felt totally committed to. I fell in love with everything the material represented!

So how did you go from importing to manufacturing your own board in the UK and setting up Made of Waste?

Well, it was not exactly environmentally friendly to ship the recycled plastic all the way across the Atlantic! I needed to find a way to fabricate the material here in the UK, using our own plastic waste. I set up Made of Waste to act as an agency for recycled materials, starting with plastics. I spent a long time searching for the right machinery and sourcing the HDPE [high-density polyethylene] post-consumer waste from community recycling schemes, but I was struggling to find investment and make the right contacts within the industry. Then I met a journalist called Sylvia Katz who introduced me to an industry insider, who also happened to be chairman of the British Plastics Federation Recycling Council. He later joined Made of Waste—which became a limited company—to develop and sell the recycled plastic to architects and designers, as well as for my own use in the furniture I designed. The material attracted a lot of interest, and over the next few years, we found new material sources, including the high-impact polystyrene range HIPS from used Marks & Spencer plastic coat hangers and yogurt pots… and another one using discarded clingfilm from the catering world.

So, at that point, there was clearly an awareness from industry that plastics needed to be considered from a point of view of circularity.

Yes, but my impression was that they embraced it under duress and in response to rising public awareness of the problems of plastic waste. The industry needed to show they were doing something. The remit of the British Plastics Federation Recycling Council was to encourage plastics manufacturers to recycle, but recycling was not widely implemented as it was often more expensive than producing virgin plastic. Most recycled plastic at that time was low-grade, as it was a random mix of different polymers and often ended up in agricultural settings.

What highlights do you remember from this time?

It was very inspiring collaborating with architects and seeing the recycled plastics incorporated into different interior projects. My favourites were the bathrooms in the Eco-Logic houses in Parc de la Villette in Paris and when the architect Ben Kelly used it in The Garden for children at the Science Museum. The graphic designer Peter Saville used it in his kitchen, and it featured in the studio sets for L!VE TV with Janet Street-Porter. Early on, we took a stand at 100% Design in London, building a whole kaleidoscopic room and making all the furniture from the material. People thought it was hand-painted initially, but then they realized that the colours instead came from chipped up bottles from their local supermarkets—the blue from the Big Dom detergent bottles was particularly distinctive!

Did you feel a sense of success in achieving all of this?

Not so much at the time; it seemed such an intense period in my life. I was so busy trying to juggle everything, including my son Noah who was born in 1995. Looking back now, I'm really happy that I threw myself into recycling and had the opportunity to pioneer the use of recycled plastics in the UK. Both the design and plastics industries at that time were male-dominated, and it was strange and somewhat lonely to be a young woman amongst it, but maybe that counts as some sort of success.

Despite much public interest and publicity, Made of Waste ceased trading less than a decade after it was founded. What happened?

There were strains within the company by 1998. I favoured developing community production facilities, keeping the raw material sources and the production of the sheets as local as possible. This would enable useful things to be fabricated from local waste; a school could build new classroom furniture from the bottles they threw away, for example. I wanted the material to be accessible and inexpensive and to develop along a social-enterprise model. Gradually, I was pushed out. My business partner and the plastics factories closed ranks. Eventually, it proved too difficult to continue, and Made of Waste closed. For a long while, I felt haunted by Made of Waste and the reasons I ended up walking away. It was such a shame that it all went wrong, and I wish I had fought even harder to stay involved. The company continued trading under the name Smile Plastics, but essentially was run down. More recently, it was given to a young couple and is now thriving. So at least there is a happy ending for the material. However, the days of endlessly recycling plastics are probably numbered. Surely, we need to reduce our dependency on plastics and work towards a predominantly plastic-free world, leaving the oil in the ground.

Every day, something new happens

Manfred Diebold, Rolf Fehlbaum, and Thomas Schweikert in conversation with Jochen Eisenbrand

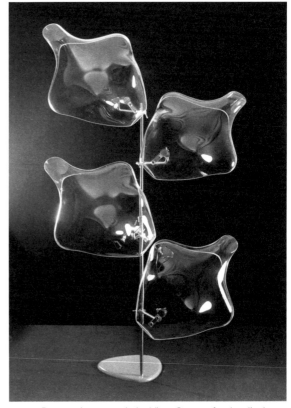

160–1 Perspex busts made by Vitra-Graeter for the display of blouses, 1956.

Rolf, when you think back to the furniture production of the 1950s and '60s, what feelings or memories do you associate with plastics?

Rolf Fehlbaum: A feeling of departure and optimism. The idea that one could shape this material in any which way—creating objects that we could have only dreamed of before—was very tempting. But it also harboured the danger noted by Charles Eames: that the ability to create anything would include the unnecessary, the arbitrary. The fact that plastic could have a problematic ecological effect never crossed our minds back then. It was quite simply a fantastic new material.

Plastics already played a role in the early days of the Vitra company.

Rolf: My father had an affinity with plastics. His shop-fitting business produced Perspex busts to present clothing on. Perspex could be shaped with very low-cost tools and without the use of complex machinery, simply by using heat. In 1952, Hans Theo Baumann and Vitra collaborated on a Perspex chair using this exact process. In actuality though, Perspex isn't a very convenient material for the furniture sector; it attracts dust and scratches easily.

Manfred, you were involved in the development of plastic furniture at Vitra from the early 1960s. What led you there?

Manfred Diebold: I had done an apprenticeship at the Raymond company in the early 1950s, and they went on to employ me as a toolmaker. At some point, I was tasked with building the first tools for the production of plastic components for the automotive industry. I then changed jobs and started working at Stara-Werke in Lörrach, where we produced flower boxes and pots from Styrofoam. Among our commissions was one for decorative busts for Vitra, and that was my first point of contact with the company.

And so, you started working at Vitra in 1962.

Manfred: One of my earliest tasks was to establish our own Styrofoam production and also to help create a plastics production process. Vitra's founder Willi Fehlbaum wanted to be as independent as possible from external suppliers. Little by little, we acquired all the necessary machinery for plastics production: an injection-moulding machine, an extruder, machines for deep drawing. Finally, we also got a large machine that could blow-mould entire mannequin bodies. Furniture production came later.

The collaboration Vitra established with Charles and Ray Eames was an important turning point in the company's history. Here again, plastic, specifically fibreglass-reinforced polyester, played an important role.

Rolf: Fibreglass-reinforced polyester can be worked manually, as in the production of boat hulls, for example. Using the process that Charles Eames had developed together with Zenith, the Eames Chair shell could be produced in large numbers. The injection-moulding technology of the 1960s, using polypropylene, was another step towards industrialization. We had asked Charles if he'd design a polypropylene chair for us, but he didn't seem interested. Since polypropylene doesn't have the same structural properties as fibreglass-reinforced polyester, the dimensions of the side profiles of the seat shell would have needed to be a lot larger; Eames didn't like that. He also appreciated the liveliness resulting from the somewhat irregular and easily visible glass fibres in fibreglass-reinforced polyester. Of course, this isn't something you get with polypropylene.

Incidentally, I recently came across Paul Scheerbart's book *Glasarchitektur*, and I found the following passage about glass fibres in applied art: "It has been forgotten by many that glass can be developed as fibres which can be spun. […] These glass fibres may lead to a whole new industry in applied art; divan covers, chair arms, etc., can be made of them." Basically, he is talking about the kind of glass that we would then use for fibreglass much later. In 1914, Scheerbart urged the industry to rethink their practice: "The industry of the future will also turn eagerly to glass fibres. For only fire-resistant materials will be used—both for divans and for flooring, where glass fibres will prove the most important material."

How was the technical know-how that was necessary in the production of the fibreglass shells transferred from the United States to Weil?

Manfred: Willi Fehlbaum's negotiations with Herman Miller granted him the license to produce the Eames shells from fibreglass-reinforced polyester, after which I was sent to Zenith in Santa Monica to be mentored by Saul Fingerhut. There,

I learned everything about how the production process worked and what we would have to pay attention to.

The first models of the Panton Chair, also developed at Vitra, were made from fibreglass-reinforced polyester as well.

Manfred: Indeed. However, unlike Eames, Panton did not want the material's structure to be visible; the surface of the Panton Chair was to be perfectly smooth. We spent a year on the first model. Panton was a nocturnal worker and would always approach me after sunset, using lamps to light the model from all sides in order to detect any deformations or alterations.

Even the first models that were presented in a 1967 edition of the magazine *Mobilia* were hand-made samples made from fibreglass-reinforced polyester. My team included 25 people who had worked on mannequins, so we knew how to make things in a single mould. But still, the production was extremely time-consuming.

And then you discovered Baydur polyurethane as an alternative.

Manfred: Yes. We saw a car bonnet made from Baydur at the plastics fair in Düsseldorf, and Willi Fehlbaum asked me to visit Bayer to find out more. I explained our product idea for the Panton Chair,

and I was told the reaction of the two components would have to take place in an aluminium or steel mould. In addition, the mould would need to be able to be heated and subsequently cooled down. Four weeks later, I'd built a plastic mould, and I drove back to Bayer. I had added some clamps for the mould to withstand the pressure, but when we injected the Baydur, we had to take cover—it went everywhere, the pressure was way too high! So, we cleaned the mould and then screwed it shut all the way around. With the second injection, it held, and we got a chair out of it that you could sit on. It was only then that Bayer realized what their material could actually do.

We started producing the Panton Chair in series in 1968. However, each one still had to be sanded down, filled in, and then painted.

So, there was still a lot of handcrafting that went into it.

Manfred: Which begged the question of how to produce it in large numbers, because demand was really picking up. And then BASF approached us, saying: "We believe that we're able to produce the chair through injection moulding with Luran." We then produced a prototype, tested its stability, and finally decided to risk it, even though the ageing resistance of this particular polystyrene was unknown to us. This version was produced from 1971 onwards.

162–1 Display-window bust by Vitra-Graeter made from Vitralon, 1956.

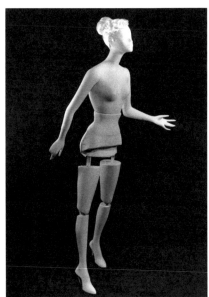

162–2 Mannequin made from Vitralon, 1956.

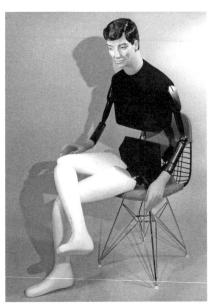

162–3 "Playboy" mannequin made from Vitrapor, wood, and foam, 1965.

Conversations

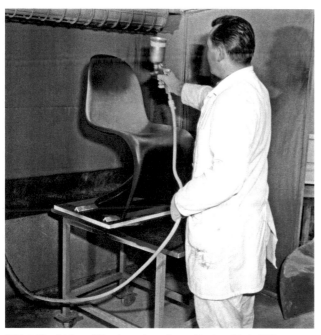

163–1 Varnishing of Baydur polyurethane Panton Chair, 1971.

163–2 Detail of the seat shell of the glass fibre-reinforced polyester chair by Ray and Charles Eames, 1948–50.

Due to the melt-in pigment of through-dyed Luran the Panton Chair no longer required a time-consuming handcrafted finish, which might indicate at least one of the motives for producing plastic chairs. Aside from the new design possibilities, the production costs are low, especially in large quantities.

Rolf: In this regard, Robin Day had made significant progress in the early 1960s with his chair for Hille. The shell was made by injection moulding polypropylene. As a consequence, it was very cheap and really stirred up the market. You could even say it marked the end of the Eames fibreglass chair as seating for the masses in halls and auditoriums.

Another important development in the 1970s came with the all-plastic chair, the Monobloc, produced from a single mould. I was fascinated by what this cheap chair had to offer: it can be quite comfortable, precisely because it is a little wobbly and flexible. But using the price point as the only guiding principle resulted in poor quality. The Monobloc became a chair that looks unsightly quickly and will end up in landfill rather sooner than later. Used in this way, plastics are problematic from an ecological standpoint, while products like the Eames Shell Chair or the Panton Chair— which remain in use over many decades—make the use of plastic more ecologically reasonable.

If we look at the role plastics play today in furniture production, there are entirely different challenges. Thomas, you are Technical Lead in Sustainability & Research at Vitra. How do you approach the topic of plastics?

Thomas Schweikert: The first task for my team and I was to look into bioplastics. What properties do bioplastics need to have? What would be desirable, and what are the exclusion criteria for their use? We carried out extensive research and developed an evaluation matrix which listed factors such as raw material, availability, price, recyclability, process capabilities, mechanical properties, and so on. Processability on a standard injection-moulding machine, for example, was rated highly, because significant investments would have to be made if that wasn't possible. Colourability was rated lower down the scale, because bioplastics don't have to look exactly like petroleum-based ones. We decided to exclude plastics that are made from food crops. And in this way, we gradually filled the matrix. When finally we evaluated it, we weren't left with a single material that seemed suitable for long-lasting furniture components. Nevertheless, we decided to test three different materials in order to collect practical, experience-based data. These were non-biodegradable materials, though: two types

164–2 Detail of Jasper Morrison's EVO-C cantilever chair, 2020.

164–1 Jasper Morrison and Thomas Schweikert with a development model of the EVO-C cantilever chair made from polypropylene, 2020.

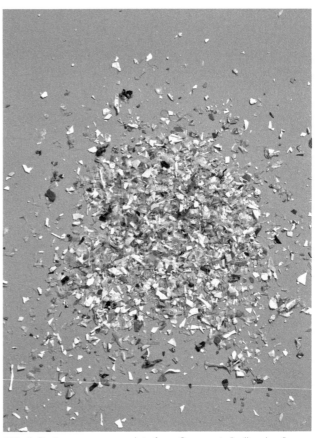

164–3 Edward Barber and Jay Osgerby, Tip Ton Re chair made from polypropylene sourced from Germany's "yellow bag" scheme, 2011/2020.

164–4 Post-consumer recyclate from Germany's "yellow bag" scheme, which Vitra uses to manufacture the Tip Ton Re chair.

of polyethylene made from by-products of cane sugar processing and a polyamide made from castor oil. Unfortunately, the results weren't satisfactory, and we decided to refrain from using bioplastics for the time being. What we learned from this experience though is that we should instead focus on circular economies and recycling, that is, keeping high-quality, petroleum-based plastics in the cycle for as long as possible.

How do differences in material quality play into this?

Thomas: Generally, we can say that the more diverse the source material of a recycled product is, the less possible it is for us to exactly define its properties. With many high-quality PIR [post-industrial recycled] grades, the primary material is almost completely pure, and so the properties of the resulting material are also quite stable. This becomes a little more difficult in the area of PCR [post-consumer recycled] grades. A valuable resource in Germany is the "yellow sack", a bin bag that is used to collect plastic packaging. However, since these bags contain different types of plastics, they have to be sorted in the recycling process by type and ideally also by colour. Here, it's crucial to work with the right companies that have mastered this process.

What does it mean that post-consumer recycled materials have to be compounded in order to be used in furniture production?

Thomas: The source plastic has to be optimized for the production process, and its properties must be altered in such a way that it can be used for durable and high-quality furniture components. During compounding, the regranulate is melted down, additives are mixed in, and it's then granulated again. In this way, UV resistance as well as flow and mechanical properties can be improved, and the plastic can also be coloured to any desirable tone. Frequently, glass fibres are added to the plastic as well, to provide more stability and improve pressure resistance, tensile strength, and scratch resistance. In this way, we are able to realize significantly thinner sections with improved stability and even save plastic at the same time.

Do you still generate plastic waste during production?

Thomas: We are very conscious of our supply chains and want to ensure that no plastic goes to waste. Our manufacturers themselves even grind down flawed elements, overflows, or sprue parts and add the material to the next injection-moulding process. You can only do this to a certain extent, however, because the material can be damaged during the first moulding process. This is therefore only done to a small extent in components we produce that are subject to significant static loads. Anything that isn't ground down is collected and handed over to a recycling company to be reprocessed, and then it re-enters the cycle.

Will plastic remain a useful material in the furniture sector in the future?

Thomas: We're convinced that plastic as a material still has its place in furniture production. I think the question is rather one of how plastic is being used; it has to be done sensibly and responsibly. When I look at the Panton Chair or an EVO-C by Jasper Morrison, I see an extremely efficient way to produce well-designed objects of outstanding quality at a reasonable price. One thing that will be of the essence in the future is to create a system and infrastructure that ensures any and all plastic products can be appropriately recycled and reused. Switching from a linear economy to a circular one is one of the most important challenges of our time.

I really enjoy working in this area, because it is significantly dynamic. Every day, something new happens—so many new ideas, concepts, and technologies emerge… like a new beginning. I find being involved in this change very fulfilling, because the responsible use of plastics will continue to influence the designs of the future.

We have to look at the whole cycle and not only at the product

Eric Klarenbeek and Maartje Dros in conversation with Corinna Gardner and Mea Hoffmann

166–1 Klarenbeek & Dros, Mycelium Project, 2013, various samples of mycelium printing and a materials overview.

166–2 Klarenbeek & Dros, Mycelium Chair, first generation, 2013.

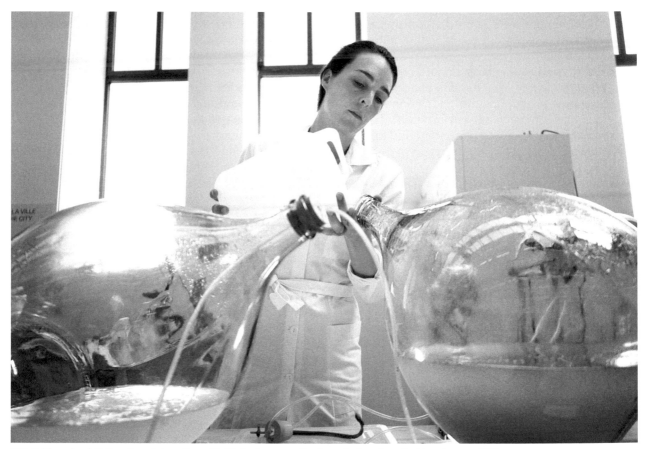

167–1 Klarenbeek & Dros in collaboration with Atelier Luma, cultivation of microalgae for biopolymers, 2017.

Who are Klarenbeek & Dros, and how did it all begin?

We're a design studio based in Zaandam in the Netherlands, and we work at the intersection of innovation, social design, and biomaterials. Our background is in identity- and public space design, and we're passionate about introducing new ideas. Often working in an art context, we bring innovative materials and 3D printing to the public, employing these as a tool for local fabrication and creating circular networks—to be socially and ecologically responsible is also very important to us.

In 2005, we began working with robotics and combined this with biotechnology, largely from a materials perspective; and then in 2010, we started collaborating with the University of Life Science in Wageningen to build the first bioprinter to produce 3D-print living mycelium cells, which solidifies biomatter through growth instead of using traditional binding agents. We were curious about which plant cells or other cells would reunite after being 3D printed, and that was the beginning of working with mycelium, combining biotechnology and robotics. And with this, we

learnt we had to go beyond our studio's facility— work towards scaling up and building our own infrastructure for production—to have an actual ecological impact. We then initiated the shift in the mushroom industry from which mycelium derives, moving from a focus on food to look at growing materials as well.

Through this work, we learnt more about propagating microorganisms such as mycelium and (secondly) algae, both of which start growing, roughly speaking, in a Petri dish. In 2015, we shifted radically towards algae and started to develop biopolymers that could be used as a replacement for traditional plastics. Mycelium is bio-compostable, but it requires specialist handling and its own infrastructure for growth (and production). Algae, in contrast, only requires lab facilities at the embryonic stage, when you propagate it, but once fully grown and harvested it unlocks the ability to extract is components and convert it into a thermoplast. At this stage you can process it like any other polymer, which in turn opens it up to the possibility of use for 3D-printer filaments, injection moulding, robotic printing, and traditional methods from the plastic industry.

When working with mushrooms, we were always asked about transport, carbon dioxide (CO_2), and depletion of the food supply, as mushrooms are land-based organisms. Naturally, this pushed us towards looking at water-based organisms and sea-agriculture, as we are based in the delta area of the Netherlands. Observing the works carried out on dikes and seeing how climate change is altering water levels went hand in hand with thinking about new production methods connected to, and in harmony with our environment. These factors were key to our development and our move towards algae and algae-based materials.

How do you bring together these insights on local context, materials, and technology?

We want to create change and take responsibility for our environment. We come from different islands [Maartje comes from a very historical island, Texel, and Eric from a totally designed island, Almere]. Our work is, in that sense, in balance. The idea that a small island needs to be responsible for its own environment and must build everything that is needed has shaped us. We need also to be mindful of background, historical context, and previous generations, and combine this with new ideas and new visions and innovation and with nature. Learning from history gives us new approaches to the future—taking what we already know and learning from it to see how we can turn the tide now. We developed the biopolymers over seven or eight years. But we're designers, and we wanted to start making things; we wanted a material that could, for example, grow new seating or make things for public spaces that are at one with nature, and this initial intuitive choice for binding carbon in our built environment still seems more relevant in terms of ecology (in comparison to shorter cycles such as food and fuel).

This is what happened with algae. When we started, algae farms were being scaled up for food, pharmaceuticals, and biofuel production, but we seemed to be the only ones interested in algae as a material. In the beginning, we started to propagate algae ourselves, growing it in the city of Amsterdam. Just as we had with mycelium, we wanted to learn about the processes and understand the potential. And then, with a sense of our position and role, we set up a seaweed circle—a network of strategic partners. We now have the same production infrastructure for seaweed that we initiated with mycelium.

There's a laboratory where scientists focus only on propagation. It's 15 kilometres from our studio, so very nearby. Then there are farmers who cultivate it in the North Sea—an architect and eco-enthusiast who wanted to boost biodiversity and an innovative circular farmer with a pilot processing plant for splitting wet from dry streams. Seaweed is over 80 per cent water, and you need to dry it, but the water extracted contains valuable nutrients, phosphates, nitrates, and minerals. These are very effective for helping plants grow, so you can use seaweed culture to boost agriculture. The wet juice has been used in this system of circular agriculture by several ecological farmers for a couple of years now, and the dry biomass comes to our studio where we convert it into biopolymers. What we do first is to make a granulate, and from that, we make products using injection moulding and robotic printing and produce filaments for 3D printers.

Our ambition is to scale up, so we've started a company. One of the first products we've tested is a decomposing plant pot. A farmer is growing tulip bulbs in pots that we've injection moulded for him. The pot remains in the soil and will feed the plant with its minerals and eventually fully decompose. We will monitor how quickly they decompose and whether they are successfully fertilizing the plants. Decomposition also means that the pots and the soil they contained can be worked into the land, and so there are no plastics, no waste, while also diminishing transportation and waste-disposal costs. This is a very practical, modest application, but it puts ideas for new fully circular supply chains in motion.

Tell us more about your role as designers and change-makers. You support the arts, but how do you see that scaling up?

As designers with vision who are sensitive to change, we often come up against the fact that we lack closed-loop and socially embedded production cycles that aren't based on exploitation of either people or nature. So first, we try to understand processes and what is necessary to overcome the challenges facing us as we create a new set up. And then we reach out to the possible players in this new envisioned field, which can vary from individuals to companies, acquaintances, farmers, or highly interesting, versatile producers. With their expertise, we try to implement our vision, educate each other, and then work together towards these new infrastructures for production. We concentrate on our work, but we need to collaborate with a lot of pioneers, experts, and hobbyists to realize our ideas, and they too can get inspiration.

169–1 Klarenbeek & Dros, algae for biopolymers.

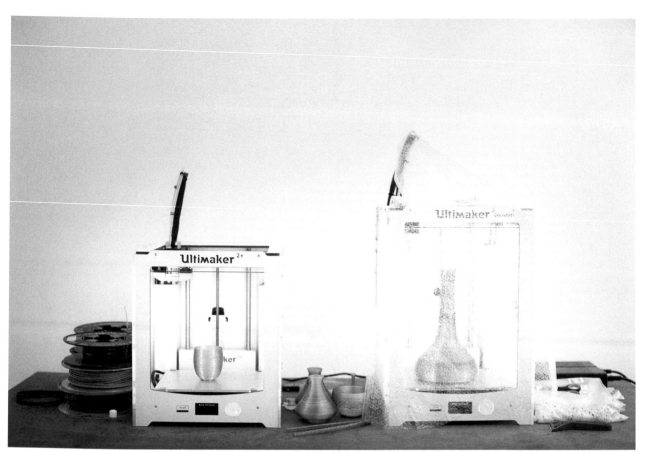

170–1 Klarenbeek & Dros, 3D-printed vases made from algae-based biopolymers.

And secondly, if you want to create an impact by means of ecological benefits, you can do this with art and design that expresses new possibilities—same as with education, what we experienced with our social design students at the Design Academy in Eindhoven with our mycelium chair, for example, where the reach was global, and we still get daily requests from students and businesses, eager for information. Art and design can have a very strong message; it communicates on a deeper, more emotional level that embraces people, creates community, and inspires change. As designers, we start with questions or problems, but we don't like to call them problems, rather possibilities or new ways to understand characteristics. What is important is that we pose perspectives on how things can develop in a nice way, a shared way. It's also about aesthetics and showing how something can connect with both its makers and users and need not be either harmful or scary.

So, if you look at the plant pots: they smell like the sea, like seaweed. That's okay for a plant pot if it is only to be placed in the soil and feed the plants as it decomposes—we quantify the positive benefits for the plants. But it's different for a chair in your house, and as designers, we must ask of every new idea we develop: What are the possible applications? How could it be used?

Which is a nice full circle back to this idea of public and identity, isn't it? It's about these objects working in context and being seen to work within context across their life cycle.

Yes, that's something we are always working on. To really introduce new materials successfully at scale, is always about getting the right certification. To do this, we actively work with research centres to validate the new materials, to get the right technical data sheets for production, et cetera.

This isn't the sexiest part of being a designer or artist, but it is a necessity, particularly for biopolymers. At this moment, there's a huge focus in the Netherlands and all over the world to push these types of materials, to integrate them into the built environment and in people's everyday lives.

All of this needs careful calculation. Transport plays a big part when it comes to climate impact, and because it is so problematic, it makes sense that we have to look at the whole cycle and not only at the product.

So, you take considerable responsibility in the way you work as designers.

Yes. Yes, we do. People sometimes remark, "Wow, you've been working on that for ten years. I wouldn't want that kind of relationship with my work. I'd rather have something done in a day." That's not us; we're in it for the long run. It's not about being asked "Hey, you're so creative, can you make this?" Our work requires a lot of attention, a lot of focus, and a lot of resilience to be able to achieve the goal.

We're constantly developing things; we focus not only on the scent of the material, but also on the colour, and look for a quality that can also change how we handle products and materials. We are constantly challenging ourselves, and one of the most recent elements is large-scale robotic printing. Now that we have the small 3D printers figured out, we're testing the seaweed material on a large-scale 3D printer, and it's also super nice for a company that builds robotic 3D printers to add this biomaterial to its portfolio of materials. We tested over the summer, and it was successful! And that has opened up the possibility for the seaweed biopolymer to be used by other robotic printing companies, so if they want to robot-print something on a large scale, for architectural purposes or furniture for instance, we can do it together. Another example is that recently we connected with Peter Ghyczy who designed the Garden Egg chair in the 1960s. He asked us if we would be interested in producing his chair in the seaweed biopolymer. For him, it was a new way of showing the design's intentions, a new vision of technology from the 1960s that can be brought to life again.

Designs like Ghyczy's were the early applications for polyurethane, the front runners of a new vision for what plastics could do in the future and how they could change our world. We are at a similar moment again: there are big challenges we must face and a lot of possibilities from a technological perspective, both in robotic printing as well as in new material alternatives to plastic.

Truly compostable alternatives

Amir Afshar of Shellworks in conversation
with Charlotte Hale and Mea Hoffmann

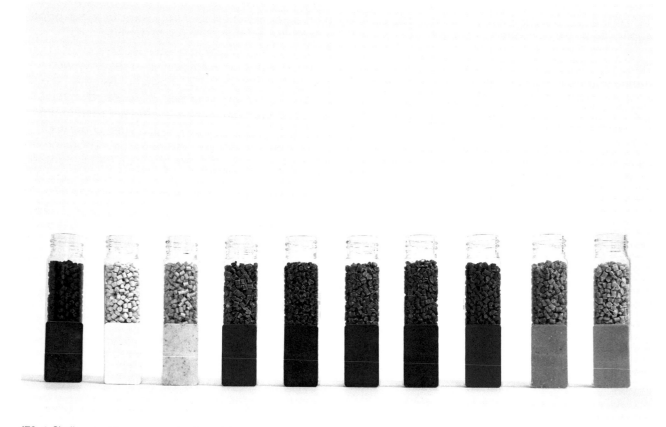

172–1 Shellworks, Vivomer natural colours, 2021.

Could you tell us about what Shellworks does, what materials and processes you use and why?

The three of us that founded Shellworks met at the Royal College of Art and Imperial College doing a dual master's called Innovation and Design Engineering, and we were fascinated by the problem of plastic pollution. Coming from three distinct backgrounds— science, engineering, and design—we thought we could bring these things together and find a solution.

From there, we created what we call truly compostable alternatives to plastic—materials that are designed to degrade in any environment without the need of special conditions like industrial composting or high humidity and temperature. Degradable plastics today come with caveats saying it will decompose but it needs certain conditions. We see that nature can do things really well; why not leverage what nature has built over millennia and try to understand how we can use it to create materials for today that will last only the duration they are needed?

We started by creating materials using a biopolymer called chitin that we extracted from crustacean shells, a waste product of seafood farming. We then got a lot of industry feedback concerning vegan solutions. And this is something that we didn't really think about, because when you think about plastic, you don't really think about it being vegan or not!

But this was a challenge for us, and then we discovered another technology. Now we use a microbe-based fermentation process, where the microbes feed on a carbon source, for example sugars or food waste, and produce a plastic-like material in their cells—just as we produce fat in our bodies. And once we take that material out, it behaves like plastic. So it felt like it was nature saying, "Here's an option that I'm okay with." The beauty of it is that the same microbes will then break it down and they're abundant within marine and soil environments. So once it's disposed of, it will break down and act in a benign way leaving no microplastics behind.

Was supply another factor in changing from chitin to microbes?

Chitin is the second most abundant biopolymer on Earth after cellulose, so it's available in the short term. But when you scale up to meet the challenges of plastic, other industries have to keep up with you. We didn't want to promote unsustainable farming just to extract chitin. It's a very interesting material, but you can scale up more rapidly when working with microbes.

Do your products aim to replicate plastic or embrace their natural quality?

We like to think of nature as the ultimate biologist, the ultimate chemist. The way that you find things in nature is so complex and beautiful and so perfectly arranged that it's difficult to replicate, so why not work with nature. Our microbially derived alternatives to plastics have great barrier properties. They're water resistant and oil resistant, and they're easily formed with current manufacturing processes.

We try to create things that might manufacture like plastic but don't necessarily feel like plastic. They have a certain weight to them; they have a certain form to them. We work really hard on the surface texture, for example, or the depth of the material. We only use natural dyes, so we like the fact that sometimes there's non-uniformity. It makes you understand that, yes, it's one of 5,000 pieces, but somehow there's a beauty to that one piece, inherently separate to its collection. And I think those kinds of action build value into things. But it's definitely something that we question all the time.

How far along are you with this process in terms of developing products?

We're already shipping products to a couple of different companies in the beauty space. That's where we've focused, because when people think of single-use plastics, they usually think of food packaging. And rightly so; it's something that is used very quickly. Yet people don't really focus on beauty products, because they're used for a longer period of time. But here, there is also plastic packaging that is ultimately going to be disposed of. The issue within the beauty industry—like with lipstick holders, one of the things that we have now developed—is that they're conventionally made up of around four or five different types of plastic that all tuck inside each other, which pretty much makes it impossible to recycle them even with the best intentions. Our solutions in contrast to this are all mono-material.

Could you tell us about what "truly compostable" means and some of the challenges or questions around certification?

Compostability is an interesting one, because a lot of products at the moment are certified as home compostable. We did internal testing first with wormeries and different disposal and home composting methods to make sure that our products achieve that. But it's a difficult balance to strike, because there's a lot of performance attributes that you're trying to meet: you want it to be shelf-stable for a duration of time; it needs to be shipped in containers that come to quite high temperatures; other products shouldn't interact with it. So, it's definitely a challenge balancing those different parameters.

Understanding what happens during the breakdown process is important too. There's a misconception that you can have a natural product that is shelf-table for many years and performant against formulations, but will completely disappear in a few months when

disposed of, that's simply not possible, at least for now. PBAT, a kind of petroleum-based plastic that's got a lot of interest recently, will degrade in nature very, very quickly. The problem is that it degrades down to microplastics, and much faster than other conventional plastics, like LDPE. But at the same time, if you were to put that into a home composting certification test, it might actually pass. So, we have to question: are those tests currently working in the correct way, or do we need to re-evaluate them? And what does "home compostable" actually mean?

With this confusion so abundant, you're also paying a lot of attention to communication and education. What role can designers play in creating awareness?

We always like to make the process and what goes into it clear to anyone. One of the key drivers of the company is to be as transparent as possible, because we recognize that we're in this situation partially because of plastic, but also partially because of greenwashing.

In terms of education, we have visual content that we're putting out; we try to look at ways to create symbols on our packaging that will then tie into a greater ecosystem. We've had decades worth of unclear symbols on bits of plastic. It can say that plastic number, whatever it is, is recyclable, but when it gets to the recycling facility they might just say, "Well, we don't deal with that here, so straight to landfill." Other symbols might seem to be about recycling, but ultimately they just mean this company's paid not to have to deal with recycling, which we see as the plastic industry's equivalent of paying for your sins. So, we're trying

174–1 Shellworks, Vivomer pellets, 2021.

174–2 Shellworks, Vivomer in orange, 2021.

175—1 Shellworks, jars in blue hues, 2021.

175—2 Shellworks, product line up, 2021.

to navigate that landscape carefully, but I think it's a combination of building the right platforms and cultivating the right relationships.

How do you select your partners and approaches?

I think because we're in the early days right now, we like to work with people whose true driver for choosing to work with us is that they want to push a sustainable agenda. We try to avoid people who are using this as a kind of springboard for marketing their one "sustainable" product, whilst the rest of their practices are unsustainable. I think it's also about understanding what's happening today and looking ahead, not looking for a quick Instagram pump. Maybe we start with a bottle cap but then work to do part of a range and then expand that range.

Which industries do you think are most focused on change?

It seems that everyone's focus on sustainability is stronger since the pandemic. Perhaps being at home means seeing how much plastic you're using, especially with the nature of sterility, testing kits, and PPE. Our focus for now is on the personal care and beauty industry, where there is a big pull to moving to what they call "clean beauty"—removing a lot of different kinds of ingredients that are detrimental to the environment with packaging being the last hurdle. But our intention is that, as we can bring the cost of our offerings down, we can start to move into other industries.

What do you think are the biggest challenges and opportunities in bioplastics at the moment?

I definitely don't think that there's a silver-bullet solution. It's going to be a collaborative approach, because, for one, it's a massive problem, obviously. And secondly, there's so many different types of plastic that you can't just have one bioplastic to replace everything. So, I think the approach is going to be a multipronged approach, and it is not only going to be a materials approach; it's going to be a communications approach and a usage approach. Whether we can move away from single use is something to think about. And legislation is a complicated one too.

How do you feel about the future of plastics?

We are very positive. We don't want people to feel guilty about the way that we've all dealt with plastics. It's been an available material. In theory, it's a great material—it's been too good, so we've used it for everything. But now, there must be a better way to do things. Let's embrace it and work together collaboratively to try to find a solution which is ultimately going to be useful to everyone.

We're looking to nature

John McGeehan in conversation
with Jochen Eisenbrand

176–1 John McGeehan mounting an enzyme crystal on an X-ray diffractometer.

176–2 Doctor Rosie Graham manipulating tiny crystals of an enzyme under the microscope.

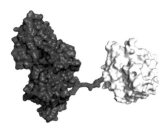

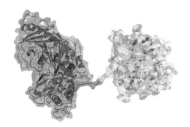

177–1 A PETase enzyme in blue is linked with a MHETase enzyme in red, to create an enzyme that is faster at breaking down PET bottles than the natural one.

177–2 A view of the internal structure of our PETase-MHETase chimeric enzyme.

Please tell us a about your research on enzymes.

We have been working on discovering enzymes from nature, bringing them into the laboratory, and evolving them for industrial purposes for quite some time. Our common theme is to study enzymes that break apart polymers, molecules that are ubiquitous in biology, from the DNA that encodes our genome, to cellulose that stores energy in plants, and chitin that provides the shells of many organisms. Understanding how these polymers are made, and then broken down again, will provide insights into how to break down man-made plastics. We can already use enzymes to break down cellulose into sugars, proving a feedstock for biofuels, and enzymes are widely used in the food and pharmaceutical industries.

When did you start your research on plastic-eating enzymes?

In 2016 a Japanese group published a paper in the journal *Science* on a remarkable bacterium that can break down plastic and use it as an energy and carbon source. We decided to work on this to see if we could understand how the enzyme works and then figure out how to make it faster. Could this be a potential naturally evolved solution for the plastics problem? We published our first work in 2018 and it took off in the slipstream of the David Attenborough BBC TV documentary series *Blue Planet II*, and fortuitously in the same week as *Earth Day*. Basically, all the planets aligned and we captured global interest. Over the subsequent years, the UK government has funded our research, providing a grant of six million pounds to help us create the Centre for Enzyme Innovation [CEI] at the University of Portsmouth, now with a team of 30 researchers.

What plastics are your current focus?

We are currently focusing on polyethylene terephthalate, commonly known as PET. It is the plastic that you will find in single-use drinks bottles and food packaging, easily recognized by the number 1 in a recycling triangle label. But that's just the tip of the iceberg. Most PET can actually be found in textiles, and clothing made with these polyesters is normally very poorly recycled.

Could you describe your general approach?

We're looking to nature, we have people out in the field actually scraping around in rubbish dumps, out in the oceans, on beaches… places where you would find plastic, searching for new enzymes and then bringing those back to the laboratory. The idea is a really simple one, in that nature recycles everything incredibly efficiently, it doesn't waste a single piece of energy, so we can learn from these processes.

For example, one of my colleagues, Professor Simon Cragg, is a marine zoologist who is leading a project in Southeast Asia looking at places such as mangroves and coral reefs. Environments such as rainforests and mangroves have high rates of microbial carbon turnover, with enzymes playing a key role in these natural cycles. The microbes are breaking down the plant material and turning it over in the soil and then regrowing. There is a whole natural recycling process taking place. Unfortunately, the roots of the mangroves also act like giant sieves for plastic bags and the other plastic rubbish that becomes an environmental problem. We are looking at this to see whether the microbiology at these sites is adapting to this plastic insult and evolving new enzymes. And the evidence is yes, they are, and that's a really exciting finding.

What other types of fieldwork are you doing?

We're also doing controlled experiments where we take an area, map it out, and introduce a whole row of different plastics in the environment which we then monitor every month to see what's happening to it. We can then identify microorganisms that are growing on the plastic, and then hopefully the enzymes they produce.

Then what happens when you take the enzymes found in nature to the lab?

My specialist area is taking these natural enzymes and engineering them to work faster in the laboratory, adapting them for industrial recycling. The original bacterium that our people have found in the rubbish dump actually produces two key enzymes: The first one, PETase, starts to break down the PET bottles, then the next, MHETase, takes the products from the first enzyme and breaks them down further, all the way to the original building blocks. We joined the two enzymes together in the lab and found that the larger enzyme works about six times faster than the original one. This shows the potential for engineering enzymes further.

When you heat PET bottles up to around 65–70 degrees centigrade, they start to become soft and malleable. The enzymes can then access the bonds holding the plastic together more easily and this dramatically speeds up the breakdown. The trouble is that enzymes naturally tend to fall apart at these temperatures. Thus, our team, and indeed many other teams, are looking in places such as hot springs, gathering hundreds of enzymes from all around the world to see which can work efficiently at these hotter temperatures.

What technology are you using to alter or join the enzymes?

We use a technology called X-ray crystallography, where basically we take the enzyme, purify it, and make crystals—in much the same way as you can make salt crystals by evaporating water from a salty solution. We then fire powerful X-rays at the crystals, using large facilities such as the Diamond Light Source. This allows us to generate these beautiful three-dimensional pictures of what the enzyme actually looks like. Once we know that, we can start to understand how it works, alter its shape and make it faster, to attack and break down our man-made polymers.

The great thing about this is that the technologies are quite mature. The pharmaceutical industry has been doing this for many years as have the food and drinks and the biofuels industries. All those enzymes that are in your laundry detergent originally came from natural sources, but were then evolved to work well in a washing machine. The technology to make enzymes at scale is available now, meaning we can move forward quite fast.

What are the advantages of this kind of biological recycling in comparison to mechanical or chemical recycling?

When you break down plastic bottles mechanically and melt them, they can start to lose some of their material qualities, becoming more brittle and less clear. But if you use enzymes, you can actually break down that plastic to its original components, which are identical to those produced from oil and gas. You can then make plastic that is of a virgin-like quality, even suitable for food use.

We believe that biological recycling with enzymes has a real advantage by lowering energy use across the supply chain and greenhouse gas emissions compared to current fossil-based production routes. Technologies such as pyrolysis require high temperature and pressure, employing extensive energy use. Enzymes operate at much cooler temperatures.

We need to be aware that real waste streams are contaminated and mixed. The good thing about enzymes is that they don't care, they're highly selective. You can select enzymes to only pull out the monomers from one type of plastic and then put in enzyme number two, potentially to get the monomers for the second plastic. Other options could be to use cocktails of enzymes for mixed waste. We are testing these now.

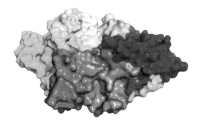

179–1 The MHETase enzyme shown in multiple colours to illustrate how if folds into a 3D structure.

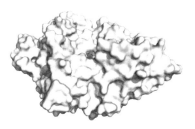

179–2 The MHETase enzyme shown as a surface representation.

However, I believe that we will actually need a combination of many technologies including chemical recycling, mechanical recycling, and the types of bio-recycling that we are proposing. There is not one solution, because plastics are made up of such a diversity of different materials. Polypropylene, for instance, is going to be a major challenge to break down with enzymes, so we need to match the technology to the waste stream. I am hopeful that the most innovative advances will come by working together and combining these technologies.

How do you make your research applicable for industry?

Industry doesn't necessarily want enzymes alone, they want integrated solutions that can be adapted to their current recycling facilities and supply chains. They also want to know how much it costs and what benefits it will give them. Last year our local enterprise partnership, Solent LEP, was awarded a one-million pound investment to build an industrial-engagement hub and bio-cycling lab on site, so that we can take real waste streams, test them, and develop processes quickly. The enzyme lab will feed enzymes into this new facility. We'll then take those building blocks and remake plastic out of them again and again. This will allow us to refine the process and help to calculate the costs, energy savings, and reductions in greenhouse gas emissions. Our new laboratories are due to open early in 2022.

Do you think we'll be able to do without plastic at some point in the future?

There are certain plastics that we just don't have good alternatives for at the moment, and some uses such as medical devices, where plastics outperform other materials. Of course, there are also many areas where plastics are vastly overused, and single-use plastics and fast fashion need to be reconsidered carefully. Opinions vary, and some will say that we need to stop all production of plastics immediately, but in reality, plastic production worldwide is likely to grow. I am certainly an advocate of the reduction of single-use plastics, and I think we can all take personal responsibly to help with this, but the main issue with plastics is taking better care of what happens to them at their end of life. A reduction in the number of different types of plastics would certainly help to simplify recycling. In addition, some research groups are working on recycled plastics by design. These cleverly designed plastics combine high performance during their lifetime but have the ability to be safely deconstructed and recycled at their end of life. I believe that there is still much to be learned from nature and I'm hoping that the current trend of researchers collaborating across the globe will help us to find real solutions for our plastics pollution crisis.

Calling it out was really important

Dianna Cohen in conversation with
Corinna Gardner and Mea Hoffmann

180–1 PPC Scientific Advisor Doctor Sylvia Earle, Mission Blue, Coco Islands, Myanmar.

Conversations

How did you go from exploring plastic in your artistic practice to co-founding the Plastic Pollution Coalition?

I grew up by the beach in Southern California with a deep love of the ocean. But I also grew up thinking of myself as an artist. Then my mum died of breast cancer the year before I graduated high school. So I set out to become a biology major and do preventative cancer research. Having very sadly lost my mother to cancer, I wanted to study it and figure out how to prevent it.

In the science department at UCLA, people often said to me, "Your drawings are so good, you should become a scientific illustrator." I felt offended because they only saw this quality in me. I knew art was a bigger part of myself—I had been making it my whole life. So I transferred to the art department, and as soon as I did that, the world opened up.

And what happened then?

I needed to earn a living and started by selling paintings of flies and insects, and then went into working in collage and using brown paper bags. At some point, working with an artist friend of mine in the Belgian countryside, a homeopathic pharmacy gave me a plastic bag with an image of a dandelion printed on it and the name in Latin, *Taraxacum officinale*. I had an epiphany—plastic! I sewed part of this bag into an artwork and I then really started thinking about plastic; it was so seductive, and it was all around.

My pieces became larger, and friends started mailing me beautifully coloured or interesting plastic bags from all over the world. I began receiving giant boxes of bags; I think I became people's de facto upcycling or downcycling friend.

But after a number of years, some of the bags in my pieces began to fissure and break apart. I realized that my artwork is ephemeral. Like us, it's alive, it's organic. I started learning more about plastic. I was kind of celebrating this material when I originally started working with it: the variety of bag colours, and all the different printed texts and images on them.

The deep irony is that, in the late 1970s, plastic bags were introduced in the US as better than paper, with the marketing that choosing plastic over paper, saved trees. And these bags were printed with trees or flowers or animals or nature scenes.

That was an important switch, but many of us became wary soon after.

Yes, I educated myself about the material and learned that plastic doesn't break down, it breaks apart—and it's primarily made from oil. I think your average person still has no idea about this fact. I was also seeing more and more plastic at the beach and in the water. In my mid-20s, I became a certified diver, and I kept seeing more and more plastic. I'd put it in my little mesh bag during dives. I had this feeling that we all needed to be picking up rubbish from the water and the beach.

I heard a lone voice at that time, Captain Charles Moore, out there yelling, "There's a Great Pacific Garbage Patch. Hey, people wake up!" I called him up. He was very abrupt and said, "You can't clean this up." I then had the opportunity to meet him in person. I told him I wanted to go out to the Garbage Patch with a cargo ship, some decommissioned fishing trawlers, and a chipping machine that can take up to 50 per cent organic matter. I wanted to collect it, chip it, cold-mould it, and make bricks and artwork out of it. I would bring a bunch of surfers, actors, musicians, and friends from Los Angeles with me to help raise awareness about what's happening in the ocean. And again, he said to me, "You can't clean it up; it's in the entire water strata, spread over 2,000 square miles. It's a Sisyphean task, and I am not sure we should be focusing on just cleaning it up. We need to work out where it's coming from."

Every time I had conversations like this, I'd go back to the drawing board. I began to meet other people who were also looking at the problem, not just focusing on clean-up, but rather trying to think about the upstream source points. Where's the stuff coming from? Who's creating it? What's it made of? Whose responsibility is it? Where is the legislation that might change what's happening with it?

Coming together, we realized we needed to create a coalition, an alliance that would bring together disparate, diverse groups and people who were all looking at the issue at different points along the cycle. We spent days together discussing what to call ourselves. Finally, we settled on Plastic Pollution Coalition. We decided it was an important name, because people weren't calling this stuff plastic, and they weren't calling it pollution. They were calling it "marine debris". "litter", "rubbish", "waste", and "garbage". If you call it those things, then you manage it as those things.

182–1 Dianna Cohen, *PostConsumer Mandala*, 2001. Plastic bags, plastic handles and thread, collection of the artist.

Calling it out was really important, and that's still a core part of our work—educating and encouraging people to call it what it is: plastic, single-use plastic, plastic that has been designed with intended obsolescence, microplastics, microfibres, nanoplastic washing out from synthetic clothing. Plastic packaging too euphemistically goes to the "landfill", as if that's something real! And incineration, which we euphemistically call "waste to energy" and "waste to fuel".

What we've learned over 12 years at Plastic Pollution Coalition is that plastic pollutes our environment and our bodies through the entire life cycle. From the well head or from extraction, through manufacturing, to use, to end of life. Throughout this entire chain, it releases greenhouse gases, dioxins, and particulate pollution; it releases microfibres and microplastics—it's toxic. It leeches small amounts of plasticizing chemicals into our food, our beverages, our beauty, health, and childcare products....and into us.

It's fascinating to hear your views of shifting perceptions and terminology. How do we address the ongoing confusion and lack of transparency?

It was and is greenwashing. It just came up again, because we've had an "oil spill" on Huntington Beach. Think about the BP Oil Spill. Adding the word "spill" to the end of something that's a disaster is the cleverest act of marketing crisis comms I've ever seen! We're all familiar with what a spill is. A spill happens with a glass of iced tea; go grab a sponge and wipe it up. Disaster to spill—it's brilliant to me, but totally diabolical. Plastic was never "disposable", and it never will be. The words society uses to speak about materials are tricky, slippery, and important.

In the last few years we've been part of forming another global movement—Break Free From Plastic. As part of this, we spent time in Houston, Texas, on the Gulf Coast, where there are 66 miles of oil and petrochemical refineries and processing plants, and in between are these tiny little estuaries and inlets where people still have shrimping boats and fish. I don't even know how to describe the sweet and toxic smell. I met with groups that we now work with, allies who are part of the Coalition and of Break Free, fence line and front line organizations on the ground contending with this. Communities are being poisoned—people are suffering from all different kinds of asthma, cancers, and reproductive health issues.

183–1 Dianna Cohen, *Wave Lens*, 2005. Plastic bags and thread, collection of Jackson Browne.

183–2 *PPC REFUSE* artist print series, artwork by Raymond Pettibon.

Yes, these are challenges many are only seeing now.

Right, and I've also come to realize more recently that our global use of and dependence on plastic directly contributes to the climate crisis and disproportionately impacts BIPOC communities and front line communities. We collaborate with these groups and try to help uplift and amplify their work and the need for change. At Plastic Pollution Coalition, we're working toward a more just, equitable world, free of plastic pollution. We ask where we can be effective, where the upstream source points are, and how we can create effective change. We've found those pressure points to be policy and legislation, producer responsibility, and engagement with companies and corporations, working with schools and different institutions. And now watching students and youth ambassadors, so many of whom are climate activists working towards intersectional change—none of it's in a vacuum anymore.

One of the things I love is how much I've learned from our youth ambassadors and activists. They're so fluid in their understanding, looking at systems and the interconnectivity of everything. It's their tomorrow—it's their future. But coming back from the World Economic Forum, the UN Climate Change Conference, and places they've been invited to speak, they're frustrated. They feel rolled-out but not heard. It's great that they are invited to the table, but don't stick them at the kids' table! They need to be in every meeting, and you need to really listen to what they're saying.

You've been speaking about pollution, but the focus is also increasingly on the danger of plastic manufacture. How do we make this known?

Coming back to language, the Break Free From Plastic movement has a great new talking point: "Plastic fuels the climate crisis." The double entendre for "fuels" is so good. The movement is good on legislation too, we are pushing hard right now. The Break Free From Plastic Pollution Act 2021—a comprehensive bill that addresses plastic pollution—was put before Congress this year. What we need to know is that, as organizations divest from fossil fuels, plastic is the petrochemical industry's Plan B. The challenge is real.

Roundtables

What About Recycling?

Plastic recycling is as complex as its labeling is abstract: a number in a triangle of chasing arrows gives little clue as to what a specific material is for, what it contains, or its potential future applications once recycled.

Together with seven experts in their fields – James Wakibia, Anirban Ghose, Veena Sahajwalla, Dirk Hebel, Purnima Joshi, Vijaya Rao and Vaishali Nadkarny – we try to untangle the world of waste management and speak about where the challenges and potentials lie. We discuss the material sciences and the pioneering work to turn non-recyclable materials into recyclable ones. We project into the near future when buildings will be dynamic storage systems, talk to the citizens cleaning up a street at a time, and discuss the effects of government bans and policies. The conversations were conducted by Anniina Koivu.

In 2017, Kenya was the first country to ban single-use plastics. James, you were a key player. What was your experience of this historical moment?

James Wakibia: My experience was first hand. I became an activist out of anger; in around 2013, I started campaigning and collecting signatures that I presented to the local county parliament. I wrote newspaper pieces and ran the #BanPlasticsKE on social media. I created awareness of how plastics were affecting our environment and tried to influence some change.

In 2015, our Minister for Environment Judi Wakhungu retweeted my hashtag and wrote that she was working with industry to try to affect the ban. To test the waters, I wrote an opinion piece in the next day's newspaper suggesting that it was the government's position to move forward with a ban on plastic bags. The new hashtag I created #IsupportBanPlasticsKe reached thousands of people. On 28 February 2017, the government announced a ban on single-use plastic bags.

What has happened since the ban took effect?

James: While the approximately 100 million plastic bags issued every year have been phased out, the plastic issue has not actually been solved. Not long after the ban, someone found a loophole in the system and introduced non-woven polypropylene bags that quickly became omnipresent.

Unlike single-use plastic bags, these bags are more durable and can be used several times. They are also heavier, and it's more likely they'll cling to the ground until waste pickers collect them.

What makes the single-use plastic bag so popular in Kenya? Is there a link to the so-called *kidogo* economy where packaged products are split into smaller quantities?

James: Plastic bags have been a convenient and important means for low-income people: for example, a two-kilo sack of sugar will be split into smaller portions, which are weighed and transported in plastic bags.

But the ban did not cause the *kidogo* economy to collapse. The ban has affected every class in society, but it's true that the majority of single-use plastic bags that continue to come in from neighbouring countries—despite high fines— are used mainly by low-income people. So far, there is no valid alternative.

Has the ban triggered new waste-plastic recycling projects?

James: Various projects have deservedly attracted attention: Flipflopi is a sailing boat entirely made from plastic waste and flip-flops collected from beaches and towns along the coast; Gjenge Makers turn used plastics into building bricks; and there's the environmental NGO I'm with called the Centre for Environmental Justice and Development in Nairobi (CEJAD), which advocates for the rights of waste pickers. Waste pickers are the true environmental defenders, yet why do they get paid so little for their important work?

Can you give some numbers?

James: During a recent visit to the rubbish tip in my home town Nakuru, waste pickers told me they were selling one kilogram—about 30 half-litre plastic bottles—for eight shillings.[1] That is a lot of work for not much money.

Do pickers differentiate between the plastics they pick?

James: Waste pickers know exactly what kind of plastic gets the best price, for example HDPE or PET. They avoid PVC or low-quality plastics as well as any coloured and sprayed bottles.

No local recycler wants to recycle something already recycled because it usually means downcycling and hence a quality loss. Actually, much recycled or low-quality plastic stays on the ground.

Honestly, I don't think recycling is the sole solution to our current plastic problem. Action should be taken much earlier: the chemical industry should design new plastic materials specifically to lessen the environmental impact, then a country like Kenya will use less of the polluting kind.

Does Kenya receive waste from other countries as part of the global waste-management system?

James: No, Kenya is part of the Basel Convention's multilateral environmental agreement designed to reduce the movement of hazardous waste between nations. But, as always, there's a loophole: had Kenya agreed to receive plastic waste from, let's say, the US, the Convention would no longer be binding. Luckily, we have a very attentive society and people stand up. Like in 2020, when the American plastic lobby proposed investment in Kenya's recycling infrastructure providing Kenya accepted US plastic waste—about 500 million kilograms per year. The people of Kenya stood up and asked:

Why can't the US recycle its own waste? Does it want to use a low-income country like Kenya as a rubbish tip? They should invest in their own citizens and deal with their own waste.

Australia finds itself at the other end of the global waste scenario; China's 2018 waste-import ban hit the country hard. Until 2017, it was exporting 36 per cent of all its waste plastic to China.[2] Still today, Australia holds one of the top spots in per capita plastic waste generation.[3]

Anirban Ghose: More and more legislation is kicking in in Australia. As of March 2020, Australia can't export waste materials, including plastic. Since March 2021, single-use plastic drinking straws, stirrers, and cutlery have been banned; on 1 March 2022, polystyrene food and drinks containers as well as oxo-degradable plastics will be added to the ban. There is a clear message from the government that "business as usual" can't continue.

Crisis often creates fertile ground for change and new projects. Veena and Anirban, you and your team at SM@RT work on next-generation recycling and upcycling technologies.

Veena Sahajwalla: We work from the mindset that waste is an opportunity, not a problem. We want to challenge recycling norms and propose smart recycling that allows waste to be transformed back into valuable products. To get there,

we have to reassess what quality actually means.

In many cases, plastics do fabulous things when they have clear and important functionalities. But then there are poor-quality products too.

Human beings' drive to make things convenient has taken us to the extreme: just think of plastic drinking straws, cups, and cutlery; cheap plastic toys. Surely these are part of some of the most unhappy meals one can imagine!

The discussion must be about value. Plastic's value will increase if it is uncontaminated, high-quality material ready for recycling. Take scrap steel, it has huge value and is traded across the world as a commodity. The opposite is true of plastic.

What makes recycling so problematic?

Veena: The resin code number that is put into the triangular chasing arrows causes a lot of confusion. A number from 1 to 7—with 7 being "other"—as the sole identifier is just not enough.

In fact, the variations seem infinite. There are so many other elements, like the functional additives to the core resin that are never mentioned.

Veena: Yes, the problem lies in the complexity of the material. Let's take the different plastics that go into making a car as an example. For a one-ton car, 10 per cent of its weight, so about 100 kilograms, is non-metallic and primarily made from a variety of plastics. What if we could make all these different plastics a bit more converging?

Then deconstruction of a vehicle becomes far simpler, the material quality increases, labelling is simplified and so is the recycling.

What are the most recyclable plastics?

Veena: Today, the regular PET water bottle is fully recyclable. Even more importantly, a PET bottle was and is meant for containing water or other drink, both before and after its recycling. You cycle back to the original purpose, and it's a closed loop.

Already with the next resin code number 2, for HDPE, things get complicated. The material can contain liquids, anything from milk to chemicals. But different liquids need different additives, and so we venture into the details of chemistry very quickly. The conversation typically stops here. We hardly ever talk about the different combinations of core polymers and the numerous additives when it comes to plastics.

Why is that?

Veena: First, we need to fully comprehend how plastics vary according to their different applications. We are still learning about plastics.

So recycling is largely a matter of correct labelling?

Veena: Labelling can only start working if we also consider and communicate not only its composition but also its specific purposes. Only then will we be able to become circular and to keep a specific plastic within its original sector.

What is the key takeaway?

Veena: Stop making poor-quality products only to complain about them afterwards. Make quality products instead that are appropriate for their specific applications and try to keep a given plastic's recycling within the same sector!

What can help?

Veena: Product designers should be thinking about the lifespan of their products, recycling science needs to operate in collaboration with industry. A MICROfactory can provide the missing link to fill that gap.

Should we imagine the MICROfactory as little rubbish-processing WALL-E's, cleaning up the Earth?

Anirban: Why not! The MICROfactory model features a series of small machines and devices that use patented technology to re-form waste products into new and usable resources. They can be installed in an area as small as 50 square metres, and be set up wherever waste is stockpiled, such as a manufacturing plant or regional waste disposal site, processing waste at source and putting it back into the use cycle.

Veena: Being modular, fit-for-purpose, and flexible in size, the MICROfactory model may disrupt the current highly centralized, vertically integrated industrial model.

Anirban: A small-scale module in our university's basement converts electronic waste into new products. Smartphones or circuit boards are broken down and scanned by a robotic module to identify useful parts, which are then re-formed into valuable materials. Valuable metal alloys such as copper can be retrieved, while plastics can be converted into high-quality filaments for 3D printing.

Veena: One of the most fundamental pieces in the circular economy puzzle is the notion of re-forming. You can re-form structure, re-form products, re-form chemistry. We can help to rethink the system. "Re-form" should become the fourth R in the common phrase "reduce, reuse, recycle — and reform".

Dirk, you are advocating for reform in the building industry, taking disassembly as a starting point. You ask for a more dynamic change in how we perceive static building material and call for the renewal of outdated building codes.[4]

Dirk Hebel: Waste is a design problem. We must start to design buildings in such a way that future generations do not have to deal with our poor planning. We need to rethink materials and construction systems to allow for 100 per cent reuse and recycling at the same level of quality. In the building sector, that means getting rid of composite materials that are not fully recyclable or connection systems that are not fully demountable—avoiding glues, foams, or wet sealants.

Many people will see this as wishful thinking, but when you realize that less than 10 per cent of all deconstruction material is brought back to the market and that 90 per cent is either landfilled, burnt, or downcycled, the facts are simply frightening: where will future generations get their resources from if we are wasting them?

There's a German term for how we should design: *sortenrein*. It describes the purity of materiality, meaning that neither synthetic, mineral, metallic, or biological materials should be mixed into composites, nor should any connection system prohibit a circular reuse or recycling. The moment adhesives are added, the circular building industry the EU needs and demands is out of reach. We need to think ahead to when buildings are deconstructed and start thinking of buildings as temporary storage systems.

Like a leasing agreement?

Dirk: Imagine, after use, you could go into a building designed as a material depot, just as any other storage warehouse, and take out all materials and elements one by one, reuse, reconfigure, or recycle them. You'd have dismantled the entire structure in a matter of days. Now architecture becomes part of a sharing economy: a digitally organized, managed, and steered storage system. Companies in Germany have already developed algorithms for such a system, aware that a completely new market will develop.

Digitalization is fundamental to this vision. We need digital twins of all our buildings in the future, and these need to be accessible. The first of these platforms are already online, Madaster being one of them,[5] including material passports describing all properties in great detail.

This demands transparency—similar to, say, the ingredients listed on a chocolate bar, you'd want to know every detail of a building.

Dirk: Yes, I'd want accessible information answering questions like: what are the technical properties; is it fireproof; is it biologically or technically recyclable? Does it contain any problematic fractions we need to take care of? We need to get to that level. And these material passports could then be the ground for evaluating the circular potential of a building.

Downcycling is already common practice, so what's stopping you putting 100 per cent recyclable "storage buildings" into action?

Dirk: The construction industry currently is torn between two systems that don't match. On one side, the European Commission Action Plan introduced a way to achieve 100 per cent circularity by 2050,[6] and the German Packaging Law gives priority to recycled materials over primary sources.[7] But the building sectors' norms and codes do not fit with any of this. We need to prioritize these ecologically important questions that are also going to have a great economic impact. The Club of Rome prognosticated in the 1970s that primary resources would get increasingly expensive, but nobody believed them.[8] The incredible price increases in primaries we are experiencing right now will continue unless we change our thinking. We need urgently to activate our secondary material streams, make them more attractive from a political level also, and change our application attitude. Codes

and norms need to steer this change rather than prevent it from happening.

What about urban mining? Wouldn't that allow the reuse of existing debris?

Dirk: The current built environment was never designed or even conceived of as part of a circular system. So how could it suddenly become our hope for the future? We need to design a new generation of buildings for this; the existing urban mine should be seen as building stock to be accepted, remodelled, and extended, not demolished. The most sustainable building is the one that already exists.

Purnima, Vijaya, and Vaishali, with a group of ten other volunteers you took matters into your own hands and started an award-winning community project in Pune, India, called the Resource Recycling Centre (RRC). One street at a time, you have been teaching residents about material recycling.

Purnima Joshi: Yes, we always start with people. First, the RCC helped residents to take ownership of their streets by organizing collective cleaning Saturdays. We put out a guide to becoming an active citizen; it takes as little as speaking to your neighbour or picking up the phone and reaching out.

Today, we work with community leaders, ward officers, the municipal corporation, people in charge of utilities (sanitation, street lighting, water, electricity), the traffic police, the department of forests and parks, recyclers, NGOs, and a range of manufacturers.

Next, we organized e-waste bins and found a proper vendor

authorized to recycle waste. Every fourth Sunday of the month we spoke to residents in the local park about how harmful e-waste is if not managed properly.

Next on the list was the poor-quality kind of plastic that no one seemed to want.

Vijaya Rao: At one time, we did not use plastic at all, but nowadays every spice and condiment is sold in flimsy plastic bags. No recycler is interested in them! It was specifically this poor-quality plastic that we wanted to find a new purpose for. Eventually, we found out about Rudra Environmental Solutions and met with Dr. Medha Tadpatrikar.[9] Rudra transforms poor-quality plastic into fuel (something between kerosene and petrol), which is a cheap way for farmers to fuel their machinery.

Purnima: The RRC has also existed since 2020 as an open drop-off point for dry waste.

Nine different kinds of material are currently collected: metal, thermocol (expanded polystyrene), paper, cardboard, glass, broken glass, e-waste, and plastic. Over the years, we have collected more than 50 tons of e-waste, 40 tons of plastic, and three tons of thermocol!

Vaishali Nadkarny: Actually, we also don't call it waste, we call it a resource: we want to re-educate people to see nothing as waste and everything as a resource.

The RRC is now reaching more than 30,000 inhabitants. More and more producers and recyclers are actively participating in your project. What's the role of the municipality?

Purnima: The municipal corporation collects household waste—at least 3,000 tons in Pune daily. Of this, 50 per cent is dry waste, which is transported to waste-management plants where it is converted into Refuse Derived Fuel (RDF). There is a problem here in that everything is shredded without separation into "recyclable" and "non-recyclable" materials.

The waste-to-energy plant has not been able to handle the quantity of waste, especially because construction debris, even vehicle parts, are incorrectly sent to the plant. The large shredding blades broke down repeatedly, which meant waste processing came to a standstill until the blades were replaced.

Change comes from citizens. Unless the leader is a real out-of-the-box thinker, most government bodies aren't thinking innovatively. Otherwise… it must be citizens, like us.

Vijaya: It doesn't take much: remember to take a cloth bag to the shop and a second one to give to someone. Don't buy bottled water. I once brought my own plate, spoon, and cup to a wedding—you should have seen how the other guests laughed. They thought I was crazy. Well, one wedding at a time…

Purnima: Music is a great tool to generate awareness. Why not also about plastics and recycling? With Vijaya as our lead singer, we go around and perform with instruments made from broken combs, pistachio shells in a bottle, or rattling jars. The Indian people are crazy about music, especially Bollywood numbers. We change the lyrics, and these songs stick in people's minds.

Vijaya: Here's our version of "My Favourite Things" from *The Sound of Music*:

*Bubble wrappings on gifts
and all of our packings
Bright coloured bottles and
broken glass casings
Videos and audio tapes that
still can sing
These are a few of the
RRC things!*

*Small 'n' big thermocol
bits 'n' electronic waste
All types of metals and
scraps thrown in haste
Clothes and toys and books,
you also can bring
These are a few of the
RRC things!*

*Paper and cardboard and
all types of plastic,
Washed, dried, to see they
don't stink,
Bring all these stuffs to the RRC
The RESOURCE RECYCLING
CENTRE, you see!*

*When I see waste,
When I see plastic,
Then I'm feeling sad,
But I simply remember,
I give it to the RRC
And then I don't feel so bad!*

1. 100 Kenyan shillings equals approximately 0.80 euros; around 68 pence sterling or 91 US cents.

2. Jenni Downes, "China's recycling 'ban' throws Australia into a very messy waste crisis", the *Conversation* (26 April 2018), online: https://theconversation.com/chinas-recycling-ban-throws-australia-into-a-very-messy-waste-crisis-95522, accessed 16 December 2021.

3. Shanta Barley (ed.), *The Plastic Waste Makers Index*. Perth: The Minderoo Foundation, 2021, online: https://cdn.minderoo.org/content/uploads/2021/05/27094234/20211105-Plastic-Waste-Makers-Index.pdf, accessed 16 December 2021; and "How Much Single-Use Plastic Waste Do Countries Generate?", *Statista* (18 May 2021), online: https://www.statista.com/chart/24874/single-use-plastic-waste-generated-per-person-in-selected-countries/, accessed 16 December 2021.

4. The 2019 report of the European commission states that the building industry is responsible for 40 per cent of carbon dioxide (CO_2) and other greenhouse gas emissions, 50 per cent of all energy consumption, and 36 per cent of all waste production in the European Union. "In focus: Energy efficiency in buildings", *European Commission News* (17 February 2020), online: https://ec.europa.eu/info/news/focus-energy-efficiency-buildings-2020-feb-17_en, accessed 16 December 2021.

5. See the Madaster online registry for materials and products, https://madaster.com/, accessed 19 December 2021.

6. "How the EU wants to achieve a circular economy by 2050", *European Parliament News* (3 February 2021), online: https://www.europarl.europa.eu/news/en/headlines/society/20210128STO96607/how-the-eu-wants-to-achieve-a-circular-economy-by-2050, accessed 16 December 2021.

7. "Packaging", *Umwelt Bundesamt* (7 January 2021), online: https://www.umweltbundesamt.de/en/topics/waste-resources/product-stewardship-waste-management/packaging#packaging-in-germany, accessed 16 December 2021.

8. In 1972 the Club of Rome published the "The Limits of Growth" report, which suggested that economic growth could not continue indefinitely because of resource depletion. Founded in 1968 in Italy and today based in Switzerland, the Club of Rome consists of 100 members selected from current and former heads of state and government, UN administrators and high-level scientists, economists, and business leaders.

9. See Keshav SITA Memorial Foundation Trust, https://rudraenvsolution.com, accessed 19 December 2021.

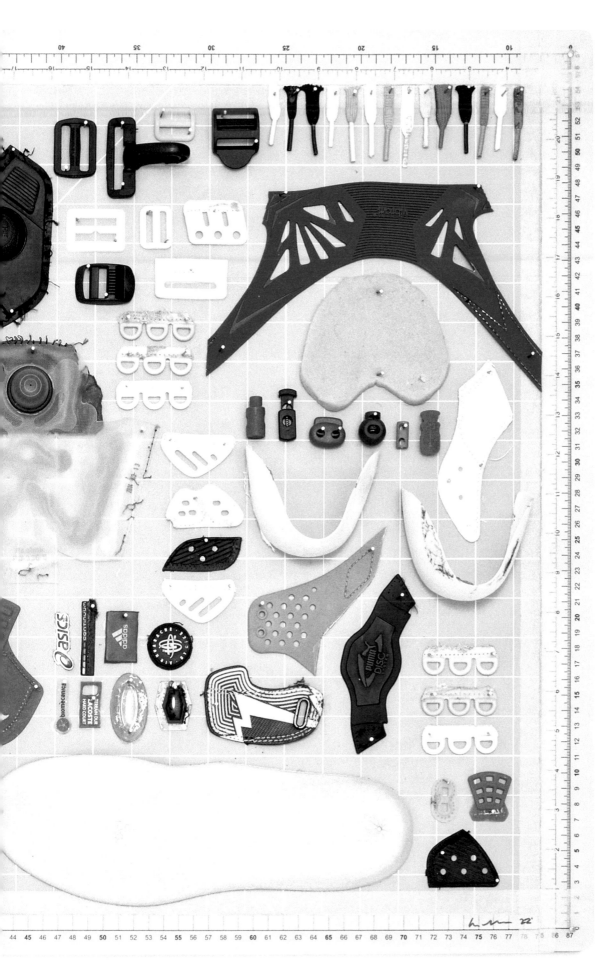

Plastic Pollution: A Tale of Social Injustice

A conversation conducted via Zoom between
Erica Cirino, Ama van Dantzig, Suzanne Dhaliwal,
and Nihan Temiz Ataş, chaired by Sumitra Upham.

Forty per cent of the UK's plastic waste is being exported to Turkey, nearly half of which is mixed plastic and thus impossible to recycle.[1] Turkey is not alone; the Global South (GS) bears the brunt of the Global North's (GN) plastic waste. While we don't like to admit it, our "recycling" is being exported, illegally dumped, and burnt year-round, leaving populations to shoulder the economic, social, and environmental costs.[2] As we continue to perpetuate these same harmful waste management systems, the GS adapts through developing eco-intelligent ways of repairing and reusing waste—not as an act of "innovation" but as a means of survival.

This phenomenon isn't new. Claiming access to Indigenous land through extraction and pollutant-dumping is part of colonialism's long history of environmental violence towards marginalized peoples. This discussion positions plastic within the colonial system of invasion, extraction, settlement, and racialization to demonstrate that class and race determine who endures the effects of hazardous waste.[3] It took place on 18 October 2021, a week before COP26.[4] Many of the issues raised here were absent from the dialogue at this global UN summit.

Collectively, the work of these women interrogates the oppressive environmental systems that dehumanize socio-economically vulnerable Black, Indigenous, and POC communities, and campaigns for climate literacy and social justice above all else. In this conversation, we speculate on the tools needed to restore endangered land, to mobilize and resist oppression, and to decolonize and demystify climate knowledge. We wrestle with the idea of "innovation" and question whether progress could rather lie in the design of care, empathy, and active listening.

How does your work connect to the plastic crisis?

Nihan Temiz Ataş: It's great to be talking with a group of women—not the norm when discussing plastic pollution! I am Greenpeace Mediterranean's Biodiversity Projects Lead. I live in the GS, surrounded by three seas in a country that is subsequently one of the most polluted in the world, where one in every two fish contain microplastic.[5] We have been the top destination for European waste export since 2019.[6]

My work investigates plastic export bases, and I campaign to end the practice of sending waste to developing countries and for the implementation of the European Commission's Single-Use Plastics Directive,[7] a legislation (2019) to prevent and reduce the environmental impact of certain plastic products.

Erica Cirino: I'm the author of *Thicker Than Water: The Quest for Solutions to the Plastic Crisis* (2021), a comprehensive story of plastic and its far-reaching justice implications that many ignore.[8] For example, in Louisiana, we have an 85-mile stretch of land called "Cancer Alley", where almost every household has been effected by cancer as a direct result of exposure to the toxic waste from chemical plants.[9] Communities worst-effected by plastic pollution are mostly Black, Asian and Indigenous. For them, pollution is more than just a blight on Earth. It's life or death.[10]

Ama van Dantzig: I run a social innovation agency called Dr. Monk, with offices in Amsterdam and Accra. Existing between these two locations, we are confronted with a lot of inequalities, plastic being an important part of the story.

One of the things that fascinates me is the ease with which

these material production systems are replicated—in fact, they are identical: extraction, production, dumping. They all fuel the reproduction of inequality and marginalization.

Suzanne Dhaliwal: My work is focused on the stage before plastic—oil and heavy oils. I'm the director of the UK Tar Sands Network, which looks at the extraction of tar sands oil in Canada. I'm interested in the social-justice implications of extraction and the Indigenous rights that are violated as a result.

The rising interest in the climate crisis post 2018 was accompanied by a decline in climate literacy. While we see a focus on reducing plastic and using fewer drinking straws, our actions and their impact on front line struggles remain disconnected. I'm interested in increasing climate literacy to demonstrate where plastic comes from and how it connects with oil extraction. I want justice and remediation for territories that have been impacted by extraction.

Let's spend some time thinking about how we got to where we are today. How has colonial history impacted plastic and the ubiquity of this pollutant?

Erica: Plastic's colonial history became apparent to me while writing *Thicker Than Water*. Throughout history, we've been marketed this material by plastic corporations persuading us that's it's ok to waste. That why it's so ubiquitous: "This is how you use a plastic cup… it's great, you just throw it away". In reality, our waste systems aren't adequate for managing waste at this scale, especially plastic that doesn't degrade. It's been a case

of very wealthy, mostly white, people making a lot of money from plastic whilst other people, usually people of colour, suffer from the effects of its non-circular lifecycle and lack of disposability.

It's important to look at who's selling plastic to us, to question how they are benefitting and what their value systems are. Do they believe in justice and a safe environment for all? I think there's a lot that would need to happen, accountability-wise, in order to repair, remediate, and build equity for these front line communities who suffer disproportionately as a result of plastic.

Suzanne: This is echoed in the history of the oil industry which dates back to 1492, when the american landscape became something to disrespect and extract from. Back then, Crown treaties severed relationships that existed within that landscape, only to then violate those treaties in order to extract bitumen, for instance.

In Canada, there's a violent history of extracting bitumen and shifting relationships with it. As we know, bitumen isn't actually oil. It contains hidden dangerous variables that we know very little about. In Canada, bitumen was used for waterproofing canoes, and then suddenly it became an adhesive, and our relationship with it, and the whole map of Canada, changed. Now the region has the second fastest rate of deforestation in the boreal forests, and communities have been moved to reservations. This picture of oil really mirrors what has happened with plastic—we've been sold a product that cannot be cleaned up.

We need to remember that the oil industry is dependent on plastic and gather the data to

demonstrate how this symbiotic relationship works. With the oil surplus from global transport on hold during the pandemic, the plastic industry came up with new ways of producing, so that, as the world is pushed to reduce its dependence on fossil fuels, it can increase its plastic use.

Ama: Since around 2010 in Ghana, we've been celebrating finding oil: economic progress is coming, we're going to be rich. But oil is never sold on the people's terms, it's sold on the terms of the buyer and the big capitalist players, replicating the same colonial systems. We chose to believe an empty promise, and now there's plastic everywhere. We have choked gutters, washed up mammals and marine life on the coast, and no one is talking about it.

Plastic has become very visible on Ghana's streets since 1983 when I was born. We used to buy drinking water in cups, before people started getting sick, and consequently we saw a huge rise in the popularity of plastic sachets of water. That created the illusion of plastic being a "clean" product, the idea that without plastic, it's dirty. It's false information.

We've not been given the space or education to understand what happens to this material after use—we go straight to the market to buy more. When I was younger, we used to buy products wrapped in leaves. Now, buying something in an open market in Accra without getting a black polythene bag is unthinkable.

Nihan: I totally agree with your point about hygiene. Amidst the pandemic in Turkey, the plastic industry advised using disposable plates, at home and when eating out. They are trying to build a narrative that plastic protects you from the virus. They know it's not scientifically proven, but their lobbying moulds public opinion.[11]

I'm angry and upset that they also made us believe the tale of recycling. Recycling gives us a sense of relief, but plastic packaging from developed countries gets dumped and illegally burned in Southern Turkey.[12] The toxic pollutants are affecting children and contaminating agricultural land nearby. But it's all still abstract to most people. We're not told that it's rare for a product to be 100 per cent plastic, and that these composite materials won't be recycled. Or that only 9 per cent of plastic produced has been recycled since the 1950s,[13] and every minute, twelve million plastic packets enter the ocean.[14] We need to be taught that recycling doesn't work, because it's opening the door to environmental racism.

I wanted to build on Ama's point around plastic stories. We know that the GS is the global repository for waste, but we are led to believe that eco-innovation occurs in the GN, where funding is more prevalent. What examples are there of innovation happening in the GS that the GN could look to for direction?

Ama: People are processing trash all the time in Ghana. The results might not be innovative, creative, or pretty, but people are constantly getting their hands dirty, cleaning up, and burning waste. What else can they do? Reusing, repurposing, and making new materials is a luxury when you have nothing. It would be dishonest for me to

tell you that there's a fantastic process of making bricks from plastic waste. It could well be happening, but it's not a sufficient response to something so horrific.

There was this story that vanished mysteriously about the Trump administration putting a lot of pressure on Kenya to either accept their plastic waste or have their trade agreements adjusted.[15] The administration has the audacity to go to Kenya, where they have implemented a plastic ban which sends people to jail for using single-use plastics, and demand they collect their trash!

Most of us here recognize that the GS is doing the GN a huge favour by taking care of the trash, and that itself is innovation, right? The ubiquity of black polythene bags in Accra isn't because people are constantly dumping their trash, but it feeds the false narrative of Africa being a dirty and disease-ridden place where people are poor and have malaria. Nobody in the GN describes the work in Ghana as innovative or something to learn from, because they care less about learning and more about producing plastic, because of the money tied to oil. This is the fundamental problem.

Suzanne: At the moment, there seems to be a high on innovation, an emphasis on quick solutions and fixes. If we think about making jackets out of bananas or pineapples, who actually benefits? The seed funding from these projects isn't going to the small-scale fruit growers. When we think about traditional ecological knowledge and the communities who've had the least environmental impact, we might think about our grandparents using ice-cream containers

as lunch boxes. Innovations like these aren't sexy, they're about caring and being economical.

In the past few years, we've heard so much about plastic drinking straws going up turtles' noses: that's the big issue that we need to address. Those campaigns are often dictated by a non-profit industrial complex, and the issues highlighted are easily solvable through small incremental changes. They're also easily communicable and unoffensive, unlike regulating the oil industry, banking, and dumping, which are more challenging and therefore rarely communicated. We should question who's being asked to change their behaviour and who isn't.

The innovation we need is ecocide for corporations that devastate territories. What would be really innovative is respecting Indigenous land rights. The fact is that 80 per cent of endangered global biodiversity lives on Indigenous land, but this and human rights laws are absent in the COP26 agreement.

Erica: True, systemic problems are where we need to start, because innovations can be a distraction. There are many competitions to find plastic replacements, but they often tap into the same wasteful mindset: disposing of something made of algae might be better, but it's still reinforcing the colonial capitalist system that is destroying people's lives by adding to the world's waste burden.

All of us here today have similar values, which is really inspiring, but a lot of people don't—largely due to brainwashing by industries and people in power whose investment in fossil fuels has been the status quo for so long.

I wonder if we could talk a bit more about education around waste-management practices and how this is shaping the narrative of the crisis.

Erica: A global education campaign to tell people the truth about plastic and waste is essential, because that's where behavioural change will happen.

I actually live in a town with an incinerator. Local trash is brought to my town, incinerated, and then sent to another town on Long Island to be landfilled. Near the landfill is a mostly Black and Brown community with widespread pollution in their soil, air, and water from my community's incinerator ash, and people don't know. And that's just on a micro-scale—I live on a highly populated island, but it's a small geographic area. Imagine the impact on a macro-scale.

Suzanne: As we've said, how many of us actually know where our recycling goes? This is how corporations skirt around and export accountability, and then we're all left feeling guilty. Maybe hope and innovation comes from educating our children about what happens when you dispose of plastic.

This comes back to transparency and listening to the communities who are raising the alarm. There's an initiative called Bucket Brigades, people who measure the impact of pollution in their local areas to determine what action needs to be taken. Of course, we need scientists and thinkers like Erica painting this bigger picture too.

Another area to discuss is developing love for spaces that we feel propelled to keep clean and protect.

Ama: Yes, and really being able to empathize with the situation is important, because most of the time people just walk by and ignore it.

The value in the beach cleanups we did in Accra was not just picking up plastic, it was in interacting with the local communities and hearing about their struggles.

Pre-plastic was not that long ago. Remembering who we are, our history and traditions, is important. Ghana is a young country; we only gained independence in 1957. In the colonial period, we destroyed so many eco-friendly systems that worked perfectly well. Now there's a powerful opportunity to remember what was done in the past.

What impact does language have on our portrayal of the crisis? And what strategies and systems are needed to embed Indigenous, Black, and POC perspectives in the climate debate and in decision making?

Erica: We know that systemic racism ensures communities of colour are worst affected by industrial pollution, and many of these communities, including those I've visited in Louisiana, are highly vulnerable to the devastating effects of the climate crisis.[16] The perspectives of these communities must be at the forefront, and I encourage fellow journalists to put global Black and Indigenous stories first, rather than the typical white, male-centred CEO point of view. A lot of media reporting on plastic centres the corporate agenda, even though they've been lying to us for decades about plastic and what we can do with it!

Suzanne: The non-profit industrial complex—or big greens—controls what we care about. Tar sands were big in 2002, and then they decided that it was too tied to racial politics, and instead we needed to talk about plastic straws. We need more independent activism and more tools for mapping that aren't tied to the big greens. And above all, we need to be more critical and question the agenda of these organizations. The reporting of COP26 will be determined by the Rockefeller Foundation, who will tell the *Guardian* newspaper what to say, and the whole thing is sponsored by a corporate: Unilever. We really need to think about where our climate information is coming from.

Lastly, as well as foregrounding the stories of communities of colour, we need leading writers and publications to help us tell our stories. We also need to rethink our communication tools: is a takeover of somebody's instagram account effective, or, do we need a new app that maps incinerators in communities? We've gained visibility, but now we need real innovation to help us identify what's happening in our territories, respond accordingly, and reclaim the complexity of the climate crisis.

1. Anon (Greenpeace UK report), Part II: "Turkey, The Top Destination for UK Plastic Waste", in *Trashed: How the UK is Still Dumping Plastic Waste on the Rest of the World*. London: Greenpeace UK, 2021, online: https://www.greenpeace.org.uk/wp-content/uploads/2021/05/Trashed-Greenpeace-plastics-report-final.pdf?_ga=2.101278273.1309246628.1637581585-454501566.1632556314, accessed 2 December 2021, p. 12.

2. Erin McCormick et al., "Where does your plastic go? Global investigation reveals America's dirty secret", the *Guardian* (17 June 2019), online: https://www.theguardian.com/us-news/2019/jun/17/recycled-plastic-america-global-crisis, accessed 2 December 2021.

3. Robin D. G. Kelley, "What Did Cedric Robinson Mean by Racial Capitalism?", *Boston Review* (12 January 2017), online: https://bostonreview.net/articles/robin-d-g-kelley-introduction-race-capitalism-justice/, accessed 2 December 2021.

4. The 26th United Nations Climate Change Conference (COP26) held at the SEC Centre in Glasgow, Scotland, 31 October–13 November 2021.

5. Cem Çevik and Sedat Gündoğdu, *Plastikten Kurtul: Oltaya Gelme*. Istanbul: Greenpeace Mediterranean, 2019, online: https://www.greenpeace.org/static/planet4-turkey-stateless/2019/10/33abcb16-mikroplastik_rapor_final_rev.pdf, accessed 2 December 2021; "44 percent of fish in Turkish waters contain microplastics", *Hurriyet Daily News* (25 October 2019), online: https://www.hurriyetdailynews.com/44-percent-of-fish-in-turkish-waters-contain-microplastics-report-147934#:~:text=ISTANBUL,report%20prepared%20by%20Greenpeace%20Mediterranean-.&text=In%20other%20words%2C%20approximately%20one,contain%20microplastic%2C%E2%80%9D%20it%20said, accessed 2 December 2021.

6. According to Eurostat, the country took in 11.4 million tons of waste from EU countries last year, three times more than in 2004. See: Selin Uğurtaş, "Why Turkey became Europe's garbage dump", *Politico* (18 September 2020), online: https://www.politico.eu/article/why-turkey-became-europes-garbage-dump/, accessed 2 December 2021.

7. "Single-use plastics", *European Commission* (2 July 2019), online: https://ec.europa.eu/environment/topics/plastics/single-use-plastics_en, accessed 2 December 2021.

8. Erica Cirino, *Thicker Than Water: The Quest for Solutions to the Plastic Crisis*. Washington, DC: Island Press, 2021.

9. Written by UN Experts, E. Tendayi Achiume et al., "Environmental Racism in Louisiana's 'Cancer Alley', Must End, Say UN Human Rights Experts", *UN News* (2 March 2021), online: https://news.un.org/en/story/2021/03/1086172, accessed 2 December 2021.

10. *Neglected: Environmental Justice Impacts of Marine Litter and Plastic Pollution*. Nairobi: UN Environment Programme, 2021.

11. See "Oceanic Global Covid-19 Fact Sheet" (6 December 2020), online: https://oceanic.global/wp-content/uploads/2020/08/OG-COVID-FACT-SHEET-UPDATED-3.pdf, accessed 21 December 2021.

12. See Anon (Greenpeace UK report), Part II: "Turkey, The Top Destination for UK Plastic Waste".

13. "Only 9% of the world's plastic is recycled", the *Economist* (6 March 2018), online: https://www.economist.com/graphic-detail/2018/03/06/only-9-of-the-worlds-plastic-is-recycled, accessed 2 December 2021.

14. Helena Spiritus (ed.), *Ghost Gear: The Abandoned Fishing Nets Haunting Our Oceans*. Hamburg: Greenpeace Germany, 2019, online: https://www.greenpeace.de/sites/www.greenpeace.de/files/publications/20190611-greenpeace-report-ghost-fishing-ghost-gear-deutsch.pdf, accessed 2 December 2019.

15. Hiroko Tabuchi, Michael Corkery, and Carlos Mureithi, "Big Oil Is in Trouble. Its Plan: Flood Africa With Plastic", *New York Times* (30 August 2020), online: https://www.nytimes.com/2020/08/30/climate/oil-kenya-africa-plastics-trade.html?searchResultPosition=19, accessed 10 January 2022.

16. Robert Brulle and David Pellow, "Environmental Justice: Human Health and Environmental Inequalities", *Annual Review of Public Health*, vol. 27 (2006), pp. 103–24.

A World Post-Plastic?

The consensus of this roundtable is that widespread awareness of the plastic pollution issue has already been achieved—to the point where people feel comfortable to call each other out, online and in-person, for consuming plastic irresponsibly. Solutions for alternatives to plastics are already here too, thanks to a thriving global eco-innovation scene. So, what's stopping us from leaving our disastrous relationship with plastics behind? Is a new, globe-spanning wonder material the answer? Or would it be healthier to return to a more resourceful way of living and to embrace vernacular materials that are more suited to local conditions and climate?

Riya Patel in conversation with Mark Buckley, Liang-Jung Chen, Cyrill Gutsch, and Chineyenwa Okoro Onu.

Is all plastic bad?

Mark Buckley: Any material in the wrong place can cause problems. The material itself isn't the problem, it's just the wasteful way that we use it. We need plastics in lots of ways: in medical settings, in cars, planes, electricals. It's a versatile material, it's lightweight, it's durable. We just don't need it in our food, the ocean, or our air. We need to use this material less, and in a way that doesn't ever create waste.

Chineyenwa Okoro Onu: If you think about the usability of plastic, you realize it wasn't bad until it became a menace. It became a problem when we realized the challenges of recycling, collection, sorting, biodegrading—when we realized what a mess we had created with our own hands. We turned a beautiful innovation into a complete disaster.

Cyrill Gutsch: But technically, it is bad, although that's an extreme position to take against plastic. It's shedding off micro particles, it's letting off gasses, things we don't want in our atmosphere, and it's leaching chemicals. Unfortunately, we are totally addicted to plastic right now. That's why it's not as easy as it sounds to say plastic is the devil, and we need to get rid of it. It also allows for safety in some areas. It has fostered innovation and democratized comfort—most plastic products that used to be made from other materials are now affordable.
    At Parley, we believe plastic is a design failure. It was great for a moment, but not anymore. We are producing too much, and we're not able to manage it and the huge negative impact. That means we need to invent new

materials with the same properties, the same price—rethink all these things we are so used to. To replace plastic as we know it today will take ten to 20 years. In the meantime, the first step is to recycle. And go heavily into eco-innovation.

Chineyenwa, eco-innovation is the subject of your work at Waste Or Create. Could you tell us a bit more about that?

Chineyenwa: Yes. So, coming up with new products using waste plastic, charcoal dust, coconut husk is a big part of what we do. And redesigning existing products to make sure they don't go back into the waste stream. We began from working to educate in schools and with young entrepreneurs, then started moving towards designing from scratch. It's so exciting to do, because there's always a loop!
    It's about educating and inspiring people to look in that direction, asking why people are not doing it already, why there is a limitation to eco-innovation. I think that's a conversation most people don't want to have just yet, because it's expensive to be an eco-innovator. It can cost four times your existing budget to design something with resources that are already just there. Just because a product is made from waste material, recycled or not, doesn't limit its value. But we can show that by buying it, you are saving the environment too—kudos to you, superhero! Then we ask: what can we do to scale this up?

What should the alternative materials in a post-plastic future be like?

Cyrill: I think we have to finally accept that we are not as

awesome as we thought. We are being humbled. Our seemingly amazing technology has come with a big price. The encouraging thing is that there are a lot of innovators who have been working on solutions that we are now ready for, solutions that are closer to nature. Nature is the ultimate hi-tech—packaging like a banana peel or the skin of a grape that's super thin but still keeps the flesh inside fresh. The next step forward is really collaboration with nature.

Liang-Jung Chen: I agree with Cyrill that we need to invent new materials, but we also need to take advantage of existing materials. I co-founded a project called The Misused that challenges the existing approach to product design. It invites the public to repurpose everyday hardware items into sensible homeware products through a series of creative exercises, such as research, reconfiguration, sourcing local materials, democratic fabrication, and more. The Misused tackles "functional fixedness", a type of cognitive bias that involves a tendency to see objects as only working in a particular way. We would like to liberate people's imagination and to promote critical thinking about our surroundings. The outcome is a collection of both practical and thought-provoking homeware products that can be made by anyone, anywhere, and anytime, with just a twist of creativity required.
    We promote "upcycling intelligence" so that the new generation can be equipped with resourcefulness in all aspects of their everyday lives. My stand here is to advocate for sensibility through playful engagement—sustainability doesn't have to be stoic! As a creative practitioner,

I would like to think my role in this conversation is as a strategical agent who accelerates the process of executing the vision.

Mark, what kind of future would the Ellen MacArthur Foundation like to see?

Mark: When thinking about the future, what's exciting is that we have so many of the solutions already at hand today. We launched our *Upstream Innovation Guide* last year with over 100 examples of organizations making the change to eliminate the packaging we just don't need. And innovating to make sure the packaging we do need is reusable, recyclable, compostable, and kept in circulation. I think a key perspective is to look upstream to solutions in the design and production stages. If you came home to find your apartment flooding, you probably wouldn't just grab a mop and start mopping up the floor, you'd look for the source of the leak and turn the tap off. That's what we need to do with plastic. We need to fundamentally redesign how we deliver products to users, without creating waste.

Cyrill: I know that example of the faucet inside out, but I don't agree. It's not spilling water, it's toxic chemicals. And if I see those substances going into nature, then I have to jump in both directions. I think a burning house is a better example. Yes, I can look into constructing a new house that won't burn, but at this moment the house is burning. I need to save lives.

Mark: We totally need the downstream innovation too. The sorting, the collection, and better infrastructure to do that.

Obviously, there is a huge quantity of plastic, and we'll only really solve it in the long term if we don't use plastic in such a wasteful way.

Cyrill: But Mark, if you are looking for the ultimate solution, it's not in fighting symptoms. I agree with you that the ultimate solution is actually changing the core of the problem. It just doesn't mean that one has to be prioritized over the other.

Mark: Absolutely. We need people innovating at all stages of the plastic life cycle. Whether it's in design, sourcing, production, use, or after use. We see so much emphasis on better sorting and collection to fix the problem downstream. We're 40 years on from that little recycling symbol on the corner of most packaging, but only 2 per cent of plastic packaging gets made back into similar quality packaging. We're never going to fix it with more recycling. We have to go upstream and design-out waste from the start.

If we could reach a stage where we stop producing virgin plastic, would recycled plastic be enough, and would industry support this?

Cyrill: We have convinced Adidas to move completely to recycled materials and invest heavily in alternatives to plastic. But they are competing against companies that are not doing that. The only way to really change the trajectory here is to put laws in place. And you would be surprised how fast solutions sprout when companies are not allowed to make products in the same way anymore.

But you can't just put a law in place and then ask the economy to do something impossible. You saw that in India, when they tried to get the plastic ban through. It backfired. Therefore, you need frontrunners in the private sector, eco-innovation champions, to deliver the proof of concept; and lawmakers have enough examples to show industry that it's possible now.

Where do consumers come into this? With social media, we hold the power to make brands take responsibility; we have a direct way to communicate what we want our future to look like, what we want our products to be.

Cyrill: If companies hear that their customers want something else, they will change. And that's the only reason, to be honest, that the industry is now moving. Companies that laughed at me nine years ago are now saying "What can we do?" Because sustainability—although I don't like the word, I prefer eco-innovation—that's the new luxury. Purpose is the new luxury.
And social media? As great as it is, it's not always helpful. It's a hype-based machine. Often ill-informed individuals propagating what they believe is the right thing; but who are the people I can get real advice from as a consumer? It's such chaos. We need trustworthy authorities—that's the missing link right now.

Chineyenwa: Right. Everyone knows it is the new hype to greenwash products and services. This is where we need more regulation. Sorry if I'm calling out names, but the likes of Colgate, Unilever, Nestlé, they have zillions of products out there, but they opt to produce just one line that's eco-friendly. I don't accept that! You have the necessary resources, why aren't you using them? Make the investment that's required! And don't greenwash. That becomes a challenge to the individuals who are taking the time, effort, and resources to do things ethically.

Mark: What people can do is learn what types of innovation can have the biggest impact on the problem, and that isn't just tinkering with existing problematic packaging. When you buy something, do you think there's a need for the packaging? Tesco eliminated the shrink-wrap they used to put around their multibuy tins, now you just get the multibuy discount at the checkout. Apeel is an amazing company that, like Cyrill said, looks at how fruit and vegetables in nature take care of packaging themselves. Inspired by the science behind fruit skins, they've created an edible coating they apply to fruits and vegetables, which keeps them fresh for up to two to three times longer.

So, to really understand whether packaging needs to be there. If it does, could it be reusable? For example, are you throwing away the same cleaning detergent bottle every time you purchase the product? And lastly, what does good packaging look like? Can it be recycled or composted easily, is it made of one material? The more we can all understand what good packaging and real innovation looks like, the more we'll be able to see where companies are genuinely trying to make efforts to do something better, or if they're just on a campaign to sell more stuff.

The Ellon MacArthur Foundation's network includes some major players that can make these kinds of changes upstream. What's the feeling there?

Mark: In terms of the whole system change needed—so customers only have good choices—the Foundation's Global Commitment is a voluntary agreement that has signatories representing over 20 per cent of all the plastic produced globally. There are really ambitious targets for reduction and reuse by 2025 involving many big fast-moving consumer goods companies (FMCGs) and retailers, and we need to see bolder action from them in order to meet those targets. And finally, we need to go beyond voluntary cooperation and create a UN treaty on plastic pollution, to level the playing field.

Do you think societal change will shape our relationship with plastics in the future? Knowing its impact, will it become socially unacceptable to use plastics irresponsibly?

Cyrill: I think we're already there. People don't want to be associated with plastic. The only problem is they don't know what is and isn't made from it. I was in a shop and the salesperson was totally convinced there was no plastic in the duvet, only polyester. I'm like, that's plastic! Plastic is such a big category that people don't know what it is, where it is, when they are consuming it. Plastic is dead already; the trust is cracked. That makes it easy, but also opens the door for alternatives that are not always better, to be honest. So, we are in a very complicated area. We know what we don't want, but

what we do want is undefined. And that brings us again to the definition of good and bad. What is wrong and what is right?

Chineyenwa: That definition is important. I used to love getting a manicure. But someone asked me once, you're talking to us about change, but do you know your nails are made of plastic? I started looking for eco-friendly nail products! Where am I going to find those in Africa? I stopped having my nails done. And since then, I locked my natural hair too, because when I washed off the products I was using on my hair, all of which contained synthetic plastics, we know full well where they were ending up…

It takes a lot of work from you, the individual, to make these decisions. Is it eco-conscious because it's wrapped in paper, because it *looks* eco-friendly? At this point, the plastic manufacturers are becoming so creative about putting this thing in your face! So, it's about educating the consumer about what they can do. Honestly, some people want to make a difference, but they just don't know how.

Can the designer step in then? If the consumer can't always make an informed choice?

Liang-Jung: The best thing we can do as creative individuals is to push the boundaries in every project. And to initiate our own projects if the potential is there. I see myself as a bridge between technology, policy, and community. To optimize my creative strengths and to come up with a design, campaign, or a scheme in an approachable way that implements the policies. Like with the workshops we do for The Misused, the feedback we get is overwhelmingly positive, and people tell us that it has shifted their perspective. A simple idea, yet the impact can be unexpectedly influential. You never know if you don't take the first step.

Cyrill: Yes. It's about education, inspiration, and empowerment. But also, collaboration, since as a designer, you are not always equipped to make expert decisions about materials. Or at least, you need to know where to go to ask or who to consult. A designer should always be flanked by a material scientist.

We also have to allow ourselves to play. To pivot and jump and test things out. Without that we will not find a solution. We will just be anxious all the time about making something that is wrong. Failure is the best ingredient for true innovation.

Mark: You asked if this is a problem for designers, hopefully this is a massive opportunity for designers! The new solutions we seek must be better than single-use plastic. They need to delight consumers and be convenient and seamless. And they must use technology in clever but responsible ways. So, it's the job of designers to make this new future exciting, something that people want to live in and enjoy.

Designers are also amazing facilitators. As so many of these challenges are systemic, it can't be one brand or retailer that makes a change; it will need the whole value chain to transform for these solutions to be possible. That's going to need a lot of facilitation!

How can a post-plastic future be inclusive?

Cyrill: I think the colonialism of our technology needs to end. Solutions should come from everywhere, not only places that are known for their industrial achievements. The strategy we promote at Parley is AIR—avoid, intercept, and redesign. That's the strategy which we implement at the governmental level, with companies, and even for individuals. And how you bring it to life individually depends on how you are set up.

And the second piece is funding—supporting and funding eco-innovators. And that means serious cash. We are collaborating with the World Bank, because we want to channel cash to eco-innovators in all the regions. We need billions to be put into the hands of people, because some will invent amazing stuff. And I doubt it will be 3M and DuPont, because they might just be protecting the technology that they already own.

Chineyenwa: When you look at the conversation now, it's all about renewables, not looking at infrastructural development and local entrepreneurship. We need a 360-degree educational approach. It's not about whether you are an engineer or a local farmer. It's that this education needs to be across every part of the value chain. And encourage investors! Because some innovators might not have the track record or finance, but they have a viable solution to the challenges we must meet, which needs nothing more than 10–20,000 dollars to get it from seed to growth.

Who wants the last word on what our future world should look like and how we get there?

Cyrill: I think it's all about creativity, collaboration, and eco-innovation.

Liang-Jung: We need to pick up vernacular materials again. The plastic problem is a by-product of capitalism and consumerism, and our desires are shaped by globalization in unhealthy ways. We should scale back and constantly re-evaluate our desires. It is essential to cultivate alternative ways of living according to each local community, based on their geography, climate, habits, and even religion. It's like biodiversity. Lifestyle diversity is also vital, and thus material diversity.

Mark: But it's also a global problem. Plastic in your air will be in my air, and in your ocean will end up in my water. And it's not just a pollution problem, it affects biodiversity, it's intimately linked to climate. To fix it, there's not one blanket solution; we're going to need lots of different solutions. A circular economy for plastics, or for any material, will only be possible if progress is distributed and inclusive and diverse. And this is an approach that is going to require creating locally relevant solutions that work in that context with the materials, people, lifestyles, and environments that are there. We need innovation locally all around the world to tackle the problem from all angles.

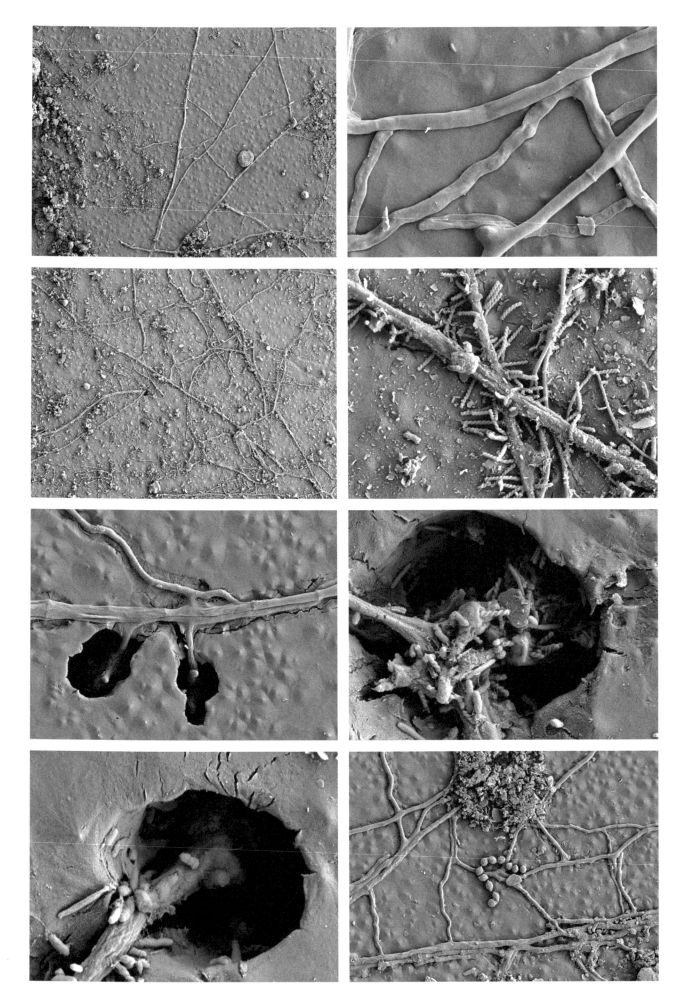

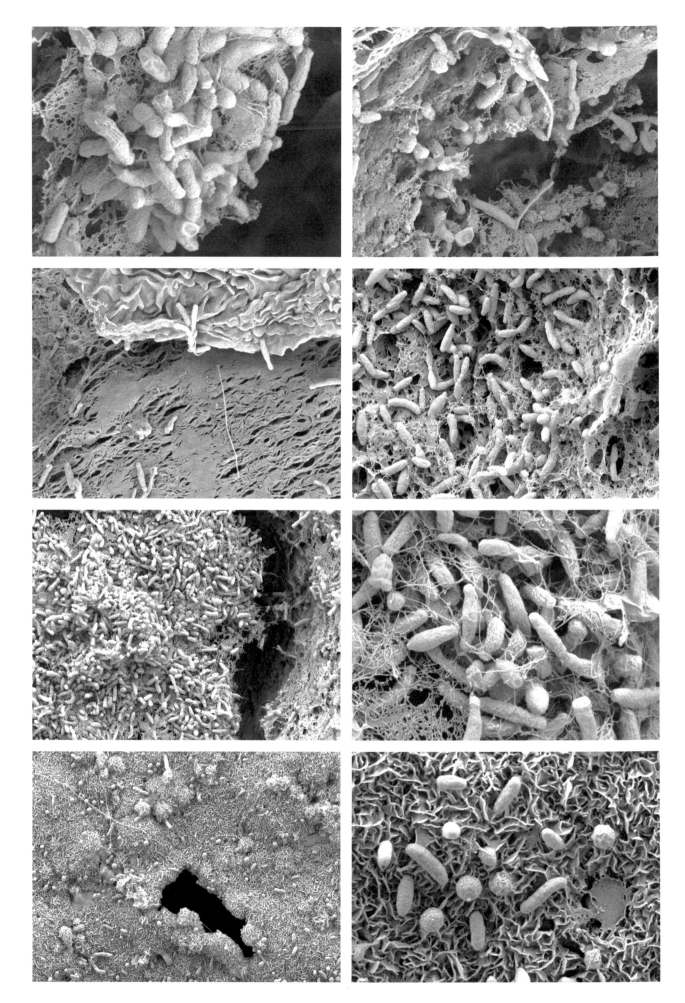

Plastic Data

Oil and plastic

Global oil/plastic production

In comparison to global oil production and its increase in the second half of the twentieth century, the increase in the production of plastics by the petrochemical industry seems deceptively minimal. Still, both developments are closely intertwined. With the recent spread of electrically powered mobility and the subsequently decreasing demand for fuel, the production of plastics has become a more important outlet for the petrochemical industry.

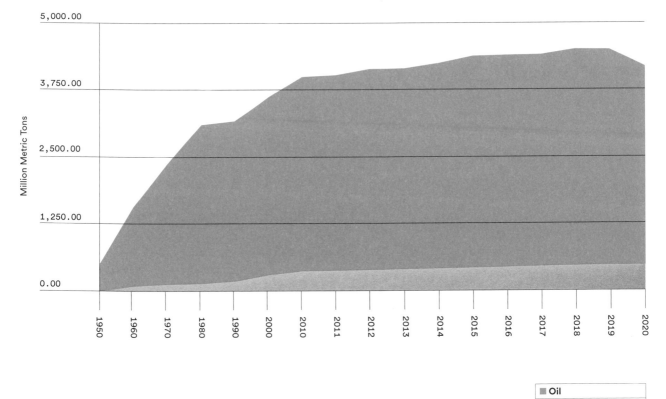

Source: "Plastics – the Facts 2020", *Plastics Europe*, online: plasticseurope.org/knowledge-hub/plastics-the-facts-2020/, accessed 11 January 2022.

At the current rate of consumption, plastic production is set to quadruple by 2050. BP expects plastics to account for 95% of net growth in demand for oil (2020–40).

Sources: Minderoo Foundation, *The Plastic Waste Makers Index*; and Carbon Tracker Initiative, *Annual Report 2020*, online: carbontracker.org/reports/the-futures-not-in-plastics/, accessed 11 January 2022.

Global plastics production

The chart shows the increase in global plastics production, measured in metric tons per year, from 1950 to 2020. In 1950, the world produced only two million metric tons (Mmt) per year. Since then, annual production has increased nearly 200-fold, reaching 368 Mmt in 2019. This is roughly equivalent in mass to two-thirds of the world's population.

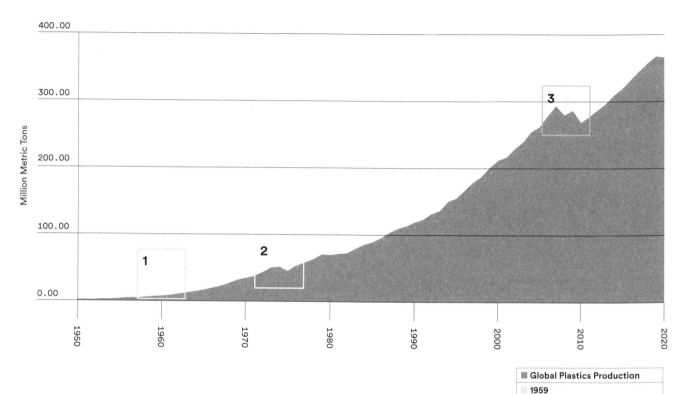

Million Metric Tons

400.00

300.00

200.00

100.00

0.00

1950   1960   1970   1980   1990   2000   2010   2020

	Global Plastics Production
	1959
	1973
	2009

Throughout history, oil production and prices have fluctuated repeatedly, causing significant short- and long-term effects on global politics and the global economy. Here are three milestones.

1959

In 1959, US President Dwight Eisenhower imposed a Mandatory Oil Import Quota Program, a system to restrict oil imports to no more than 9% of domestic consumption. in order to prevent a dependence of the US on imported petroleum supplies.

1973

The 1973 oil crisis was initiated with an oil embargo of the OPEC (Organization of Arab Petroleum Exporting Countries). It was targeted at nations that supported Israel during the Yom Kippur War. By the end of the embargo in March 1974, the price of oil had quadrupled. The 1979 oil shock caused a second drop in oil production in the wake of the Iranian Revolution.

2009

This brief downturn in annual oil production in 2009 and 2010 was predominantly the result of the 2008 global financial crisis.

Sources: Hannah Ritchie and Max Roser, "How much plastic does the world produce?", *Plastic Pollution* (2018), online: ourworldindata.org/plastic-pollution; "Annual production of plastics worldwide from 1950 to 2020 (in million metric tons)", *Statista*, online: statista.com/statistics/282732/global-production-of-plastics-since-1950; Council of Foreign Relations, "Oil Dependence and U.S. Foreign Policy 1850–2021", online: cfr.org/timeline/oil-dependence-and-us-foreign-policy, all accessed 11 January 2022.

Global plastics producers

Twenty firms produce 55% of the world's single-use plastics

Single-use plastics account for over one-third of plastics produced every year and for the majority of plastic thrown away the world over: more than 310 million metric tons (Mmt) in 2019—almost all of which is burned, buried in landfill, or discarded directly into the environment.

Of approximately 300 polymer producers operating globally, 20 plastic producers account for more than half of single-use plastic waste generated globally—and the top 100 account for 90%. Their choice to continue to produce virgin polymers, rather than recycled polymers, will have massive repercussions on the extent to which plastic is collected, is managed, and leaks into the environment.

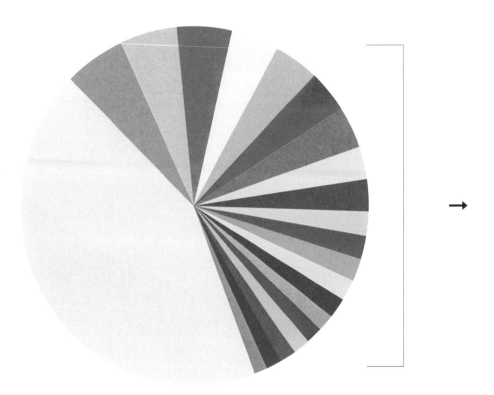

Source: Minderoo Foundation, *The Plastic Waste Makers Index* (2000), online: https://www.minderoo.org/plastic-waste-makers-index/, accessed 11 January 2022.

The ten biggest plastics companies by global annual turnover

The global plastics market was valued at US$580 billion in 2020 and is expected to grow considerably over the next decade, with rising demand for plastic materials in the construction, automotive, and electrical & electronics industries. These ten companies are the world's biggest plastics producers.

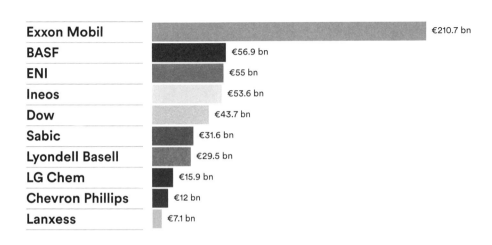

Company	Turnover
Exxon Mobil	€210.7 bn
BASF	€56.9 bn
ENI	€55 bn
Ineos	€53.6 bn
Dow	€43.7 bn
Sabic	€31.6 bn
Lyondell Basell	€29.5 bn
LG Chem	€15.9 bn
Chevron Phillips	€12 bn
Lanxess	€7.1 bn

Sources: Heinrich Böll Foundation and Break Free From Plastic, *The Plastic Atlas* (Berlin: 2019), online: https://www.boell.de/sites/default/files/2020-01/Plastic%20Atlas%202019%202nd%20Edition.pdf; and Ian Tiseo, "Global plastics industry" (22 November 2021), *Statista*, online: statista.com/topics/5266/plastics-industry/#topicHeader__wrapper, both accessed 11 January 2022.

      Plastic Data

The top 20 single-use plastic producers

Exxon Mobil

5.9%
4.55 Mmt*
United States

Dow

5.6%
4.32 Mmt
United States

Sinopec

5.3%
4.09 Mmt
China

Indorama Ventures

4.6%
3.55 Mmt
Thailand

Saudi Aramco

4.3%
3.32 Mmt
Saudi Arabia

Petro China

4.0%
3.08 Mmt
China

Lyondell Basell

3.9%
3.00 Mmt
Netherlands

Reliance Industries

3.1%
2.39 Mmt
India

Braskem

3.0%
2.31 Mmt
Brazil

Alpek SA de CV

2.3%
1.77 Mmt
Mexico

Borealis

2.2%
1.70 Mmt
Austria

Lotte Chemical

2.1%
1.62 Mmt
South Korea

Ineos

2.0%
1.54 Mmt
United Kingdom

Total

1.9%
1.47 Mmt
France

Jiangsu Hailun Petrochemical

1.6%
1.23 Mmt
China

Far Eastern New Century

1.6%
1.23 Mmt
Taiwan

Formosa Plastics Corporation

1.6%
1.23 Mmt
Taiwan

China Energy Investment Group

1.5%
1.16 Mmt
China

PTT

1.5%
1.16 Mmt
Thailand

China Resources

1.3%
1.0 Mmt
China/Hong Kong

* Mmt: Million metric tons (1,000,000 × 1,000 kg)

Source: Minderoo Foundation, *The Plastic Waste Makers Index*, 2021.

Global plastics production

Global plastics production

After World War II, plastics manufacturing grew steadily in Asia: Japan became the main producer of PVC and Hong Kong the world's leading producer of plastic toys and flowers by the 1970s. Since the 1980s, production has moved to mainland China, with Vietnam, Malaysia, Thailand, Indonesia, and the Philippines rapidly growing into important plastics exporters too.

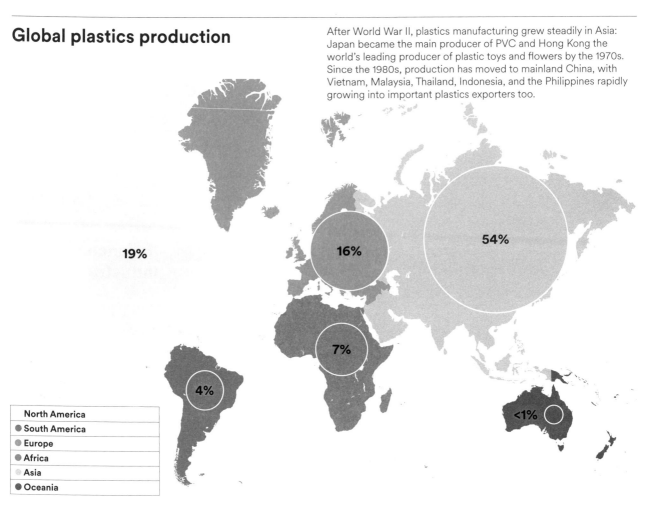

North America
- South America
- Europe
- Africa
- Asia
- Oceania

Source: Heinrich Böll Foundation and Break Free From Plastic, *The Plastic Atlas*, 2019.

Top ten oil-producing countries

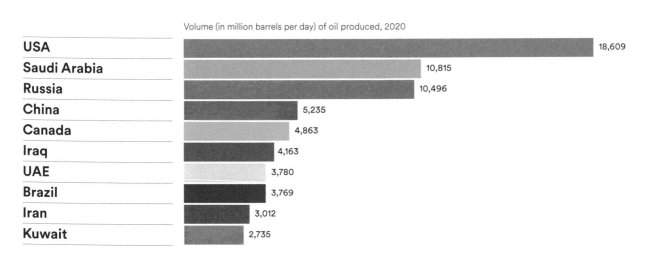

Volume (in million barrels per day) of oil produced, 2020

Country	Volume
USA	18,609
Saudi Arabia	10,815
Russia	10,496
China	5,235
Canada	4,863
Iraq	4,163
UAE	3,780
Brazil	3,769
Iran	3,012
Kuwait	2,735

Source: EIA – Energy Information Administration, "Annual petroleum and other liquids production" (May–September 2021), online: eia.gov/international/data/world, accessed 11 January 2022.

Plastic Data

Global bioplastics production

The global production capacity for bioplastics was 2.1 Mmt in 2020—an increase of 8% on the previous year's total—of which 42% was of bio-based/non-biodegradable and 58% of biodegradable bioplastics. Their share in global plastic production was, however, still less than 1%. The global distribution of bioplastic production is very similar to that of oil-based plastic, with the exception of South America developing fastest in this new segment.

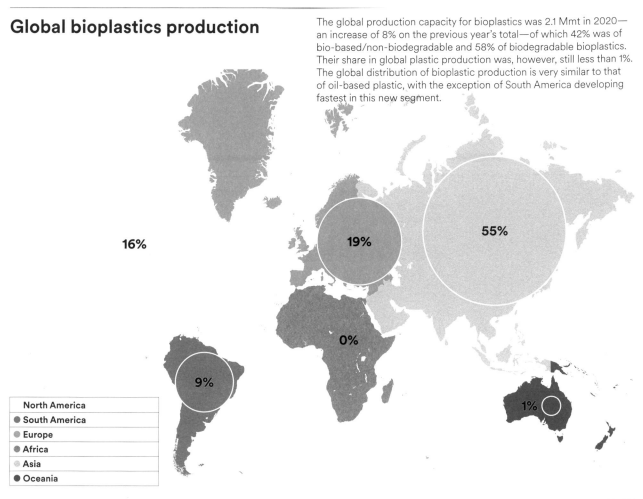

16%

19%

55%

0%

9%

1%

North America
● South America
● Europe
● Africa
● Asia
● Oceania

Source: Heinrich Böll Foundation and Break Free From Plastic, *The Plastic Atlas*, 2019.

More than half of all the plastic ever produced has been made since 2000.

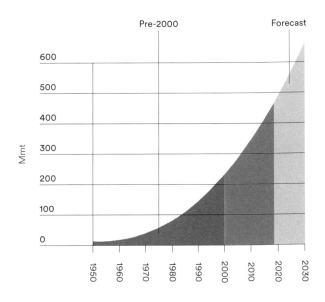

Pre-2000   Forecast

Mmt

600

500

400

300

200

100

0

1950 1960 1970 1980 1990 2000 2010 2020 2030

What do we use plastic for?

Use of plastics by industrial sector

Usage by industrial sector in 2017. Each symbol represents 1 million tons, total volume 438 million tons.

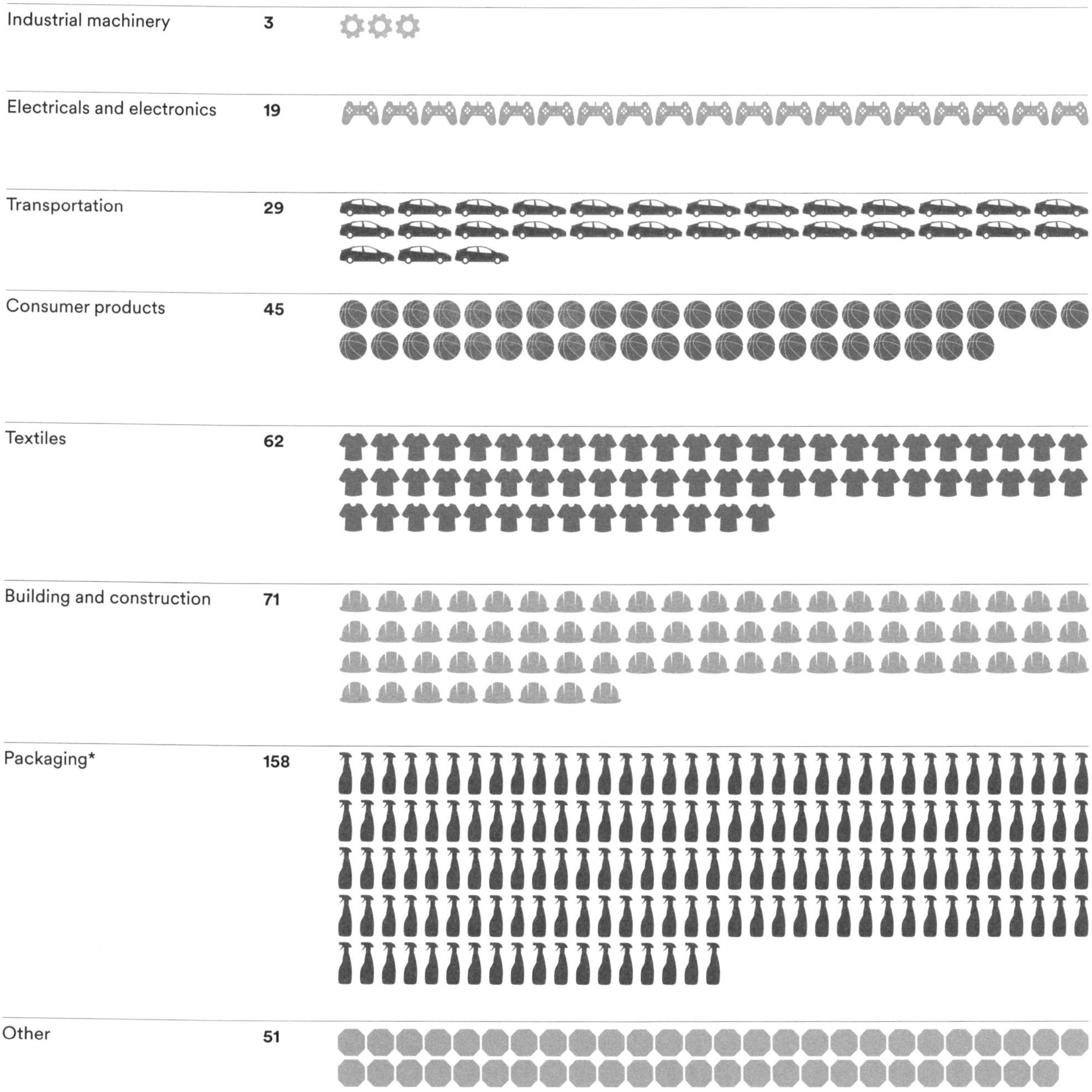

Industrial machinery	3
Electricals and electronics	19
Transportation	29
Consumer products	45
Textiles	62
Building and construction	71
Packaging*	158
Other	51

* mostly single-use

Source: Heinrich Böll Foundation, Berlin, Germany, and Break Free From Plastic, *The Plastic Atlas*, 2019, p. 15.

Plastic Data

Single-use plastic product categories (million metric tons), 2019

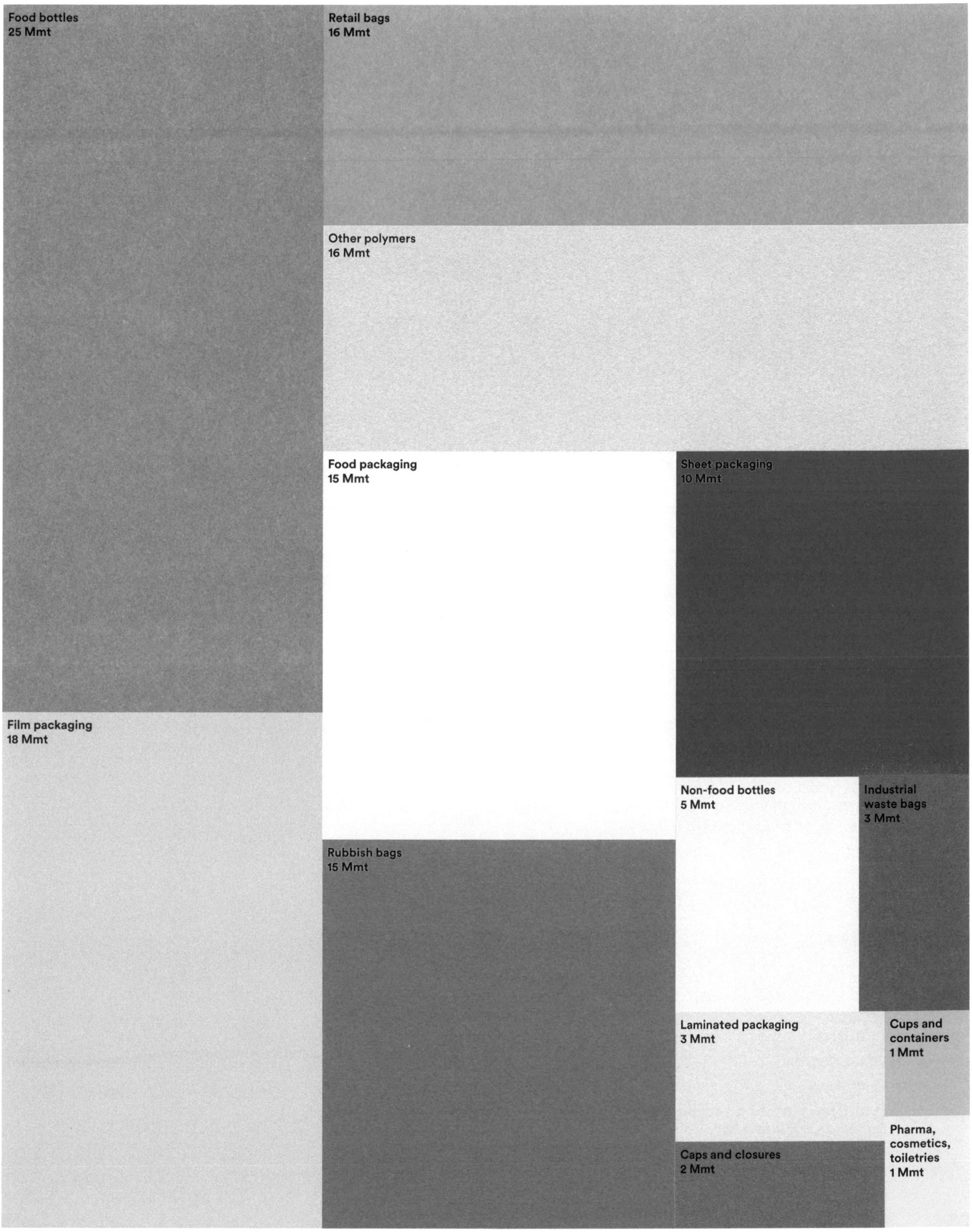

Food bottles
25 Mmt

Retail bags
16 Mmt

Other polymers
16 Mmt

Food packaging
15 Mmt

Sheet packaging
10 Mmt

Film packaging
18 Mmt

Non-food bottles
5 Mmt

Industrial
waste bags
3 Mmt

Rubbish bags
15 Mmt

Laminated packaging
3 Mmt

Cups and
containers
1 Mmt

Caps and closures
2 Mmt

Pharma,
cosmetics,
toiletries
1 Mmt

Global plastic-waste streams

Main global plastic-waste flows before China's ban

On 27 July 2017, China issued an import ban on 24 types of solid waste including plastic waste. This abrupt ban prompted changes in how global plastic-waste trade-flow patterns, as well as plastic waste-treatment systems in both the short- and long-term, are now managed and will be in the future.

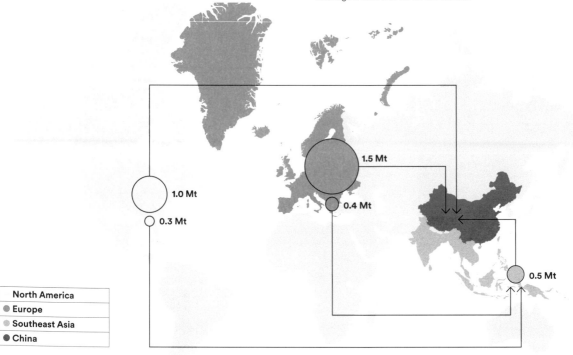

North America
● Europe
○ Southeast Asia
● China

Source: Woldemar d'Ambrières, "Plastics recycling worldwide: Current overview and desirable changes", *Field Actions Science Report Special Issue 19: Reinventing Plastics* (2019), online: journals.openedition.org/factsreports/5102?lang=fr, accessed 11 January 2022.

Exports of plastic scrap to China

Before the ban, China was the world's main importer of plastic waste and the largest producer of plastic. With annual imports of 8.88 Mmt of plastic waste, with as much as 70.6% of this buried or mismanaged, a series of environmental problems were triggered.

━━━ Total
┄┄┄ Hong Kong*
━━━ Japan
    USA
━━━ Germany
━━━ Thailand
━━━ United Kingdom
━━━ South Korea
········ In 2017, China set stricter requirements for imports of plastic waste.

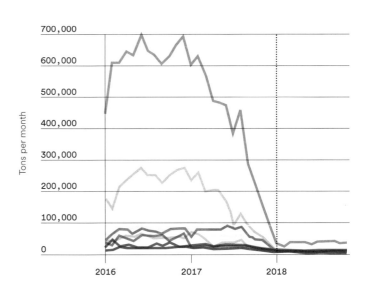

* Figures for Hong Kong are high because it is a transhipment point for global waste.

Sources: Zongguo Wen et al., "China's plastic import ban increases prospects of environmental impact mitigation of plastic waste trade flow worldwide", *Nature Communications*, no. 12 (18 January 2021), online: nature.com/articles/s41467-020-20741-9, accessed 11 January 2022; and Heinrich Böll Foundation and Break Free From Plastic, *The Plastic Atlas*, 2019.

European Union exports

After the China ban, the exports of four countries—Japan, the USA, Germany, and the UK—accounted for 46.1% of the world's trade-flow of plastic waste (globally: 7.8 Mmt). Malaysia, instead of China, became the primary export destination for most countries (12.2% of the total) along with other South Asian countries and Turkey.

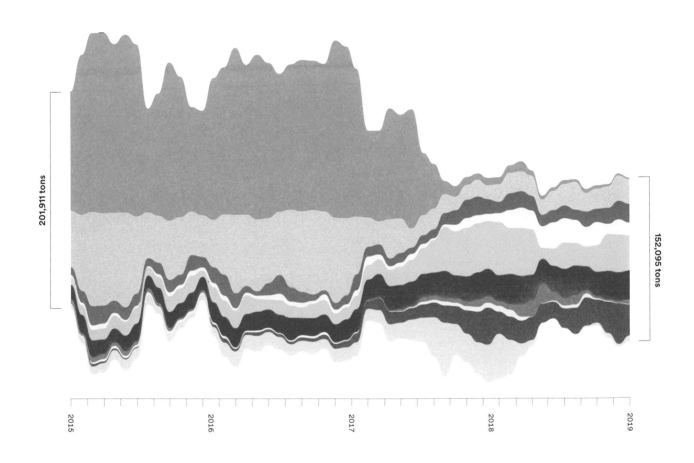

	China	Hong Kong	India	Indonesia	Malaysia	Other	Taiwan	Thailand	Turkey	Vietnam
	↓	↓	↑	↑	↑	↑	↑	↑	↑	↑
2015	1,658,970.6	775,557.8	139,628	32,640.2	137,876.8	177,742.4	31,548.3	15,414.4	19,377.7	88,760.7
2018	64,662	211,530	158,250.9	190,933.2	404,123.9	301,135.8	99,071.8	39.676.4	270,339.8	187,378.3

Sources: European Environment Agency, "Extra-EU-28 plastic waste trade by receiving country" (10 December 2019), online: eea.europa.eu/media/infographics/extra-eu-28-plastic-waste/view, accessed 11 January 2022; and Wen et al., "China's plastic import ban increases prospects of environmental impact mitigation of plastic waste trade flow worldwide".

Plastic in the water

Plastic emissions from the rivers to the world's oceans

Rivers are a major source of plastic waste into the oceans. Approximately 1,000 rivers are accountable for nearly 80% of global annual river plastic emissions, which range between 0.8–2.7 Mmt per year, with small urban rivers amongst the most polluting.

Source: International Union for Conservation of Nature (IUCN), "Marine plastic pollution" (2021), online: iucn.org/resources/issues-briefs/marine-plastic-pollution, accessed 11 January 2022.

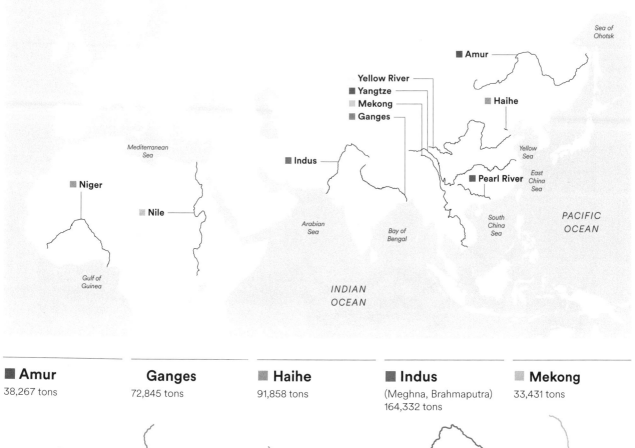

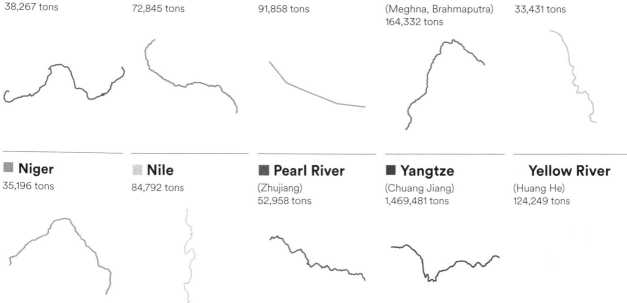

Amur
38,267 tons

Ganges
72,845 tons

Haihe
91,858 tons

Indus
(Meghna, Brahmaputra)
164,332 tons

Mekong
33,431 tons

Niger
35,196 tons

Nile
84,792 tons

Pearl River
(Zhujiang)
52,958 tons

Yangtze
(Chuang Jiang)
1,469,481 tons

Yellow River
(Huang He)
124,249 tons

Sources: The Ocean Cleanup, "River Plastic Emissions to the World's Oceans" (2022), online: theoceancleanup.com/sources/; and see also Christian Schmidt et al., "Export of Plastic Debris by Rivers into the Sea", *Environmental Science & Technology* (UN Environment Programme, 2017), online: unep.org/interactive/beat-plastic-pollution/, both accessed 11 January 2022.

Ocean plastic distribution

At least 14 Mmt of plastic end up in the ocean every year, and plastic makes up 80% of all marine debris found—from surface waters to deep-sea sediments.

Heinrich Böll Foundation and Break Free From Plastic, *The Plastic Atlas*.

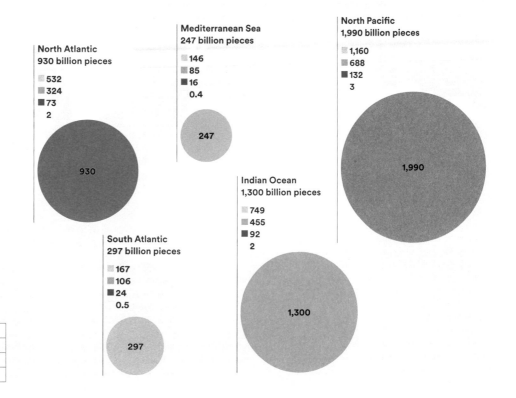

Mediterranean Sea
247 billion pieces
- 146
- 85
- 16
- 0.4

247

North Pacific
1,990 billion pieces
- 1,160
- 688
- 132
- 3

1,990

North Atlantic
930 billion pieces
- 532
- 324
- 73
- 2

930

Indian Ocean
1,300 billion pieces
- 749
- 455
- 92
- 2

1,300

South Pacific
491 billion pieces
- 269
- 176
- 44
- 1

491

South Atlantic
297 billion pieces
- 167
- 106
- 24
- 0.5

297

- Small microplastics
- Large microplastics
- Mesoplastic
- Macroplastic

The Great Pacific Garbage Patch

Orbiting around 32°N and 145°W, half-way between Hawaii and California, the Great Pacific Garbage Patch is the largest of five offshore plastic-accumulation zones in the world's oceans. With an estimated surface area twice the size of Texas (or three times the size of France), it has gathered more than 1.8 trillion pieces of plastic—a plastic count that is equivalent to 259 pieces of debris for every human being living on the planet.

Source: The Ocean Cleanup, "What is the Great Pacific Garbage Patch?", online: theoceancleanup.com/great-pacific-garbage-patch/, accessed 11 January 2022.

Small microplastics
0.33–1.00 mm

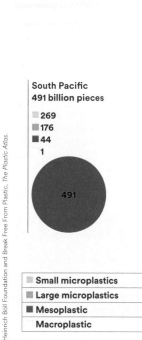

Microbeads or micro-exfoliates are small plastic granules found commonly in personal-care products such as toothpaste and facial cleansers. These smallest of microplastic particles have been identified as having the highest potential for causing damage to marine ecosystems.

Large microplastics
1.01–4.75 mm

Small particles produced unintentionally (i.e. from degradation and the manufacture of plastic objects).

Mesoplastics
4.76–200 mm

Mesoplastics are large plastic particles such as virgin resin pellets.

Macroplastics
> 200 mm

Macroplastics are large plastic debris such as plastic bottles.

Source: National Oceanic and Atmospheric Administration (NOAA), "What are microplastics?", *National Ocean Service*, online: oceanservice.noaa.gov/facts/microplastics.html; and UN Environmental Programme, "Plastics and Microplastics" (2015), online: wedocs.unep.org/bitstream/handle/20.500.11822/28420/Microp-las-en.pdf?%20sequence=1&isAllowed=y, both accessed 11 January 2022.

Global regulation of plastics

Global regulation of plastic

Africa stands out as the continent with the largest number of countries that have instituted a total ban on the production and use of plastic bags and other single-use plastic items. Other continents and countries have followed, implementing new laws to regulate or ban the use of single-use plastic items. So far, North America has introduced regulations mostly at the state or city level.

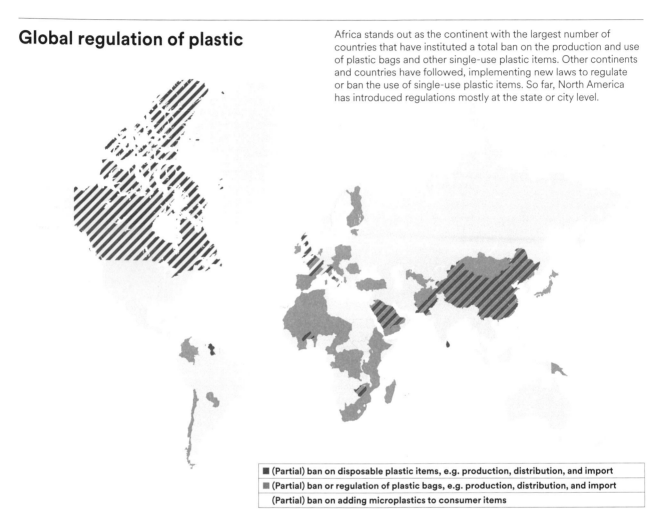

- ■ (Partial) ban on disposable plastic items, e.g. production, distribution, and import
- ■ (Partial) ban or regulation of plastic bags, e.g. production, distribution, and import
- (Partial) ban on adding microplastics to consumer items

Source: Heinrich Böll Foundation and Break Free From Plastic, *The Plastic Atlas*, 2019, p. 43.

Around the world, almost one million plastic bottles are purchased every minute.

Source: Simon Scarr and Marco Hernandez, "Drowning in plastic: Visualising the world's addiction to plastic bottles", *Reuters Graphics* (4 September 2019), online: https://graphics.reuters.com/ENVIRONMENT-PLASTIC/0100B275155/index.html, accessed 21 January 2022.

Estimated number of new regulations on single-use plastics entering into force at the national level worldwide

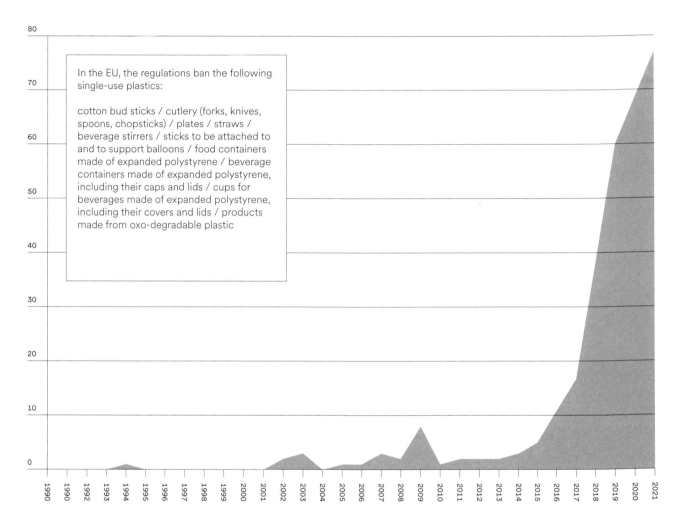

In the EU, the regulations ban the following single-use plastics:

cotton bud sticks / cutlery (forks, knives, spoons, chopsticks) / plates / straws / beverage stirrers / sticks to be attached to and to support balloons / food containers made of expanded polystyrene / beverage containers made of expanded polystyrene, including their caps and lids / cups for beverages made of expanded polystyrene, including their covers and lids / products made from oxo-degradable plastic

Source: UN Environmental Programme, *Single-use plastics: A roadmap for sustainability* (5 June 2018), online: https://www.unep.org/resources/report/single-use-plastics-roadmap-sustainability#:~:text=The%20bene-fits%20of%20plastic%20are,lightweight%20and%20easy%20to%20make.&text=It%20looks%20at%20what%20governments,consumption%20of%20single%2Duse%20plastics.

On 2 July 2021, the Directive on Single-Use Plastics took effect in the European Union (EU). The directive bans certain single-use plastics for which alternatives are available. A "single-use plastic product" is defined as a product that is made wholly or partly from plastic and that is not conceived, designed, or placed on the market to be used multiple times for the same purpose.

Source: "EU restrictions on certain single-use plastics", European Commission, https://ec.europa.eu/environment/topics/plastics/single-use-plastics/eu-restrictions-certain-single-use-plastics_en, accessed on 26 January 2022.

How virgin plastic is made

How plastics are produced

1. Extraction of raw material

Crude oil and natural gas, but also coal are extracted from the earth's reserves. These are a complex mixture of thousands of compounds that then need to be processed.

2. Refining processes

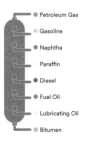

The raw resources are transformed into different elements. The refining process transforms crude oil into different petroleum products—these are converted to yield useful chemicals including 'monomers' (a molecule that is the basic building blocks of polymers). In the refining process, crude oil is heated in a furnace, which is then sent to the distillation unit, where heavy crude oil separates into lighter components called fractions. One of these, called naphtha, is the crucial compound to make a large variety of plastics. However, there are other means, such as using gas.

3. Cracking

Naphtha has to be cracked to release valuable hydrocarbons. Heat breaks down the bonds of long-chain molecules, resulting in short-chain molecules and producing monomers: ethylene, propylene, butadiene, and benzene, along with many other by-products like hydrogen. These various elements create different types of plastics after further processing.

4. Polymerization

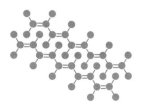

Catalysts and high pressure are applied to create long-chain molecules with new properties. Two different types of polymerization are used: addition polymerization is when one monomer connects to the next (dimer) and the dimer to the next (trimer), and so on. This reaction is achieved by introducing a catalyst, typically a peroxide. This process is also known as chain-growth polymerization as it adds one monomer a unit at a time. Common examples of addition polymers are polyethylene, polystyrene, and polyvinyl chloride. Condensation polymerization involves joining different monomers by removing the small molecules such as water. This is known as step-growth.

5. Antioxidants and stabilizers

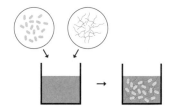

In this step, chemicals are added to plastics to prevent them from degrading, including for the prevention of UV damage, oxidation, and thermal degradation. The process can also involve antioxidant stabilizers to meet the legal standards of food safety, thus the same plastic can contain several different antioxidants and stabilizers to fulfil different requirements.

6. Extrusion and pellets

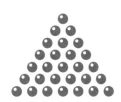

The resulting polymer is then fed into an extruder where is it melted and fed into a form to create a long rod of material. This cools to the resulting plastic which is then cut into small pellets ready for manufacturing. These pellets are then reheated to bond them together and then shaped, using various manufacturing techniques, into their desired forms.

Moulding methods

Injection moulding

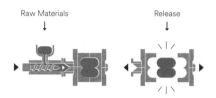

Plastic injection moulding (PIM) accounts for about 80% of durable everyday plastic items. Injection moulding uses a mould or die made from aluminum or steel. The mould, consisting of two sides, the core and cavity, is placed into a plastic injection-moulding machine. This machine heats the raw plastic-resin pellets until they are molten, injects them into the empty mould cavity under great pressure, and then ejects the finished part. The advantage of PIM is uniformity and efficiency at low cost. Moulds, however, can be expensive and complex to make, depending on the part geometry.

Blow moulding

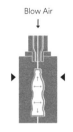

A moulding process in which heated plastic is blown into a mould cavity to create a hollow object. The defining characteristic of blow moulding is its use to create hollow objects. Raw plastic is first heated; it is then formed into a parison, which is then secured to the top of the mould. Air is then blown down onto the plastic parison, thereby stretching it across the interior walls of the mould cavity. This process is used to make plastic drinks bottles.

Extrusion moulding

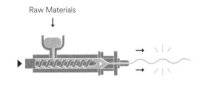

The extrusion process is used for high-volume processes during which plastic is melted and formed into a continuous profile. Extrusion is typically used for items such as pipes and tubing. The extrusion process begins with feeding plastic material (pellets, granules, flakes, or powders) from a hopper into the extruder barrel. The material is then gradually melted by the mechanical energy generated by turning-screws and heaters inside the barrel. The molten polymer is then forced into a die; this shapes the polymer which then hardens during cooling.

Compression moulding

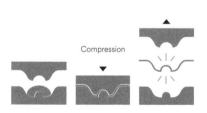

Compression moulding is a method in which the moulding material, generally preheated, is first placed into a heated mould cavity. The mould is then closed with a top force or plug member, to force the material into contact with all areas of the mould. Heat and pressure are then maintained until the material inside the mould has cured.

Calender moulding

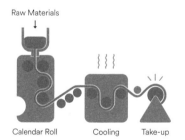

This technique applies heat and pressure in an extruder while also feeding the resin into heated calendering rolls to stretch it. This method is used mainly for PVC and also for making plastic film and sheeting.

Vacuum forming

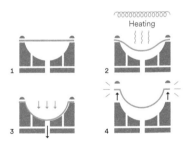

Sheets of resin are heated to a soft consistency and a vacuum is applied to force the material into the mould. Vacuum forming is used for producing containers.

Sources: The British Plastics Federation, "How Is Plastic Made? A Simple Step-By-Step Explanation", online: https://www.bpf.co.uk/plastipedia/how-is-plastic-made.aspx; and see also the OMV Group [video], "Petrochemistry: How plastic is made from crude oil" (18 February 2021), https://www.youtube.com/watch?v=6qQS4VMeh1s, both accessed 21 January 2022.

What happens to our plastics?

Plastic recycling worldwide

India is the world's most prolific plastic waste recycler, recycling 60% of its plastics. India is followed by South Korea (45%) and the European Union (30%). In the United States, the plastic recycling rate is only 9%.

India	S. Korea	EU	China	Japan	Morocco	Mexico	S. Africa	Brazil	Australia	Argentina	USA
60%	45%	30%	25%	25%	25%	24%	20%	19%	14%	11%	9%

Sources: Roland Geyer et al., "Production, use, and fate of all plastics ever made", *Science Advances*, vol. 3, no. 7 (2017), online: https://www.science.org/doi/10.1126/sciadv.1700782; The Ellen MacArthur Foundation (eds), *The New Plastics Economy: Rethinking the Future of Plastics* (2017), online: https://ellenmacarthurfoundation.org/the-new-plastics-economy-rethinking-the-future-of-plastics; see also "Plan For Plastics: The Circular Solution / Plastic Recycling Report", *Veolia* (2018), online: https://www.veolia.co.uk/insight/plan-plastics, all accessed 21 January 2022.

United States municipal plastic waste streams

- Landfill
- Incineration with energy recovery
- Recycled

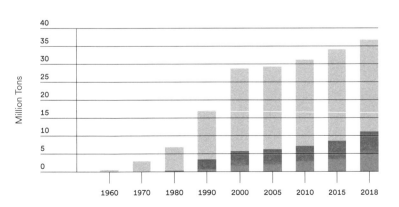

Sources: Heinrich Böll Foundation and Break Free From Plastic, *The Plastic Atlas*, p. 36; US Environmental Protection Agency, *National Overview: Facts and Figures on Materials, Wastes and Recycling* (2021), online: www.epa.gov/facts-and-figures-about-materials-waste-and-recycling/national-overview-facts-and-figures-materials, accessed 26 January 2022.

Waste treatment by type of recovery and disposal in Europe, 2018

The first EU directive on the regulation of landfill of waste was introduced in 1999 with the aim to prevent, or reduce as much as possible, any negative impact from landfill on surface water, groundwater, soil, air, or human health.

In 2018, an amendment to the Landfill Directive introduced a landfilling ban for separately collected waste and limits the share of municipal waste landfilled to 10% by 2035.

■	Recovery – Recycling
■	Recovery – Backfilling
■	Energy recovery
▨	Disposal – Landfill and other
■	Disposal – Incineration without energy recovery

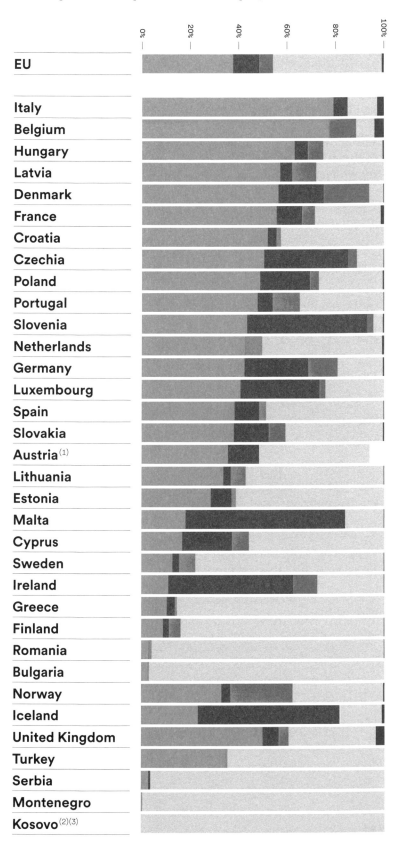

1. No data available for energy recovery and incineration without energy recovery.
2. No data available for incineration without energy recovery.
3. This designation is without prejudice to positions on status, and is in line with UNSCR 1244/1999 and the ICJ's opinion on the Declaration of Independence of Kosovo.

Source: Confederation of European Waste-to-Energy Plants (cewep), "Landfill Taxes and Bans", online: https://www.cewep.eu/landfill-taxes-and-bans/, accessed 26 January 2022.
Source for graph: "Waste treatment by type of recovery and disposal, 2018", *Eurostat*, 2018, online: ec.europa.eu/eurostat/statistics-explained/index.php?title=File:Waste_treatment_by_type_of_recovery_and_disposal,_2018_(%25_of_total_treatment)_30-04-2021.png, accessed 26 January 2022.

Recycling plastic

What are SPI codes?

In 1988, the Society of the Plastics Industry (SPI) established a classification system to help people recycle and dispose of their plastics responsibly. Today, manufacturers follow this coding system and place a number, or SPI code, on each product, usually moulded into the bottom.

Source: Plastic Soup Foundation, "Recycling codes", online: plasticsoupfoundation.org/en/plastic-problem/what-is-plastic/recycling-codes/, accessed 11 January 2022.

Global production

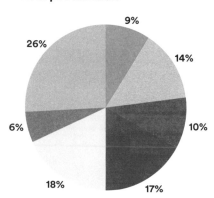

9%
14%
26%
10%
6%
18%
17%

Ways to identify plastics

Several simple tests can distinguish between the common types of polymers so that they may be separated for processing.

The water test: After adding a few drops of liquid detergent to some water put in a small piece of plastic and see if it floats.

The flame test: Hold a piece of the plastic with tweezers or on the back of a knife and apply a flame. Does it burn? If so, what colour?

The scratch test: Can a sample of the plastic be scratched with a fingernail?

Type	SPI Code	Name	Properties	Common Uses
PET	1 PET	Polyethylene Terephthalate	Clear, tough, solvent, resistant, barrier to gas and moisture, softens at 80 °C	Soft drink and water bottles, salad domes, biscuit trays, food containers
HDPE	2 HDPE	High-Density Polyethylene	Hard to semi-flexible, resistant to chemicals and moisture, waxy surface, softens at 75 °C	Shopping bags, freezer bags, milk bottles, juice bottles, ice cream containers, shampoo bottles, crates
PVC	3 PVC	Polyvinyl Chloride	Strong, tough, can be clear and solvent, softens at 60 °C	Cosmetic containers, electrical conduit, plumbing pipes, blister packs, roof sheeting, garden hose
LDPE	4 LDPE	Low-Density Polyethylene	Soft, flexible, waxy surface, scratches easily, softens at 70 °C	Cling film, rubbish bags, squeeze bottles, mulch film
PP	5 PP	Polypropylene	Hard, but still flexible, waxy surface, translucent, withstands solvents, softens at 140 °C	Bottles, ice cream tubes, straws, flower-pots, dishes, garden furniture, food containers
PS	6 PS	Polystyrene	Clear, glassy, opaque, semi-tough, softens at 95 °C	CD cases, plastic cutlery, imitation glass, foam meat trays, brittle toys
OTHER	7 OTHER	All Other Plastics	Properties depend on the type of plastic	Automotive, electronics, packaging

Test	PET	PP	PS	PVC
Water	Floats	Floats	Sinks	Sinks
Flame	Blue flame with yellow tip, melts and drips	Yellow flame with blue base	Yellow, sooty flame – drips	Yellow, sooty smoke. Does not continue to burn if flame is removed
Smell after burning	Like candle wax	Like candle wax – less strong than PE	Sweet	Hydrochloric acid
Scratch	Yes	No	No	No

Source: Practical Action, "Recycling Plastics", The Schumacher Centre (2009), online: file:///C:/Users/Mandi/Downloads/530485a2-16b8-45da-9ddf-75d30a000075.pdf, accessed 11. January 2022.

A circular plastic economy?

To reach a circular plastic economy the current, still mostly linear plastic economy would need to change at both ends, from the source material to the recycling of waste. It also takes a combination of different approaches that complement each other.

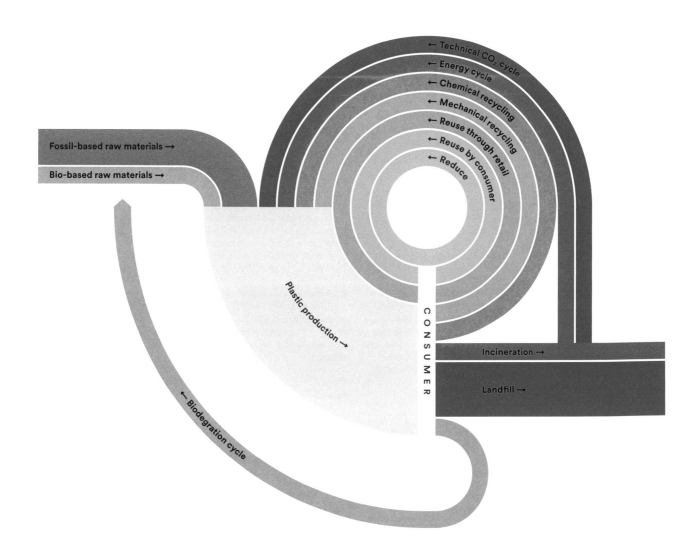

Fossil-based raw materials →

Bio-based raw materials →

← Technical CO₂ cycle

← Energy cycle

← Chemical recycling

← Mechanical recycling

← Reuse through retail

← Reuse by consumer

← Reduce

Plastic production →

C O N S U M E R

Incineration →

Landfill →

← Biodegration cycle

Source: https://news.cision.com/vtt-info/r/vtt--a-circular-economy-of-plastics-will-reduce-plastic-pollution-and-slow-down-climate-change,c3115141; und https://cedelft.eu/publications/biobased-plastics-in-a-circular-economy/; both accessed 26 January 2021.

Key

Fossil-based raw materials Crude oil and natural gas are not available in unlimited quantities as fossil-based raw materials for the production of plastics and hence are not circular. **Bio-based raw materials** Bio-based raw materials are renewable, but should not, however, compete with food crops. **Reduce** Reducing consumption of plastic—especially single-use plastic—is the most effective way to reduce plastic waste. **Reuse by consumer** Reuse of products whether for their original purpose or a different one, requires them to be durable and repairable. **Reuse through retail** Reuse of products using a deposit-and-return system requires standardization and the appropriate infrastructure. **Mechanical recycling** Mechanical recycling preserves the chemical structure of plastics but shortens the polymer chains, which reduces the quality of the material. **Chemical recycling** Chemical recycling breaks plastics down into their basic chemical building blocks so that new plastic of the same quality can be made, but this consumes a lot of energy. **Incineration** Incineration to generate thermal energy is the most common, but ecologically unfavourable way to recycle plastic waste. **Technical CO₂ cycle** Theoretically, the CO₂ produced by waste incineration could be used by the chemical industry to produce new plastics. However, CO₂ only decomposes at very high temperatures above 2,400 °C. **Biodegradation cycle** A biodegradable cycle could be achieved with plastics based on renewable raw materials. However, most biodegradable plastics still require industrial composting.

Authors and Collocutors

Johanna Agerman Ross (JAR) is Curator of Twentieth-Century and Contemporary Furniture and Product Design at the Victoria and Albert Museum, London, and co-curator of *Plastic: Remaking Our World*.

Jane Atfield is a designer and educator based in London who founded Made of Waste in the early 1990s and has worked as a design consultant for IKEA and Habitat. Pieces of her furniture are held in the collections of the Crafts Council, the Victoria and Albert Museum, and the Vitra Design Museum.

Nihan Temiz Ataş is Biodiversity Projects Lead at Greenpeace Mediterranean and is based in Turkey. Her work investigates plastic export bases, and campaigns to end the sending of waste to the Global South and to implement the European Union's 2019 Single-Use Plastics Directive.

Lauren Bassam (LB) is Assistant Curator at V&A Dundee and co-curator of *Plastic: Remaking Our World*.

Mark Buckley is Circular Design Network Manager at the Ellen MacArthur Foundation. There, he helps to operate the world's leading circular-economy network of businesses, institutions, governments, cities, universities, and innovators. The Foundation also generates research, explores opportunities across stakeholders and sectors, and supports learning opportunities.

Connie Karol Burks (CKB) is Assistant Curator at the Victoria and Albert Museum, London.

Liang-jung Chen, an interdisciplinary artist and designer based in London, is deeply interested in material culture. Her work, including the project, The Misused, is informed by research on the everyday politics within artefacts.

Erica Cirino is a science writer, author, and artist exploring the intersection of the human and nonhuman worlds. Her book *Thicker Than Water: The Quest for Solutions to the Plastic Crisis* (2021) documents plastic across ecosystems and shares stories from the primarily Black, Brown, Indigenous, and rural communities disproportionally harmed by industrial pollution.

Dianna Cohen is co-founder and CEO of Plastic Pollution Coalition and a leading activist against plastic pollution. A Los Angeles-based visual artist, she has been the recipient of the Global Green Environment Award, the Snow Angel Award, and SIMA's Environmentalist of the Year.

Ama van Dantzig is co-founder of Dr. Monk, an international social-innovation agency headquartered in the Netherlands and Ghana. Combining sustainability, international cooperation, art, and media, the agency develops concepts and co-creates initiatives to influence the way people think and act, fostering a fairer, cleaner, and more beautiful world.

Suzanne Dhaliwal is a climate justice creative, researcher, environmental justice lecturer and campaigner, and trainer in creative strategies for decolonization. In solidarity with frontline Indigenous communities, she co-founded the UK Tar Sands Network, which challenged BP and Shell investments in Canadian tar sands and spurred the international fossil fuel divestment movement.

Manfred Diebold worked for Vitra between 1962 and 1988 and led the implementation of all Eames chairs and Action Office products and developed a new technique for the upholstery of office chairs. He was instrumental in the realization of the Panton Chair.

Jochen Eisenbrand (JE) is Chief Curator at the Vitra Design Museum, Weil am Rhein, and co-curator of *Plastic: Remaking Our World*.

Rolf Fehlbaum was CEO and Chairman of Vitra and founded the Vitra Design Museum in 1989. At the Vitra Campus, Weil am Rhein, he forged relationships with leading designers and developed projects with Tadao Ando, Frank Gehry, Zaha Hadid, Nicholas Grimshaw, Álvaro Siza, Herzog & de Meuron, and SANAA.

Susan Freinkel is an American journalist of science, health, and the environment living in San Francisco, California. She is the author of *Plastic: A Toxic Love Story* (2011) and *American Chestnut: The Life, Death, and Rebirth of a Perfect Tree* (2007).

Corinna Gardner (CG) is Senior Curator of Design and Digital at the Victoria and Albert Museum, London, and co-curator of *Plastic: Remaking Our World*.

Peter Ghyczy studied architecture at the Technical University of Aachen alongside serving as assistant to German architect Rudolf Steinbach. After graduating, he worked as a designer for Elastogran, a producer of polyurethane in Lauenförde, Germany, where he designed the foldable plastic Garden Egg chair in 1969. In 1972, he founded his own company for which he designed furniture and lighting.

Cyrill Gutsch is founder of Parley for the Oceans, a collaboration network for creators, thinkers, and leaders. Initiatives include the Parley Global Cleanup Network, which works to protect marine environments from threats including plastic pollution, as well as an ongoing partnership with Adidas to phase out single-use plastics and microbeads.

Charlotte Hale (CH) is Curator at V&A Dundee, and co-curator of *Plastic: Remaking our World*.

Dirk E. Hebel is Dean of the Faculty of Architecture and Professor of Sustainable Construction at the Karlsruhe Institute of Technology. He is a member of the Academic Committee of the non-profit Holcim Foundation and principal investigator at the Future Cities Laboratory established by ETH Zurich and Singapore's National Research Foundation.

Mea Hoffmann (MH) is Curator at the Vitra Design Museum, Weil am Rhein, and co-curator of *Plastic: Remaking Our World*.

Sandy Jones (SJ) is a design historian who trained at the Royal College of Art and the Victoria and Albert Museum, with a particular interest in graphic design. She began her career in the design industry running brand identity and product innovation programmes for organizations such as British Airways, the BBC, and Unilever.

Purnima Joshi is a communications consultant and a founding member of Team Swachh Kalyani Nagar, an active citizens group in Pune, India, and Swap, a platform for hyperlocal exchanges of pre-owned household items. She is passionate about creating engaged communities as the basic units of a healthy, vibrant democracy.

Eric Klarenbeek and Maartje Dros (Klarenbeek & Dros) have been collaborating since 2014 on research and design projects that strive to achieve new local economies and production chains, material development, and durable design objects. Their most recent work, the Seaweed Circle, introduces a seaweed-based production network around sea-farmed biopolymers known as Weedware.

Anniina Koivu (AK) is a freelance design writer, curator, consultant, and teacher. In her role as a co-Curator of *Plastic: Remaking Our World*, she is representing the Museum of Art, Architecture and Technology, Lisbon.

John McGeehan is a Professor of Structural Biology focused on the global challenge of plastic pollution. He co-founded and serves as Director for the Centre for Enzyme Innovation at the University of Portsmouth and leads a team of scientists researching natural enzyme discovery and engineering.

Mark Miodownik is Professor of Materials and Society at University College London who, for more than 20 years, has championed material science research that links the arts and humanities, medicine, and society. Fellow of the UK Royal Academy of Engineering, he is also the author of the *New York Times* bestseller *Stuff Matters* (2013).

Nanjala Nyabola is a writer and researcher based in Nairobi, Kenya, focusing on the intersection of technology, media, and society. She is the author of *Digital Democracy, Analogue Politics: How the Internet Era is Transforming Politics in Kenya* (2018) and *Travelling While Black: Essays Inspired by a Life on the Move* (2021) and co-editor of *Where Women Are: Gender & the 2017 Kenyan General Elections* (2018).

Chineyenwa Okoro Onu is founder and Managing Director of Waste Or Create, Africa's first eco-innovation centre. Through the centre's educational and practical solutions, she plays a critical role in preparing future generations for responsible participation in building a sustainable and inclusive green economy.

Riya Patel is a freelance London-based architecture and design writer. Formerly curator of The Aram Gallery, an independent platform for experimental design, and senior editor at *Icon* magazine, she has written for *Wallpaper**, the *Independent*, *Architects' Journal*, *Frame*, and *Disegno* amongst other publications.

Helen Pickles (HP) is Project Officer at the Highland Folk Museum where she is responsible for researching, documenting, and digitizing the shinty collections. Prior to this, Helen worked at Kenwood House in London, English Heritage, and the British Museum taking care of diverse collections.

Veena Sahajwalla is an inventor and Scientia Professor of Materials Science at UNSW Australia, where she is also Director of the Centre for Sustainable Materials Research and Technology (SM@RT). In addition, she is a councillor on the independent Australian Climate Council and was a judge on the ABC show *The New Inventors*.

Thomas Schweikert has worked for Vitra since 1993. From 2004 to 2020, he was head of Development for Vitra Home, and he became Technical Lead Sustainability & Research in 2021.

Shellworks is a biotech start-up based in London that works towards delivering sustainable solutions without compromise. Co-founded in 2019 by Insiya Jafferjee and Amir Afshar, Shellworks develops truly compostable alternatives to plastic via microbial fermentation.

Sumitra Upham is a curator and writer based in London with an interest in material cultures and social justice. Currently Head of Public Programmes at the Crafts Council, she was also Curator of the 5th Istanbul Design Biennial led by Mariana Pestana.

James Wakibia is a Kenyan environmental activist and photojournalist advocating for better management of plastic waste and a ban on single-use plastic. He is Executive Director of the non-profit Eco Rethink Organization, and his slogan is "Less Plastic is Fantastic".

John Williams (JW) is a Collections Moves Officer at the Victoria and Albert Museum specializing in furniture and product design. Prior to working in design, he managed large-scale technology projects.

Illustration Acknowledgements

2–1 © Vitra Design Museum, photo: Andreas Sütterlin

14–1 ↵

40–1 © Victoria and Albert Museum, London

42–1 Vitra Design Museum Archive

43–1 ↵

43–2 Science Museum / Science & Society Picture Library

43–3 Courtesy of Michigan State University Libraries

44–1 Museumsstiftung Post und Telekommunikation

46–1 Science Museum Pictorial / Science & Society Picture Library

47–1 ↵

48–1 Courtesy of the George Eastman Museum

49–1 National Science & Media Museum / Science & Society Picture Library

49–2 Courtesy of the George Eastman Museum

50–1 amsterdambakelitecollection.com / Reindert Groot

50–2 ↵

51–1 ↵

52–1 Courtesy of Stiftung Eisenbibliothek, Georg Fischer AG, Schlatt, Switzerland

53–1 Photo: Jochen Eisenbrand, courtesy of ETH-Bibliothek HDB

54–1 Courtesy of Hagley Museum and Library

55–1 Courtesy of the Science History Institute

56–1 Vitra Design Museum Archive

56–2 © General Motors LLC

57–1 Vitra Design Museum Archive

58–1 © The Henry Ford

59–1 © VG Bild-Kunst, Bonn 2022, Vitra Design Museum Archive

60–1 Vitra Design Museum Archive

62–1 ↵

63–1 Courtesy of the Science History Institute

64–1 Courtesy of the Hagley Museum and Library

65–1 ↵

65–2 Courtesy of Exxon Mobil Corporation /

ExxonMobil Historical Collection, di_07455, The Dolph Briscoe Center for American History, The University of Texas at Austin

66–1 Photo: Museum für Gestaltung Zurich, Plakatsammlung, ZHdK

66–2 Courtesy Ville de Paris / Bibliothèque Forney

67–1 Vitra Design Museum Archive

68–1 Courtesy of the Hagley Museum and Library

69–1 Courtesy of the Science History Institute

70–1 © Getty Images, photo: Peter Stackpole

71–1 Museum of Design in Plastics, Arts University Bournemouth

72–1 Vitra Design Museum Archive, photo: Andreas Sütterlin

73–1 ↵

74–1 Courtesy of the Science History Institute

75–1 Courtesy of the Hagley Museum and Library

76–1 Courtesy of Paris Musées / Musée d'Art Moderne de Paris

76–2 Courtesy of STUDIOCANAL

77–1 © Peter Schnetz, courtesy of Coop-Himmelb(l)au

77–2 In possession of Brandes/Erlhoff; courtesy of Zamp Kampel

78–1 Vitra Design Museum Archive

79–1 Courtesy of B&B Italia

79–2 BASF Corporate History, Ludwigshafen a. Rh

80–1 Vitra Design Museum Archive, photo: Andreas Sütterlin

81–1 ↵

82–1 Courtesy of W. L. Gore & Associates, Inc.

83–1 Archivio Fotografico Alessi

83–2 © Swatch

84–1 Algalita Marine Research and Education

85–1 © Chris Jordan

86–1 Photo © Mandy Barker, mandy-barker.com

87–1 Courtesy of Kelly Jazvac,

photo: Jeff Elstone

88–1 © National Geographic; Vitra Design Museum Archive

89–1 Ross Mantle/The New York Times/Redux/laif

90–1 Courtesy of Breakfreefromplastic

90–2 © United Nations Environment Programme, 2021

91–1 © VG Bild-Kunst, Bonn, 2022 / photo: Marco Barotti

92–1 © Vitra Design Museum, photo: Andreas Sütterlin

112–1 ↵

114–1 © Victoria and Albert Museum, London

115–1 © Museum of Design in Plastics, Arts University Bournemouth / Worshipful Company of Horners collection

116–1 Museumsstiftung Post und Telekommunikation

117–1 amsterdambakelitecollection.com / Reindert Groot

118–1 © Vitra Design Museum, photo: Andreas Sütterlin

119–1 ↵

120–1 amsterdambakelitecollection.com / Reindert Groot

121–1 © Victoria and Albert Museum, London

122–1 ↵

123–1 ↵

124–1 ↵

125–1 ↵

126–1 amsterdambakelitecollection.com / Reindert Groot

127–1 © Museum of Design in Plastics, Arts University Bournemouth

128–1 © Victoria and Albert Museum, London

129–1 © Peter Ascher, Ascher Family Archive / Victoria and Albert Museum, London

130–1 © Victoria and Albert Museum, London

131–1 Reproduced by permission of the Warner Textile Archive, Braintree District Museum Trust / Victoria and Albert Museum, London

131–2 © Victoria and Albert

Museum, London

132–1 © Vitra Design Museum, photo: Andreas Jung

133–1 © Museum of Design in Plastics, Arts University Bournemouth

134–1 © Victoria and Albert Museum, London

135–1 © Vitra Design Museum, photo: Andreas Sütterlin

136–1 Google Patents/ US3180557A

137–1 © Vitra Design Museum, photo: Jürgen Hans

138–1 © Vitra Design Museum, photo: Andreas Sütterlin

139–1 © Victoria and Albert Museum, London

140–1 Courtesy The Estate of R. Buckminster Fuller / Victoria and Albert Museum, London

141–1 © Vitra Design Museum, photo: Andreas Sütterlin

142–1 © Vitra Design Museum, photo: Jürgen Hans

143–1 © Vitra Design Museum, photo: Andreas Sütterlin

144–1 © Museum of Design in Plastics, Arts University Bournemouth

145–1 Courtesy The Body Shop / Victoria and Albert Museum, London

146–1 Photo: Museum für Gestaltung Zürich, Grafiksammlung, ZHdK

147–1 Courtesy of Ellis Developments Ltd / Victoria and Albert Museum, London

148–1 Courtesy of Formafantasma / Victoria and Albert Museum, London

149–1 © Vitra Design Museum, photo: Andreas Sütterlin

150–1 © Kay Sanvito, Professorship (of) Sustainable Construction, KIT Karlsruhe

152–1 © Kunstmuseen Krefeld

154–1 ↵

154–2 ↵

154–3 ↵

154–4 ↵

154–5 ↵

156–1 Courtesy of Jane Atfield, photo: Edward Woodman

157–1 ↵

158–1 Courtesy of Jane Atfield / Victoria and Albert

Select Bibliography

Altman, Rebecca, "How Bad Are Plastics, Really?", the *Atlantic* (3 January 2022), online: https://www.theatlantic.com/science/archive/2022/01/plastic-history-climate-change/621033/, accessed 16 January 2022.

Ambasz, Emilio (ed.), *Italy: The New Domestic Landscape*, exhib. cat. Museum of Modern Art, New York, 1972.

Böhm, Karl, and Rolf Dörge, *Der Mensch und seine Welt*. Berlin: Verlag Neues Leben, 1960.

Braungart, Michael, and William McDonough, *Cradle to Cradle: Remaking the Way We Make Things*. New York: North Point Press, 2002.

Brooks, Amy L., Shunli Wang, and Jenna R. Jambeck, "The Chinese import ban and its impact on global plastic waste trade", *Science Advances*, vol. 4, no. 6 (2018), online: https://www.science.org/doi/10.1126/sciadv.aat0131, accessed 16 January 2022.

Carson, Rachel, *Silent Spring*. London: Penguin, 2000/1962.

Cecchini, Cecilia and Maro Petroni (Eds.), *Plastic Days. Materials and Design*, exhib. cat. Museo Ettore Fico Torino, Milan: Silvana Editoriale, 2015.

Clarke, Alison J., *Tupper-ware: The Promise of Plastic in 1950s America*. Washington, DC: Smithsonian Books, 2011.

Coffin, Sarah D. et al., *Feeding Desire: Design and the Tools of the Table 1500–2005*, exhib. cat. Cooper Hewitt National Design Museum/New York: Assouline Publishing, 2006.

Dessauce, Marc, *The Inflatable Moment: Pneumatics and Protest in '68*, exhib. cat. Architectural League New York/New York: Princeton Architectural Press, 1999.

Du Bois, J. Harry, *Plastics History, U.S.A.* Boston, MA: Cahners Books, 1972.

Ellen MacArthur Foundation, *The New Plastics Economy: Rethinking the future of plastics*, online: https://ellenmacarthurfoundation.org/the-new-plastics-economy-rethinking-the-future-of-plastics, accessed 1 December 2021.

Bartow J. Elmore, Citizen Coke. *The Making of Coca-Cola Capitalism*. New York / London: W. W. Norton & Company, 2014.

European Commission, "Single-use plastics" (Directive, entry into force 2 July 2019), online: https://ec.europa.eu/environment/topics/plastics/single-use-plastics_en, accessed 12 December 2021.

Fenichell, Stephen, *Plastic: The Making of a Synthetic Century*. New York: Harper Collins, 1996.

Franklin, Kate and Caroline Till, *Radical Matter. Rethinking Materials for a Sustainable future*. New York: Thames & Hudson, 2019.

Freinkel, Susan, *Plastic: A Toxic Love Story*. New York: Houghton Mifflin Harcourt, 2011.

Friedel, Robert, *Pioneer Plastic: The Making and Selling of Celluloid*. Madison, NJ: University of Wisconsin Press, 1983.

Geyer, Roland, Jenna R. Jambeck, and Kara Lavender: "Production, use, and fate of all plastics ever made", *Science Advances*, vol. 3, no. 7 (2017), online: https://www.science.org/doi/10.1126/sciadv.1700782, accessed 16 January 2022.

Gorman, Amanda, *Earthrise* (2018), online: https://www.sierraclub.org/los-padres/blog/2021/02/earthrise-poem-amanda-gorman, accessed 16 January 2022.

Hawkins, Gay, Emily Potter and Kane Race, *Plastic Water. The Social and Material Life of Bottled Water*. Cambridge, MA: MIT Press, 2015.

Hebel, Dirk E., and Felix Heisel, *Cultivated Building Materials: Industrialized Natural Resources for Architecture and Construction*. Basel: Birkhäuser, 2017.

Heinrich Böll Foundation and Break Free From Plastic, *The Plastic Atlas* (Berlin: 2019), online: https://www.boell.de/sites/default/files/2020-01/Plastic%20Atlas%202019%202nd%20Edition.pdf, accessed 16 January 2022.

Hufnagl, Florian (ed.), *Plastics + Design*, exhib. cat. Künstlerkolonie Mathildenhöhe/Stuttgart: Arnoldsche Verlagsanstalt, 1997.

Katz, Sylvia, *Classic Plastics. From Bakelite ... to High-Tech*. London: Thames & Hudson, 1984.

Koller, Theodor, *Die Surrogate. Ihre Darstellungen im Kleinen und deren fabrikmässige Erzeugung. Ein Handbuch der Herstellung der künstlichen Ersatzstoffe für den praktischen Gebrauch von Industriellen und Technikern*. Frankfurt am Main: H. Bechhold, 1893.

Krieger, Anja, *Plastisphere. A podcast on Plastic, People, and the Planet*, 2018–21, https://anjakrieger.com/plastisphere/, accessed 16 January 2022.

Loadman, John, *Tears of a Tree: The Story of Rubber—A Modern Marvel*. Oxford: Oxford University Press, 2005.

Meikle, Jeffrey, *American Plastic: A Cultural History*. New Brunswick, NJ: Rutgers University Press, 1997.

Meikle, Jeffrey, "Material Doubts: The Consequences of Plastic", *Environmental History*, vol. 2, no. 3 (1997), pp. 278–300.

Minderoo Foundation, *The Plastic Waste Makers Index: Revealing the Source of the Single-Use Plastic Crisis* (2000), online: https://www.minderoo.org/plastic-waste-makers-index/, accessed 1 December 2021.

Miodownik, Mark, *Stuff Matters: The Strange Stories of the Marvellous Materials that Shape our World*. New York: Viking, 2013.

Mossman, Susan (ed.), *Early Plastics: Perspectives 1850–1950*. Leicester: Leicester University Press, 1997.

Mossman, Susan (ed.), *Fantastic Plastic: Product Design and Consumer Culture*. London: Black Dog Publishing, 2008.

Mumford, John Kimberly, *The Story of Bakelite*. New York: Robert L. Stillson Company, 1924.

Papanek, Victor, *Design for the Real World: Human Ecology and Social Change*. New York: Pantheon Books, 1971.

Quarmby, Arthur, *The Plastics Architect*. London: Pall Mall Press, 1974.

Reichle, Ingeborg, *Plastic Ocean: Art and Science Responses to Marine Pollution*. Berlin: Edition Angewandte/Boston: De Gruyter, 2021.

Robertson, Kirsty, "Plastiglomerate", *e-flux journal*, no. 78 (December 2016), online: https://www.e-flux.com/journal/78/82878/plastiglomerate/, accessed 17 January 2022.

Rubin, Eli, *Synthetic Socialism: Plastics and Dictatorship in the German Democratic Republic*. Berkeley, CA: University of California Press, 2014.

Solanki, Seetal, *Why Materials Matter*. Munich: Prestel, 2018.

Sparke, Penny, *The Plastics Age: From Modernity to Post-Modernity*, exhib. cat. Victoria and Albert Museum, London, 1990.

Stouffer, Lloyd, "Plastics Packaging: Today and Tomorrow", Preliminary copy of a report to be presented at the SPI Annual National Plastics Conference at the Sheraton-Chicago Hotel, Chicago, Illinois, The Society of the Plastics Industry, 1963.

Synthetic Collective, *Plastic Heart: A DIY Fieldguide for Reducing the Environmental Impact of Art Exhibitions* (exhib. cat. Art Museum at the University of Toronto, 2021), online: https://kirsty-mairirobertson.files.wordpress.com/2021/06/plasticheart_diy_fieldguide-1.pdf, accessed 16 January 2022.

Tully, John, "A Victorian Disaster: Imperialism, the Telegraph, and Gutta-Percha", *Journal of World History*, vol. 20, no. 4 (2009), pp. 559–79.

United Nations Environment Programme, *Towards a Pollution-Free Planet* (2017), online: https://wedocs.unep.org/bitstream/handle/20.500.11822/21800/UNEA_towardspollu-tion_long%20version_Web.pdf?sequence=1&isAllowed=y, accessed 18 January 2022

Westermann, Andrea, *Plastik und politische Kultur in Westdeutschland*. Interferenzen: Studien zur Kulturgeschichte der Technik, Zurich: Chronos Verlag, 2007.

Wilson, Sheena, Adam Carlson, and Imre Szeman (eds), *Petrocultures: Oil, Politics, Culture*. Montreal: McGill-Queen's University Press, 2017.

World Economic Forum, *Plastics, The Circular Economy and Global Trade* (29 July 2020), online: https://www.weforum.org/whitepapers/plastics-the-circular-econo-my-and-global-trade, accessed 1 December 2021.

World Health Organization: "Microplastics in drink-ing-water" (information sheet), online: https://www.who.int/water_sanitation_health/water-quality/guidelines/microplastics-in-dw-Informa-tion-sheet.pdf?ua=1, accessed 18 January 2021.

Yarsely, Victor E. and Edward G. Couzens, *Plastics*. Harmondsworth: Penguin Books, 1941.

Index

Colophon

This book is published on the occasion of the exhibition
Plastic: Remaking Our World

Vitra Design Museum, Weil am Rhein
26 March 2022–4 September 2022

V&A Dundee
29 October 2022–5 February 2023

maat – Museum of Art, Architecture and Technology, Lisbon
Spring 2023

Further venues are planned

Editors: Mateo Kries, Jochen Eisenbrand, Mea Hoffmann
Co-Editors: Johanna Agerman Ross, Corinna Gardner,
Charlotte Hale, Lauren Bassam, Anniina Koivu
Editorial Management: Kirsten Thietz
Copy-editing and Proofreading: Amanda Gomez, Hannah Sarid
de Mowbray (English), Kirsten Thietz (German)
Translations: Herwig Engelmann, Claudia Kotte, Martin Hager
(German), Lisa Schons (English)
Index: Jutta Mühlenberg
Image Rights: Mea Hoffmann, Jochen Eisenbrand
Research "Plastic Data": Anniina Koivu, Maxwell Ashford

Design: Daniel Streat, Visual Fields
Project Management: Esther Schröter
Production: Judith Brugger
Distribution: Anton Schleidt
Pre-press: GZD Media GmbH, Renningen
Printing: DZA Druckerei zu Altenburg GmbH, Altenburg
Paper: Creative Print Champagner 350gsm (100% reclaimed
fibres, Blue Angel certified), Arena Natural Smooth 120gsm
Typefaces: Circular and Bradford, designed by Laurenz Brunner

First published by the Vitra Design Museum
Vitra Design Museum
Charles-Eames-Straße 2
79576 Weil am Rhein
Germany
verlag@design-museum.de

Printed and bound in Germany
© Vitra Design Museum 2022
The German National Library has listed this publication in the
German National Bibliography; detailed bibliographical data
is available at http://dnb.dnb.de
ISBN (English edition): 978-3-945852-47-7
ISBN (German edition): 978-3-945852-46-0

Exhibition

Curatorial Team:
Vitra Design Museum: Jochen Eisenbrand, Mea Hoffmann
V&A Dundee: Charlotte Hale, Lauren Bassam
maat, Lisbon: Anniina Koivu
Consultant curators:
V&A: Johanna Agerman Ross and Corinna Gardner with support
from Connie Karol Burks and Zoe Louizos
Project Management: Karoline Harms
Design: Asif Khan (Alex Borrell, Asif Khan, Peter Vaughan,
Mara Zuliani)
Graphics: Daniel Streat, Visual Fields
Film installation "Kalpa (aeon)": Asif Khan
Image and Film Rights: Mea Hoffmann, Lauren Bassam
Technical Director: Stefani Fricker
Exhibition Development: René Herzogenrath, Nathalie Opris
Senior Art Technicians: Harald Gottstein, Patrick Kessler,
Olaf Krüger, Niels Tofahrn
Conservation: Susanne Graner, Lena Hönig, Grazyna Ubik
Press and Public Relations / Marketing: Johanna Hunder,
Jan-Marcel Müller, Maximilian Kloiber
Partnerships: Jasmin Zikry
Education and Public Programme: Katrin Hager, Julia Beyer,
Emily Harries
Exhibition Tour: Cora Harris, Ann-Marie Wieckhorst
Publications: Esther Schröter, Judith Brugger, Anton Schleidt
Registrars: Bogusław Ubik-Perski, Ann-Marie Wieckhorst
Archive: Andreas Nutz
Visitor Experience: Rebekka Nolte
Visitor Services: Annika Schlozer
Museum Shops: Fabian Emmenecker

Vitra Design Museum

Director: Mateo Kries
COO / Deputy Director: Sabrina Handler
Head of Finance: Heiko Hoffmann

Plastic: Remaking Our World is an exhibition by the Vitra Design Museum,
V&A Dundee and maat, Lisbon

Exhibition at Vitra Design Museum:

Global Sponsors

Main Sponsors

Thanks to

Our sincere thanks to everyone who contributed to this book and to the following lenders to the exhibition:

Amsterdam Bakelite Collection
Algramo
Bananatex
Elissa Brunato
Marco Cagnoni
Design Exhibition Scotland
ETH Zurich, Institute of Biogeochemistry and Pollutant Dynamics, Department of Environmental Systems Science
Everwave
Fidra
FlipFlopi
Fluid Solids
Great Bubble Barrier
Grown
Helen Kirkum
Ineke Hans
Aniela Hoitink | MycoTEX | NEFFA
Innocell Project / Free University of Bozen – Bolzano
KIT Karlsruhe, Professorship Sustainable Construction
Klarenbeek & Dros
LodgeToaster
LVR-Industriemuseum, Deutsches Kunststoff-Museum, Oberhausen
Museum für Gestaltung Zürich
Museumsstiftung Post und Telekommunikation / Museum für Kommunikation Frankfurt
Museum of Design in Plastics
National Health Service Scotland
Notpla
Ocean Cleanup
Precious Plastic
Rhino Machines
SeaCleaners
Shellworks
SHIFT GmbH
SMaRT Centre, UNSW Sydney, MICROfactories
Studio Mandin
Studio SMELT
Solubrand
SubCom
Sungai Watch
Texfad
The Tyre Collective
TrinamiX
University of Portsmouth, School of Biological Sciences, Institute of Biological and Biomedical Sciences
UTOPLAST
Victoria and Albert Museum, London
Waste2Wear

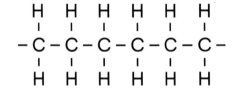

Structural formula of polyethylene (PE). Plastics are made up of small molecules (monomers) that connect to create large molecules (macromolecules) and are hence called polymers. Most plastics are composed of carbon (C) and hydrogen (H) as their main chemical elements.